Dedication

For Matthew Palmer in Eger

Transylvania and Hungary

By

Daniel Marder

ISBN: 1-4107-6385-4 (e-book)
ISBN: 1-4107-6386-2 (Paperback)
ISBN: 1-4140-2640-4 (Dust Jacket)

Library of Congress Control Number: 2003096004

This book is printed on acid free paper.

Printed in the United States of America
Bloomington, IN

1stBooks - rev. 02/13/04

Translyvania Voyage Beyond the Trees

TRANSYLVANIA: VOYAGE BEYOND THE TREES

Contents

A List of Selected Photos

ix

Preface

A quarter moon, the arc of the Carpathian mountains, separates Transylvania from Moldavia in the north and Wallachia in the south.

The first invaders to overcome the mountain obstacle were the Romans, who probably chased the natives they called Dacians into the heights, and were themselves chased into the Hungarian Pannonia by later invaders. The Great Migrations lasted longer in this land than any others in Europe. Scythians and Tartars were still intruding and plundering in the 13th century while the rest of the continent was settling into states. By the 14th century, Wallachia and Moldavia were developing a national consciousness; they became principalities under Ottoman domination.

Transylvania lies beyond the forested plain of Hungary, the Eastern province of the Magyars who called it Erdèrly, the land at the foot of the forest. It became an autonomous principality under the warring suzerainty of Ottomans and Habsburgs. When the Habsburgs gained control of Transylvania, the principalities of Wallachia and Moldavia sought Russian protection. In 1859, after the Crimean War, they were allowed to merge into a nation and named it Romania, after the rumani (Wallachian peasants.) Transylvania remained autonomous, satisfying the Habsburg Emperor with annual tributes. It was a remote and mysterious land of myth and mystery, vampire and werewolf, shrouded in a heavy curtain of woods. Tales and legends still exude like stale vapors from the medieval churches, ruined watch towers, castles, caverns and ancient mines.

But it is also a place of brutal, brooding schisms. Transylvanian Hungarians always regarded Romanians as peasants, including their noble class. In the 18th century, a Wallachian child was not permitted to attend a Hungarian school and the Wallachian clergy were compelled to carry the Calvinistic bishop on their shoulders to and from the Hungarian church. In 1920 when the Treaty of Trianon wrenched Transylvania from the Austrian-Hungarians and joined it with Romania, the tables were turned. The long belittled Romanians sought revenge on the arrogant Hungarians whose gendarmes had robbed and beaten them.

Revenge is a Romanian virtue; whoever desires respect must keep in mind past injuries and show resentment on fitting occasions. Reconciliation is opprobrious and forgiveness degrading. During my visit to the land beyond the forest, I pondered parallels with the late Yugoslavia. For me, the schisms of Transylvania symbolized those of Bosnia, Serbia and Croatia, bloodied countries where I had resided.

Though we are on a journey through Transylvania, this account cannot ignore some recent events in the greater Romania. In December 1989, the people in the town of Timisoura rioted against their dictator, Nicolai Ceausescu, who had gone seeking oil in Iran. Hurrying back, he ordered deadly force, which spilled much blood but did not suppress rioters. The rebellion spread. A few days later the dictator was executed with his wife, Elena, for "crimes against the people."

One crime was nepotism on an unprecedented scale. At least 27 Ceausescu relatives held influential positions. As Chief of Party, Elena had dictated organizational and personal changes, and as Head of the National Council of Science and Technology, she set economic goals and policy. Playboy son Nicu headed the Union of Communist Youth, and brother Iliu was Deputy Minister for National Defense. Equally offensive was Ceausescu's ostentation. While the streets were unlit, apartments unheated, bread lines interminable, the much decorated Great Conducator, as he was pleased to be called, could be seen passing in his presidential limousine en route to one of his mansions. The scepter in his hand would beat in time to the national anthem.

But the most pernicious crime against the people was the ubiquitous Securitate. Relative to the country's size, these secret police were the largest force in Europe. One was posted at every working place. The Securitate assured Ceausescu that his good people were pursuing proper roles in his vaunted "social construction." Representing their aspirations, the Great Conducator exploited the country's rich resources and nearly enslaved them.

Evidence of his mania was apparent from the moment he took over the presidency in 1965. Proclaiming Romanians descendents of the Romans, he instituted a national rebirth. He borrowed heavily to industrialize, and fostered massive migration to create an urban proletariat essential for Communist society. In 1967, his monomania ballooning, Ceausescu defied the Soviets by pursuing relations with West Germany and Israel.

The next year he denounced the Soviet move on Czechoslovakia, the "Prague Spring," and refused the Warsaw pact permission to hold maneuvers on Romanian soil. In 1970, claiming status as a developing nation and announcing "a new economic order," he gained a place at the conference of non-aligned nations.

He was rewarded for these moves with credits and technology to modernize his economy. In 1975, President Nixon visited Bucharest where he paid homage to Ceausescu as an international statesman and declared Romania a most favored nation. Whereupon Romania's debt soared out of control. Desperate to pay his bill so he could borrow more, the Great Conducator took draconian measures. He slashed imports, curtailed consumption, drove workers to ever higher export quotas, restricted energy use, and cut prices to foreign markets. Abroad, Romania's reputation was rotting. Ceausescu tried to arrest the decay by stifling emigration. Visa applicants were assigned menial jobs or fired. He assuaged the people's hardships by accusing the West of economic imperialism and stressing purification of the Romanian people, which made them spartan enough to withstand his severities.

Ceausescu became obsessed with Romaniazing the population. Ethnic minorities, especially in Transylvania, were considered foreigners. They were to be segregated unless they homogenized. Hungarian and Saxon street names were changed to Romanian, history texts were revised, publishing and teaching in Hungarian were curtailed, Hungarian and German TV suspended. But in his drive to purify his people, the Great Conducator was not above accepting hard currency. German Chancellor Willie Brandt paid handsomely for exit visas to ransom some 11,000 Transylvanian Saxons. Jews were also sold - - to Israel.

The power vacuum left by the Ceausescu executions was immediately filled by the Central Party Secretary, Ion Iliescu, and his National Salvation Front. Announcing a more democratic regime, Iliescu put the Securitate under military control, suspended food exports, and lifted the harsh energy restrictions. He then set about manipulating the political infrastructure, rearranging the postal service, the municipal administrations, and local police into management groups that would assure his National Salvation Front a landslide in elections which he then announced. He prevented the opposition from campaigning in the workplace, had the postal system intercept opponent's literature, and took charge of the media which misrepresented opposing platforms and backgrounds. Police acted as thugs, assaulting the opposition.

Today the people in Transylvania, as well as greater Romania, live cagily. A monstrous bureaucracy confounds, diverts, and finally brutalizes every aspect of life, particularly minority life. With sardonic humor, Hungarians combat frustrations, postponements, mistrusts, fears, and official schizophrenia. Long hours are spent in food lines, at ritual political meetings, and in the inferno of public transportation. Yet they make jokes and laugh. Hungarians are reputed for mirth. The Great Conducator may be gone, but clowns still conduct the kindergarten.

This work began with notes recorded in the environs and homes of Transylvanians called Szèkleys. They arrived with the Magyars in 896 and remained while the tribes moved on to establish modern Hungary. Often, historians refer to them as "Szecklers," as distinguished from other Magyars who returned from Hungary and settled in the land beyond the forest. I write more about these people and the particular histories I have come to know than about the beauteous and moody mountains, forests, streams and valleys. The intention is to reflect the experience itself and avoid excesses of scholars and dewy-eyed travelers. The people I met were not the usual fragments of nobility or others of high ranking, nor the bottom rungs, but those from the middle of the social spectrum, including former peasants.

Some names are disguised.

Daniel Marder

1. Matt, Reka, and a Ru-manian

"Transylvania will kindle your fire." This from a young assistant to his retired senior. On an extended mountain walk, I had confessed my weariness with scholarship. Thirty years of it! My young English colleague was confident my creative juices could still be excited. In Egar, Matt and I were guests of his young lady and her family. Kauty was the third fiancée the Englishman had managed in six years as a vagabond instructor in Hungary. He had also reached the last stage of his doctorate on the design of three Gothic churches in Transylvania. This static pursuit belied his vitality.

Matt exuded innocent wonder and curiosity instead of the reserve expected of a transplanted Englishman. He listened well; Hungarians were affected by his sincere interest, his empathy, and genuine sense of caring . Often he was taken for Magyar, having mastered the language, acquired the culture, and studied the history. He no longer counted expenses in quid but in forints.

Every year he bicycled home across Hungary, Austria, Germany and France, the last time with Kauty. And everywhere, Hungarians were

1

charmed with his knowledge and preference for their native ways, in spite of his unshaven face, unkempt hair, and blunt opinions.

The baroque city of Eger should have stirred my creative juices but instead only dilated my pedantic veins.

I stood on the restored fortifications where the town women repulsed the Turks in 1552 by dowsing their heads with boiling water as they climbed the walls; I duly recorded as historical mementoes the minaret marking the Turks farthest thrust north and the Romanesque remnants in the rebuilt Cathedral. Perhaps Eger"s famed Bulls' Blood wine could have stimulated the appropriate energy, but suffering late onset diabetes, I refrained.

I was in Hungary to teach at L. Klossuth University in Debrecen on the Alfold, the great eastern plain. Stimulation was everywhere. A visiting professor from Oklahoma, I still hadn't seen the Hortobàgy, most romantic puszta (prairie), where Hungary's lassoing cowboys roam.

So why Transylvania? Why another country before I explored this one. I suspected my young friend, also visiting faculty, simply wanted companionship as he pursued his own agenda in the medieval churches. It was a fabled land. I was curious.

In Debrecen, Reka Ruark gave us messages for her publisher friends in Koloszvar, Miklós and Irina. Reka was a Hungarian English professor married to an American Fulbrighter. "Koloszvar is Cluj to the Romanians." She considered it the cultural capital of Erdèly. "That's the Szèkely name for Transylvania. If you use it in public, you could be arrested."

"And Szèkely?"

"The purest Hungarians." She was effusive. "Romania's Magyar minority, most noble, most innocent, unspoiled by the excesses of western civilization." Szèkelys arrived from somewhere in the East with Arpàd in 896 and stayed when the Magyar Chieftain led his tribes to the Alfold plain and Pannonia to establish the Hungarian nation. Reka claimed that when King Stephan returned to Transylvania, the Szèkelys had already settled the empty land, and received their king with open arms. They fought with him in 1003, when he slew Guyla the Vlach, the original Romanian according to Reka, actually Wallachian. But according to most histories, Romanians were originally Dacians who inhabited the forests when the Romans arrived.

For one brief year, 1600, the Vlatch king, Michael the Brave, campaigning for the Orthodox Church against the Protestants, uniting Wallachian, Moldavia, and Transylvania into a single state, prefiguring modern Romania. But the Hapsburg Emperor, Rudolph II, could not tolerate such independence. Michael was doomed to be murdered. This occurred the following year by order of the Emperor's commissioner, General Gorgio Basta. A fury of Jesuit proselytizing followed, accompanied by severe prosecution of Vlachs, an earlier ethnic cleansing. The pieces were not put together again for three and a half centuries, when the Treaty of Trianon created the country of Romania in 1920.

"Romanians blame Szèkelys for the Vlach repression, but they took no part," Reka insisted.

Matt considered Reka a nationalist and enjoyed a bit of playful goading. "Aren't they known as valiant fighters?"

"Hungarian heroes."

"Heroes are usually vicious savages."

She customarily ignored his "immature" remarks. "Irina and Miklós publish the only literary journal left in the country, actually, the only journal in Hungarian. The Romanians are determined to eliminate all Szèkely culture, their language, their schools, theatre, newspapers, everything. They want all residents in the country to read only Romanian."

"Racial purity?" Matt's question suggested the stance of Hungary's own national party.

"Szèkelys cannot even give their babies Hungarian names," Reka continued. "The government provides a list of eighty to choose from." Rehearsing injustices apparently gave her satisfaction. "I know Matt will have you stay with his friends, but that's a crime. David and I always go to the hotel."

"And pay the foreign rates," Matt said. "The hotels smell bad."

"Everything Romanian smells bad. The first thing David does in the hotel is disconnect the phone. The country's supposed to be starving, but its electrical eavesdropping is worthy of your CIA. Bring lots of food and books. Watch out for the Keystone Kops at the border. They resent

3

foreigners bearing gifts- - bribes that hurt their dignity. They threaten the big lie that they can feed themselves. And books from Hungary might reflect Hungarian myths and customs. They're rejected without being opened. We concealed ours inside our backpacks, but a hideous fat woman in a uniform found them. We were lucky it was five in the afternoon, quitting time. But she delayed our train over an hour." Reka added her derogatory pronunciation, "Ru-manians."

In spite of Reka, Matt said Transylvania was a region to be tasted and savored. Two weeks later, on the Tuesday before All Saint's Eve, we set out. Backpacks stuffed with food and books, we boarded a Debrecen train for the junction with the Baltic Orient Express coming out of Budapest.

Matt had survived five years of vagabondage by shrewd monetary manipulation. To avoid spending hard currency which Romanians demanded for railroad tickets into their country, we would ride to the border on Hungarian forints. Knowing the train always stopped for the border checks on the Romanian side, he'd run across to the Romanian station, purchase billets to Brasso with lei, and hop on before the train started up. No hitch. He had done it two years before.

Changing at the junction, we barged into a compartment occupied by a Romanian returning to Bucharest. He had been attending a Budapest institute for young entrepreneurs. In the mold of an outmoded yuppie, he wore a yellowing white shirt with cuff links and a flagrant red tie, broad stripped suit, gold bracelet and watch. Marius was his name. His English was decent and somewhat disdainful. He smoked constantly. In Budapest five days, he missed his wife and newborn, a girl. When he learned we taught at the Kossuth University in Debrecen, Marius's tone changed significantly. It became respectful if not obsequious. He was sorry that he missed Michael Jackson's Pepsi-Cola concert in Bucharest.

Matt asked what he thought of the Szèkely situation.

"Szèkelys live in Romania, should behave like Romanians"

"Ru-manian?" Matt echoed smartly. "And give up their Hungarian language?" Their culture?"

"Romanian language is better, from Roman. We are Romans." Then he drew himself straight in his seat. "Do you know, one-sixteenth of the intelligentsia in this world is Romanian?"

"Oh, I do know," Matt responded playfully, "Ceausescu said so, but you executed him. So now you believe in him?"

"Ceausescu was bad communist, steal people's bread for his own riches." Abruptly, Marius asked, "You like Clinton or Bush?" The election was upon us. "Bush is good!"

"And Clinton?" I asked.

He shrugged. "All the same to Romania."

Approaching the boarder, Matt turned edgy. He shared our scheme with Marius. "No problem," Marius had promised. When the conductor came by, a dour looking fellow with hollow cheeks, Marius engaged him in conversation. Then the conductor took Matt's lei, though we were still in Hungary, and instead of pocketing it, as I expected, punched out two first class fares good from the border to Brasso. Overwhelmed by such generosity, I offered the conductor 100 lei, which is equivalent to an American quarter. Something should have gone to Marius as well, but it might have insulted him.

Matt pulled his seat out before the light had completely faded. By flattening the opposite seat he made a bed, his dismal all-weather coat his blanket. I followed suit, my black all-weather not much better. The plush red seats in this first class compartment were patched and retorn. A shelf dangled on its hinges just below the window; beside it hung a filled ashtray and a bin overflowing with garbage. Bulbs had been removed from the ceiling fixture and the metal of the fixture itself twisted down. The linoleum covering the floor was stained and cracked; cold air came through. The compartment was icy; I couldn't doze off. Beside me, Marius sat upright, still smoking. Once in a while a lone light in the countryside shone through the greasy window.

Then the inevitable happened. I crawled over Marius to the black corridor and followed the stench to the WC. A bleak bulb showed an accumulation of excrement, urine, and newsprint, some in the bowl, some on the seat and wet floor. I turned back. We were due in Brasso at seven a.m.

2. Brasso (Romanian Brasov)

The Carpathians grew on us. Sipping at a tiny plastic cup of bitter coffee from the station kiosk, I stared at the ridges under an iron sky. I struggled to recapture their storied spirit, myths of mystery and gloom. These were not majestic Himalayas or Swiss Alps. They seemed familiar mountains, like Pennsylvania Appalachians. Eventually I was able to envision marauding tribes driving the Romans out and chasing each other across these peakless ranges - - Goths, Huns, Avars, Bulgars, Khazars, Slavs. Last came the Magyars driven by the bestial Pechenegs. Among the posters on the railroad station was a scrawl in black letters: MICHAEL JACKSON.

A busy avenue fronted the station where a more or less disheveled crowd queued haphazardly for buses. Matt, entrusted with our money, bought tickets and we lined up for number 2 which would take us to the center. Inside, the bus was stuffed, mothers holding babies stood among the workers. They pushed back to make room for the newcomers - - foreigners with backpacks. A heavy-set man in a well-worn jacket forced two young men from their seats. Grinning, he offered them with an extended arm. We sat with our burdens upon us. Matt became uneasy only when the buildings thinned and an occasional field appeared. He asked a woman standing in the aisle if this number 2 went to the center. She didn't understand Hungarian, but their dialogue was considered hilarious and the crowded bus exploded with laughter. A man said "quatro." Another said in Hungarian to follow him. We got off at a remote intersection. Our guide pointed to a bus depot across the street. Number 4 started there.

But my travel mate certainly knew where to get off. We entered a street paved with square stones worn to a shine. It was lined with decrepit shops and void of traffic. I realized we were strolling down a mall. A few shops displayed clothing, most offered trinkets, toys watches, sundries and such, all yellowed with age. Matt was upset by the Coke and Marlboro signs. "Glitzy," he muttered, "not a sign two years ago."

It was too early for crowds, but we came upon a line of people blocks long, and eventually arrived at its source - - a bread kiosk on a corner. Beside it, a truck was unloading its loaves.

The mall led to a picture postcard of a German burgh, circa 1700. The plaza was octagonal, dominated by a clock tower rising from the red tiled roof of a squat building painted rusty yellow. Matt called it "Empire gold." Apparently the town hall, it sat in the middle of the octagonal, surrounded by attractively designed paving blocks and building facades jammed together under sloping roofs. Here and there pastels relieved the Empire gold. None were over three stories. The buildings on one side backed up to the peakless Tàmpa Mountain which hovered over the plaza like the spread wings of a gigantic bat. Just behind the plaza loomed the Black Church, one of Matt's dissertation subjects. On the farther side, a blue sign slashed across a neo-classic facade, COMPUTERLAND. Another read, PANASONIC.

Pink and white table umbrellas marked a café painted peach. I dropped my backpack, ran in, and was directed downstairs. What pleasure! The white all tiles were scrubbed, the toilet bowl immaculate, soft paper, and soap!

"A Saxon town," Matt explained. "They call it Kronstadt." He had lugged in my backpack and taken a table. "Ceausescu renamed it Stalin."

8

"And now it's just Brasov."

"Brasso," he corrected.

The café was ornamented in dark wood carved with an oriental airiness . We were the only morning patrons. A wisp of a girl came for our orders. The breakfast was fixed menu. I was famished but did not realize it until I dug into the scrambled eggs and fried pork.

"We're in luck," said Matt, wolfing down his breakfast. "No meat last time."

Had they coffee? Could they offer tea?

Each time I lifted the backpack it felt heavier, but we only had a short walk to the Black Church. It was Lutheran, established in 1425 as the Gothic Protestant church. Fire blackened it in 1689. Approaching, I saw stones shrouded in scaffolding.

We entered through rotting doors and stood on a dirt floor facing a cashier's window. Katherine, the stringy woman inside the window, took a moment before recognizing Matt, then remembered the visit of his sister and parents last year. Harry showed the Palmers everything; in fact they had stayed at Harry's house. Harry Cloos was the church guide and major domo. Assuming we would also stay with Harry, she asked Matt if he still had the address. She wrote it out and added the phone number. Katherine said Harry hadn't been at work for five months. Harry was not well. Matt remembered his stomach problems two years ago. "Something more," said Katherine. She waited a moment, but Matt also waited. "I mean his head."

The Saxon population had been dwindling, she said, ever since the city was renamed Stalin. Less than 1800 now, not one in 50 were contributors. The Baptist Church was gaining dominance, Romania's second largest after the Orthodox. She worried it was time for Harry to turn over the church keys to the town council. "I"m afraid he won't be strong enough for the ceremony."

Katherine agreed to keep our backpacks while we took the incline to the top of Tàmpa Mountain. Rounding the corner, I saw MICHAEL JACKSON scrawled on the stones inside the scaffolding.

On the street a man in a brown overcoat with rotten teeth to match engaged Matt in conversation. They exchanged addresses and then he moved off to resume his stance on the corner.

9

"He asked me for a calculator," Matt explained. "I said I'd send him one."

"You mean sell him one?"

"Oh yes, if he can pay."

I hardly had time to evaluate my companion's generosity when a bare-headed woman in a nondescript raincoat crossed the street and offered her card. Had she been watching? Were we the tourists or the attraction? She had rooms to offer, clean sheets, heat, bath and television, a "palace" she called it - - 3000 lei. Matt told her we were staying at a friend's, Harry Cloos. Did she know him?

"Take the card," I urged. "We haven't called him yet."

We headed for the mountain, through a park, across a school yard, past an extended hospital, an onion-domed church, a polytechnic college, theatre, regional museum, guarded government buildings and library. Then we hiked up a climbing street with trees and lawns. The houses were large, well kept, again Empire gold. In the middle of one lawn, a cow grazed. Its keeper sat on a stool in cap and lambskin coat. And down the sidewalk came a tall young man dressed in a leather jacket and jeans. He held a husky German shepherd on a leash. The dog paused and stared at the cow, too amazed to bark.

We climbed past the ruined citadel walls to leveled ground where a tennis court had been established in front of an alpine clubhouse of brick, wood and glass. Remains of the old fortress rose beyond it. At last, we mounted wooden steps to reach the incline's station. I leaned on a rail, puffing while Matt bought tickets. The ascent was dramatic; it seemed vertical.

From the top of Tàmpa (3140 feet), the city center was no longer rusty Empire gold, but the red of its tiled roofs. And the scaffolding had evaporated from the church. Its smoky stones rose as a grey eminence, dominant as a cathedral. Through the naked fall brush we looked out upon three purple peaks. "Bruzenland," said Matt, terrain of the old German district the Saxons have tilled for nearly eight centuries. "Dracula's castle is in those woods, maybe twenty miles from here. Not the genuine article, that's in Segisvar, where he was born." I'd never thought of Bram Stoker's blood-sucking ghoul as a real person, and had no desire to search Bruzenland for his ersatz castle.

The café was closed until eleven. We looked over the parapet on its deck. I intended to sit in the glass enclosed corner of the café that jutted over the mountain. In the meantime, Matt suggested I climb the hillock to the very tip where a scrawny excuse for a flag fluttered, its blue, yellow, and red bands sewn together like an oversized shawl. "I'll take your picture for Reka."

Seized with Matt's impishness, I scrambled up and posed, the despised Romanian flag flagrantly above my head. (Reka was predictable. Back in Debrecen, she threw the photo on my apartment floor.)

The café had opened by the time I came down. We were the only customers. Matt pointed to a cluster of new high rises in the far corner of our view. "Harry lives there."

"In an apartment?"

"In a big house. Ceausescu built his greater Romania all around it. The Cloos house is generations old. Harry traces his family back to the early Saxons."

"He lives alone?"

"Never married. His parents live with him, but they're usually in Hungary on business. Mother's Szèkely."

I had a premonition that Matt had not made arrangements. "Is he expecting us?"

"I'm always welcome at Harry's."

"When your parents and sister came last year, did they just pop in?"

"Invitations weren't necessary."

"I suggest we get off this mountain and call him, if we intend on staying there."

Matt's family lived in Sussex, his mother a schoolteacher, his father an Oxford-educated librarian assigned to writing biographies of lesser historical lights. Matt's lackadaisical manners were a mystery.

Returning, we cut through a narrow lane of shops on both sides. A group of young people were spilling out of a storefront, apparently from a meeting. They filled the sidewalk and street. After we worked through them and were approaching the corner, a slick red convertible came racing around it. Instinctively I put out a hand and muttered something. The convertible whizzed by. Then the brakes screeched. The auto reversed and stopped beside us. One of the two young mugs sneered, "Something you don't like?" Good English.

"Why?"

"Your face."

"What about my face?"

"Growled at us."

I thought to say something defensive. Or insulting. But these were young Romans! Valiant tribunes of the people! Insipidly, I thought 'Discretion is the better part of valor.'

I said, "You could have hit those people ahead."

The Romans stared an interminable moment, then grumbled and crawled on. Matt roared. "Masterful!" I worried that we'd hear their brakes again.

Matt wanted a few hours to study modifications made to the church over the centuries. His dissertation plan was to deduce the original design from them, make comparisons with similar deductions from the others in his study, and draw generalizations. My watch read twelve-thirty. Katherine said the doors were locked at three-thirty. I left him there. What could he accomplish in three hours? And two years ago had he truly devoted his time in Brasso to study? Thinking of necessary visits to the other churches, I realized Matt's dissertation would require several lifetimes. With dampened spirit, I came out to the plaza.

The city hall turned out to be a museum. A large stand-up poster in front bragged about the Columbus 500 year Exhibition. Three panels on the poster depicted Columbus Braving the Ocean, Columbus Meeting the Indians, Columbus Slaying the Indians. Inside, the place was empty to the walls. A young woman in a skirt and peasant blouse managed to convey that the museum was preparing for the exhibit. She pointed to the poster, which announced the opening date: November 15. "Come back you." She sounded like an American southerner.

The plaza was fuller. I almost bumped into a man wearing a leer, an unlit cigarette dangling from his lips. Crossing to the café, I passed several pairs of strolling police with guns on their backs. I took a table under a pink and white umbrella. On one side was a sedate Chinese restaurant, on the other sidewalk vendors hawked home bottled fruits, pickles and kraut, all sorts of candies, seeds, underwear, socks and cigarettes. I asked for coffee and because the Roman language was Latin, added in Spanish, "Leche."

"Nem," the waiter answered in Hungarian, and shook his head.

A cup of tepid Nescàfe was placed before me, most of the powder floating on the top. I settled into an hour of people watching. They came past my table - - in sweat suits, dressy skirts, jeans. While some were aged, mainly I observed young couples and threesomes with sour faces, even those hand in hand. These were the lovers? A cord was strung around a large plot near the museum building, and soon joyless children were riding tricycles and scooters within it. Parents looked on, listlessly. Rain began to fall. I headed for the church.

Katherine pointed to the sanctuary where Matt was still at work. I saw him in the front pew, eyes concentrated on the vaulting, then on his paper pad, up to the vaulting, down again. A surprising number of visitors milled in the dank and dusty aisles. Also surprising were the carpets cast over everything but the stones on the floor. They draped the sanctuary, hung from the walls, the pews, cross beams and apse. One decorated the pulpit. Suffocatingly profuse. No doubt each had been a delicate Persian or Turkish design, now so faded and worn that the original colors and patterns were barely discernable. They accumulated more or less into a Moslem shroud over the Christian church. Before we left, Katherine gave me a pack of postcards she sold at the cashier's booth. Each featured a carpet in freshened condition. I recognized a few.

I lifted my backpack with a groan, put an arm through one strap and hoisted it over my shoulder. "That's no way to carry." Matt adjusted me, pulling both arms through the hoops properly. A tremendous improvement, but the pack was still heavy.

We started across the plaza in a steady drizzle, looking for the number 6 bus stop. Matt said he was sure this time. I paused at the clean windows of the Chinese restaurant, empty except for a table of five.

"Officials," Matt said

"How can you tell? Their clothes?" The men wore neutral suits and ties, the women simple dresses and coiffured hair.

"No one else can afford it."

The restaurant did give the appearance of elegance, a huge dining room with well spaced tables adorned with blue covers, gleaming crystal and silver. We hadn't eaten since early morning. The thought aroused my hunger. A serving man in a light blue suit and matching blue tie peeked out at us. "Like Chinese?" I asked Matt.

"Harry took us for dinner last time. Somewhere in the countryside."

"Have you called?"

"Not necessary."

"Don't you think we should eat before we go to Harry's?"

I moved toward the engraved glass doors, reluctantly, Matt followed. The man in the blue suit led us to a table beside the others. They were eating with little conversation, perhaps a touch self-consciously. Our clumsy entrance disturbed them. One lady stared at our rain-matted hair as we dumped our wet packs against the wall and threw our soaked coats on them. The waiter in blue meekly poured water in the crystal goblets and withdrew. "Elegant touch," I observed. Even Budapest restaurants didn't serve water.

In a hushed voice, Matt said, "Here comes Clouseau sans mustache."

The maitre'd now approaching in tuxedo and greased hair parted down the middle did indeed resemble Peter Seller's French detective. He stood beside us with pencil and pad.

"Aperitif? Hors d'oeuvre?"

"Menu?"I asked, and came to understand that dinner was "fixée," 2200 lei.

It was more than Matt could bear. Trying to make do on 8000 forints, 40,000 lei, he could not afford such profligacy - - over a twentieth spent on one meal? There were four courses plus rice. "Could we get half a meal each?" Matt asked. "Two dishes rather than four?" Clouseau pretended amusement. Appealing to the apparent lack of business, Matt persuaded him, but we would get half portions of all four dishes.

I asked for chopsticks; Matt broke up. "And you imagine Chinese cooks in the kitchen?"

The waiter in blue brought four silver-covered compotes bearing delicate meats and vegetables. The taste of ginger overwhelmed the distinctive flavor of each. I was disappointed only in the color, anticipating the usual Chinese reds and greens. The dishes were all pot roast brown. The portions were large and, hungry as we were, we could not finish. I ordered tea then waited as the place darkened. Those at the next table quietly departed. Matt and I began table-tapping. My watch read 4:30. "When did we order the tea?"

"At least twenty minutes ago."

I looked about the huge dining room for our waiter. Deserted. Throwing back my chair, I heading for the swinging doors in the rear. They opened to another large room with a serving shelf on the back wall. Also deserted. But two steaming cups sat on the shelf. I spun about and headed for our table. About half way back, I heard the maitre'd calling to me in hot pursuit. Not understanding him, I shouted, "Time's up We must go."

Matt and I were getting our coats when the waiter in blue came running up with the two steaming cups on a platter, miraculously not spilling a drop.

"Too late. Too late."

Matt paid, adding a tip that surprised the waiter and me as well.

3. Harry

Even though I was carrying it correctly, the backpack grew even heavier; we sought the number 6 bus stop in the rain, also heavier. Matt's memory was vague. We went in one direction and another, then sighted a loaded bus pulling away from a corner and headed for the spot. "Number 6?" Matt asked one of the waiting riders. She did not speak Hungarian. Another pointed in another direction, and again we headed out. It was raining hard now, and few brave souls were afoot. I was slouching under the load on my back. Again we were confused. Seeing a man with umbrella across the street, Matt ran over and asked directions for the number 6. I was fascinated with this fellow's wonderful mustache, dampened but still upturned in the Magyar tradition. "Follow me," he said, and led us to another soaked crowd on another corner. They tried to squeeze into a little space under the awning of a kiosk. There we stood, rain pouring over us, as buses came and went, 2, 8, 4, 2 again, another 4. The man we had followed got on the last 4, and I shouted to the violent air, "Traitor!"

17

Finally, a number 6 showed up. The crowd swelled and rushed it. Pushing our backpacks ahead, we fought aboard, having abandoned all hope that another 6 would ever again reach that corner.

By the time we rumbled into the newer part of town, the crowd had dissipated and we were luxuriating in roominess. With little curiosity and less desire I followed Matt off the bus and into the weather. The rain had settled into a steady drizzle. We were in a canyon of high rises, stumbling through a checkerboard of mud and cement sidewalk blocks. The weight of my pack hunched my shoulders. We were following a wide paved street with lights that rounded a corner and met another, even wider thoroughfare. Beyond was an opening into a labyrinth of lanes through a complex of apartments. We entered, and quite as expected, were soon lost.

Mercifully, the drizzle stopped while we followed our noses through the labyrinth. We emerged at last on another thoroughfare, this one with trees in a median, small lighted shops and groups of people who had emerged after the rain. They stood on corners in conversation. It was a warm neighborhood scene that might have occurred in any American city early in the century. A bus came along, number 2. I pointed to it. Matt acknowledged that we could have taken that one. Then another bus, a number 8. I could not restrain myself, "That one, too." He was talking to a group of youngsters, fifteen-years old, at most. One said he could find the address that Katarina had written down. He ran over to the older people and I began to suspect foul play, being put on by the country's smartass set, Romanians or Szèkely. As I was about to go after him, he returned and motioned for us to follow. I cautioned Matt, "This might be a set-up."

We crossed numerous streets and wound through several alleys before the young man pointed to a poorly traveled lane. "That's it!" Matt shouted in glee. I over-tipped the young man and drowned my guilt in excessive thanks.

The house faced sideways to the street. Through a piked iron fence, we entered a narrow courtyard limited by a wall that obviously cut off what had been an expansive lawn. It was now occupied by an apartment building hovering over us. On the covered porch Matt found the bell button and pushed while I leaned my pack against the wall. Again he pushed. I became a touch alarmed. Was this possible? Harry

18

not home, after all our trouble, our long bus trip and arduous search through the cement canyons? Matt pressed a third time—a fourth. I was suffering ugly thoughts of the long trip back, of tramping the streets in the rain for a place to spend the night, when a window to the side flooded with light. We were saved!

A short man with a triangular face and stubby needles of light hair filled the window. I could not make out his features for the dominant dazzle of his white teeth, too many for the mouth. His tie-less white shirt augmented the brilliance. He gave no greeting that I could determine, merely began speaking with Matt in quiet Hungarian. Harry could not see me against the wall and probably didn't know I was there. Matt's defensive tone told me the discussion was not going well. So I was not shocked when the window closed and went black.

Going through the gate, I asked, "You kept that lady's card?"

Matt nodded. Silently we trudged through the lane to the feebly lighted street and I saw the dejection in his eyes. He said, "At least Harry could have offered tea."

"What did he say?"

"Had guests, cousins, or was expecting them. I stopped listening." Matt shook his head, "Should have asked us in."

I searched for a consoling phrase, but he provided his own. "Harry's not well."

We were back on the comfortable neighborhood street. People were still on the corners. Matt asked them for the bus to the center.

4. The "Palace"

The address on the card led us across the plaza to a pair of doors fitted into an arch beside the Chinese restaurant. We were at the peach building that housed the café. The doors gave way to our nudging and we found ourselves immersed in blackness. A light came on. We were in a long alleyway. A woman in a black dress stood in the middle of the alley, holding a flashlight. From the distance she was more than attractive, a black dress clinging to her shapely body. What was she doing there? She appeared a bit unnerved. Had we interrupted romance? A Romanian rendezvous? Was she a prostitute?

Another light came on and we saw half-flights of steps leading to door stoops along the alleyway. Matt went up to her and showed her the card for the "palace." Puzzled, our mystery lady knocked at a door and a large woman in a housedress emerged. She recognized the card. We climbed endless stone steps to a landing where I had to rest my backpack. Matt offered to carry it for me, an insult. As we began the next flight, our street crone appeared at the top.

Her "palace" consisted of a hall leading to a sitting room with TV, a sleeping room and bath, which was her pride - - tub, shower and up-to-date stool. We dumped our backpacks onto the double bed in the sleeping room and were relieved to see a cot in the corner. Matt observed a third backpack on the bed. The crone threw it on the cot, explaining that a young German had taken the room, for hard currency, marks. But we could share the room. He wouldn't mind the cot. 4000 lei.

It was 3000 this morning, Matt protested. She had no recollection of negotiations that morning. The card? Many are on the street. I picked up my backpack and made for the hallway. But Matt gave in. He went to remove the German's backpack from the cot. She took it from him and replaced it, reminding us that the German boy had already paid in marks. "Then why are you still offering it?" Matt asked.

"He doesn't mind sharing."

Again I made for the hallway.

Matt insisted, "We must have the room to ourselves." He dug beneath his shirt and brought out a stack of forints. "Here," he said, counting, "a 1000 forints." It was the equivalent of 5000 lei. He returned the lei to his money belt. Watching from the hallway, I could see she was tempted. I came back. But the crone proved to be a woman of her word.

"The German rented the room. He must have it - - at least in part." Once more I feigned leaving. "Wait!" She had something else. We were live bait, not to be lost. In a flash she was on the phone. Her friend had a lovely place available on the mall. She was on her way to get us.

Our new hostess was a bent and wrinkled woman in a shawl. Coarse stockings covered her bowed legs. As we followed her down the uneven stones of the mall, I worried they would fail her. We had retraced a good deal of our morning path into the center, when she unlocked a pair of doors in another archway and led us up another endless set of stone steps. Then we passed through a door and we were outside again, in an iron walkway like an old fire escape. We passed a foul smelling cubicle built onto the outer railing, obviously a WC, and continued on past several barred iron doors, finally knocking at one of them. It was opened by a short man, bald and grizzly bearded. He was grinning with delight at the sight of us.

22

We had entered the bedroom, and even before I tossed off my burden, the bed invited my fatigued body. I wanted no conversation, just to stretch out and close my eyes. The room also contained an upholstered chair that folded out. Gracious as always, Matt said he preferred that to the double bed. A doorway led to the dining-living room dominated by a large TV screen. There was also a dining table, chairs, and in a corner, a chintz covered mattress where I assumed our hosts would sleep. On the other side of this room was the kitchen which was also the bathroom. While our hostess showed me the shower, rigged with a circular curtain within the tub, Matt and our host engaged in vigorous Hungarian conversation, punctuated with brandy; instant comrades. Next to the tub was the hot water cylinder. There was also a sink with dirty dishes and a water hose instead of a faucet, and electric stove, and a small table with one chair.

Matt's chummy chatter with our host was interrupted for showering instructions. Four fingers were held up to the hot water boiler, indicating the allotment for each shower. Two linen towels were provided to dry each of us. To be polite, I sat at the table a moment, long enough to hear a rhapsody about this old couple's successful young man in Chicago who every other month send them hard U.S. dollars.

Barely awake, I excused myself, undressed in the sleeping room, and, returning in under shorts, meandered through the conversation to the shower without embarrassment. My near nudity had no effect; they had become sprightly as the brandy bottle emptied. I twisted and turned within the curtain, distributing the thin stream of water, then rubbed my body with the linen towels until they were soaked, and went back as I came, still eliciting no attention.

I was fully unconscious when our host turned on the light for my WC lesson. Slipping on pants and shoes, I followed him out onto the narrow ironworks and sniffed the foul air, indicating I knew where it was. He followed me back and then showed me how to key both locks on the door. While we were gone, his wife had spread crisp sheets on the bed. I saw Matt unload coffee, sugar, flour, canned meats, cooking oil and such from my backpack. He gave some to our host with 1000 forints. Their alien banter was like musical accompaniment as I slipped into the sheets and floated off to oblivion.

23

But my diabetes would not allow me to sleep through. Slipping on my pants and shoes, I quietly managed the locks. My caution was excessive, Matt was totally out. On the iron balcony I stopped after a few steps toward the WC, turned to the rail, and let go, watering whatever lay below.

My backpack was so much lighter in the morning that I asked if Matt had given away all of our food. "I've got a confession. Your bag was so heavy because I packed all the eatables in it. I meant to rearrange it on the train. I did last night, what was left."

"Now it's all in your pack?"

"No trouble. Let's go" We were catching the eight o'clock for Csíkscereda and Matt's friends, the Egyed family, Edit and Imrè.

People had formed a line at the end of the mall where we waited for the bus to the railroad. It came to a head at a window about shoulder level. I watched as clear plastic bags were handed out, one to a person. Looking closer, I saw the content was nothing more exotic than a defeathered dead chicken.

The station was stuffed with travelers, many holding bouquets of fresh flowers. We joined the end of what we took for a ticket line; it barely moved. Over a window across the station I saw a sign which seemed to say First Class. No line. Matt had no confidence it was open, but I convinced him to run over and try. He returned chagrined, tickets in hand. He pulled me out of the line, and we fought through the crowd to the platform.

It was a short way to Csíkscereda, but the train stopped at every village and often in wide open fields. At each stop, people streamed off. Holding their bouquets, they trudged up the dusty roads, seemingly towards nowhere. "All Saint's Day," Matt reminded me. "Going to their parent's grave, most of them." Romanian and Szèkely alike.

5. Edit and Imrò

A very Hungarian town, Matt called it. He was reassured by the many Hungarian signs; they outnumbered the Romanian. He suspected the linguistic differences were lost on me. "No, not at all. On the contrary. In Brasso, the Romanian signs were easy to decipher."

"Ceausescu targeted this town. He was rebuilding it when the Revolution broke out. Monstrous boulevard, acres of high rise apartments, a city hall and plaza large enough to hold the entire population for his speeches, and all turned 90 degrees from the original axis. But he couldn't affect the heavy air, the rural smells and the sounds of Hungarian vowels. They impregnate the very fabric that was meant to destroy them."

We strolled through the Ukrainian market beside the station. It was a wide aisle over a block long, established by automobiles lined up side by side, hoods pointed inward, strewn with every conceivable piece of junk under heaven: plumbing tools, sinks, faucets, wiring, TV and high-fi sets, antennas, irons and board, embroideries, car jacks, toys, pickled fruits. Most cars were covered from roof to wheels.

25

"They're here a few days," said Matt, "sleep in their cars, then move onto another town." I watched as mothers were unabashedly breast feeding babes. They were dressed like working folk everywhere, some in jeans, some in plastic leather jackets. "They come for the money." Matt saw that I was incredulous. "You might think the lei is the lowest currency in Eastern Europe. It's not. Ukraine is the bottom of the ladder."

We crossed a broad avenue running along side this makeshift market. Matt was confident he knew the way to the Egyed family. Instinctively, I thought the center of town lay in the direction of the overcast mountains. Matt was showing his address book to a large, mild looking man in tennis warm-ups. He guided us through well kept streets, gradually losing confidence, until we came to a spacious corner with a traffic light. A large yard surrounded a church in that rusty Empire's gold. The man had to admit he didn't know where we were going. A couple strolled by, wheeling a baby carriage. They spoke only German.

The corner was nearly deserted; next to no vehicles were on the streets. After a while, an elderly lady in wine colored coat and hat ambled across the corner. Her leather boots, also wine-colored, were halfway to her knees. She carried a shopping bag and newspaper. Guiltily, our guide approached her. She was on her way home, surprisingly, to the very street in Matt's address book. Not far, she assured us.

Lightened as it was; my backpack had again grown burdensome. Several times, I stopped to rearrange it on my shoulders. We were passing fenced yards with trim bungalow type houses that fronted plots of acreage, farm animals behind. Encountering ditches across the road, we hopped and skirted about, our guide displaying unexpected dexterity. Piles of dirt were stacked beside the trenches. Occasionally workers appeared knee deep, some digging out, some filling in.

"Electricity," explained our guide, "We're catching up with the 20th century before its too late."

The workers were not ordinary crews. Cream-skinned children were slinging dirt alongside shriveled men and women in their seventies and eighties. She explained that the whole family had to pitch in, and was amazed to discover there was any other way. "The city supplies the wires," she said, "but not the shovels."

I waited at the gate while Matt skipped the steps to the front porch. It was only a moment before the door opened, but I'd been conditioned and was again thinking fiasco. A short, matronly figure stood in the shadow of a half-open doorway, a baby on her hip. "Matthew," he said pliantly, "Matthew Palmer?" The door finally widened, the woman's free arm reached to Matt's neck - - he was 6 feet plus - - and pulled him into a hug. "Edit!" There was relief in his voice. Then he pointed as I scampered up the porch steps, "Meet Daniel." Her unpainted face was full-cheeked, sallow, and sad. She wore an embroidered apron over a plain white blouse and black acrylic slacks. Her figure was not so matronly, now that I could see plainly, but quite shapely.

Freed of our coats and packs in the hallway, we entered an all-purpose room, an eating table and chairs in the center, surrounded by a baby crib, a corner mattress with a lacy spread, and a huge television on a table that blocked light from the single window. Edit put the baby, Erika, in the crib; Matt picked her up again and toyed with her. I feigned an interest, but Matt was sincere. He truly enjoyed Erica; he was so engrossed that Edit had to ask more than once about his parents and sister.

Imrò was working at their apartment, on private accounts. He'd be home for lunch. "Today's All Saint's, holiday," Matt announced once more. "Imrò's an accountant with the bank."

Edit went through an open door into a small kitchen stuffed with utensils and hanging clothes. She emerged with a plate full of cheese hunks, sliced salami, and bread. Then she brought a bottle of red wine from a sideboard behind the crib and three stemmed glasses with deeply cut patterns, obviously heirlooms. Needing attention, Erika began tossing toys out of the crib. Matt picked her up as I broke my rule and sipped the wine. I was not tempted to take another.

Matt asked about their apartment. On the other side of town, Edit said, among the high rises, which meant five, six stories at most. This house belonged to Imrò's folks. They were tending it while his parents were away. Imrò's father was a wood carver and cabinet maker, working in Budapest for five times what he could earn in Romania. I could sense the question brewing in my homeless colleague's mind. Edit was a step

27

ahead of him. "Why don't you stay there?" Matt played with this marvelous windfall as if deliberating, "Should we . . .?"

Perhaps anticipating her husband's arrival, Edit turned on the TV, and suddenly we were in the midst of sport - - not European, but American. I could not quite fathom what I saw: the black uniforms of the Chicago Bears and the greens of the Philadelphia Eagles thrashing about in the living room of this remote Carpathian town. "CNN," she said. In Debrecen, the best I could do was soccer from a London station.

Imrò appeared reticent, but I saw that he was pleased with our visit. A languid man, he was the exemplar of the movie westerner, tall and thin, with a sharp, angular face. Maybe a touch of Mongolian was in him. Immediately he brought out another wine; politely, I sipped again. It was rich, dry, tasting vaguely of berries. "How is that?" His English was intelligible.

I nodded and quickly covered the glass, "But enough." He said the wine was like perfume. The ubiquitous flavor was in everything good; cognac, liqueurs, ice cream. He wasn't throwing caution to the winds, but did seem grateful for an audience, as if he had been quiet too long.

Edit put plates before us and brought in platters of potatoes, green beans, and fatty sausage the color of uncooked bratwurst. Self-consciously, I plunged in, and thought of the food we'd lugged over the mountain for her. Matt made a remark in Hungarian about rationing and Edit responded, "Last year vegetables were for sale in the market; this year they forbid the sellers from Hungarian towns." Matt interpreted and she went on, "Some cities ration sugar and flour to half kilo a month, but in Hungarian towns it's a quarter kilo."

Imrò leaned over to the TV and turned up the sound. Then he leaned forward. To hear him we also had to lean. "Eavesdroppers," he said, pointing to the TV. "The regime suspect college professors and writers." His voice dropped to a harsh whisper. "Insane, this country, always. Official policy - - rub out all trace of Hungarian. No more Szèkley universities, no more Szèkley travel, no foreign visitor in Szèkley home." His mouth opened in a laughing gesture. "I tell you story. Traveler is lost. He ask Hungarian the way. A cop come by. He say, 'Why you ask him? He Hungarian. They here in Romania only one thousand year. Ask me. We here two thousand year.'"

Imrò drank more wine and, pleased with his story, launched a series of gypsy jokes, mostly concerning ignorance of civilized ways. One was about a gypsy family in the big city mistaking swans in the pond for geese, killing and cooking them. Seeming to understand her husband's English, Edit attempted a story of her own - - true, she said. Matt's translation jammed the timing, but not enough to block the effect:

"When Gheorghe Fumar replaced the Szèkley mayor of Koloszvar, he forbade the city's use of the Hungarian name. It was formally Cluj Napoca to show Roman origins, but just Cluj for normal purposes and conditions. His council outlawed Hungarian language posters and advertisements and removed the bilingual street signs. Merchants who conducted business in both languages were fined. When a new entrepreneur proposed a cable television service to be called MTV, the city council supported the mayor in rejecting it. The initials, they thought, stood for Magyar television, the state broadcasting network of Hungary.

"Fumar ran for president against Iliescu last year," Edit continued, "as a candidate of the National Unity Party. His only issue was squelching the Hungarian threat. He sees conspiracy between us and Budapest. He is sure Szèkleys consider Transylvania still a part of Hungary."

Imrò was laughing before Matt finished the translation. He slipped into Hungarian, "They shout, 'the world dozes while Hungary plots a takeover. Our beautiful women are trained to hypnotize Western leaders! We export them to the beds of foreign diplomats.'"

I gathered the Szèkley situation had begun to boil; the Romanian army had been holding maneuvers on the mountain around Father Istvàn's parish, helicopters were circling, Szèkley girls were raped, two men were murdered.

"Not unique," I said. "Crime in Debrecen has also gone up since communist times." I told them about the fifth year medical student at Kossuth University whose body was found on the grass beside the major university building. "She'd been raped and her throat slit. Ethiopian. Police discovered she had an Ethiopian boyfriend and shipped him back home. That's how they handle matters in Hungary."

Imrò held up two fingers. "We lose only two this month."

"Not counting the rapes and beatings," said Edit.

29

I asked for the WC and received a grin. Imrò took me outside and pointed to the back. Making my way to the outhouse, I passed a chained dog guarding a rusting automobile suspended on cement blocks. It fronted a withering garden on an extensive plot. The outhouse was neat, amply stocked and surprisingly free of odor.

When I returned, Imrò said he had to visit his mother's grave in the village of Gyrgyo, less than an hour's drive. Would we like to go along? "Could we visit the apartment instead?"

The car was a block away because of the trenches blocking the street. We passed the Ukraine market along the way; most of the cars were still in line, and the merchants sat chatting on the emptied hoods, drinking and smoking, some playing cards.

Lucky at last - - the apartment was located on the first floor and just a few steps to the front door. And what luxury! Matt chose the living room containing a full bed and TV; the bedroom was all mine, another full bed, wardrobe, and reclining chair. The father's master work was everywhere - - neo-classic curlicues carved into the light woods of dressers, bookcases, cupboards, bookcases, chests and cabinets.

In the morning, I found the coffee grinder and made a tasteless brew from old beans discovered in a remote cupboard corner. Outside, the mountain air was chill. We walked to a restaurant and ordered breakfast - - eggs and sausages - - in a large dining hall that had once been plush with upholstered chairs and inlaid tables. Matt was eager to visit Father Istvàn in his parish village of Csabotflava on the mountain. I wanted to see the museum in the old palace, and the new city hall in the grand plaza.

We passed another replication of the statue in Rome depicting Romulus and Remus suckling the wolf. It was near an ice palace which displayed the finest piece of sculpture I had seen in Romania, in fact Hungary. Sheer movement, energy, two aluminum hockey players racing for the puck, capturing the essence of individual competition. The police were patrolling in pairs accompanied by a machine-gun toting soldier. They seemed to be sniffing for trouble. "Something brewing here?" I asked Matt.

We peeked into a butcher shop. Salami hung from hooks behind the empty counters. A single scrawny chicken lay on a tray. "That emaciated creature is ubiquitous," said Matt. "But the last time I was here, it wasn't. The butcher shop was locked."

In a bookstore, I found a few volumes of Americans in translation: Steinbeck, Crane, London. There were shelves of English, French and Russian authors, tables of children's books, and a whole dusty corner devoted to the works of the executed dictator, Nikolai Ceausescu.

More police manned the immense plaza. Construction of the apartments surrounding it had been interrupted by the overturn of the communists. The new regime was too poor and disorganized to continue the program of bulldozing the cities and villages and constructing the monstrous housing blocks. Csikscereda, as several cities in Transylvania, is spotted with the half built high-rises that gape upon the landscape like eyes of gigantic flies, dangling wires, pipes, and plastic boards.

The city hall featured a huge balcony. From the podium, it is said, Ceausescu made his last speech before they arrested him. We approached the light brick building up stained marble steps, and entered, unmolested by the forbidding soldiers who guarded each stairway. The anticipated grandeur was dissipated by interior walls that chopped the space into offices and dingy cubicles, all crowned by a single unlit crystal chandelier.

6. Bethlen's Palace

The museum sat back on an unkempt lawn. Across the broad avenue was an ostentatious Orthodox church, white with black trim. A short tower topped by a dome anchored one corner while a much larger, exact duplicate dominated the center. An impressive structure, but Matt, a student of church architecture, ignored it.

Pressed for an opinion, he thought it gauche, like all Byzantium structures, an exaggerated imitation of the Romanesque. "Domes suppress the spirit," he offered. "Spires lift it."

Obeying an impish impulse, I snapped a photo. "Better not let Reka see that," Matt said. (When she saw it, the photo joined the Romanian flag on my apartment floor.)

The huge wooden double doors of the museum were severely scratched - - and locked. We pounded and eventually a key grated; one door creaked halfway, befitting a spook scene in a Gothic castle. A cherubic face appeared beneath a billed cap. The museum was closed, he stated in Hungarian. This news was not all bad for Matt, who wanted to get on up the mountain to visit Father Istvàn. Perfunctorily he pleaded,

33

"But we've come all the way from Hungary." The door did not fully open again until Matt informed this curator or caretaker that we were English professors visiting from the Kossuth University in Debrecen.

We stood in a vaulted vestibule. Among a pile of junk in one corner, I noticed a discarded street sign and discerned "Erdèly," the prohibited Szèkely name for Transylvania. Matt and our host were already chummy as we walked through glass doors to the courtyard, which was totally enclosed in a quadrangle of whitewashed walls; a dark wooden balcony ran on all sides. The yard, crisscrossed with asphalt paths, was as barren as the entrance lawn. I spotted another pile of junk - - rusted plows and farm tools. We re-entered the palace and climbed a flight to the galley.

One portrait attracted me because of its incongruity, the rosy face of a young girl in bloom, fresh pink effused with light; affirmation utterly out of place. Next to this sprightly sight in dark gloom hung Gàbor Bethlen himself, builder of this dismal palace.

The painting nibbled at my brain. Scholars were gathered around a table in clerical black with white lace collars, except for Gàbor in the center robed in rich rust and gold. The only light allowed by the artist - - a Gèza Dòza - - shone off the scholarly faces. Papers were scattered on the table; Gàbor held another in his hands as if reading. A prominent figure leaned over Gàbor.

Clouds lifted. "I recognize him," I announced to the empty gallery. Matt and our host came over. "That leaning figure has to be the Jesuit Györgi Kàldy, and this painting shows Gàbor Bethlen helping him translate the Scriptures into Hungarian." I had read in detail about this Gàbor or Gabriel Bethlen. He was no mere patrician but a humanist, when the very notion was still undefined. And not only had he been the Prince of Transylvania from 1613 to 1626, but also King of Hungary!

The painting symbolized the extraordinary tolerance and devotion to liberal education of this Protestant magnifico of the Reformation. His reign was the golden age of Transylvanian art, free of prejudice and full of appreciation for all human endeavor.

Bethlen typified Transylvania's schizophrenia, whether to fight with the Hapsburg Empire against the Turks or with the Turks against the Hapsburgs. The enduring conflict was interwoven with religious struggles between the Catholic Church, its Reformation, the Orthodox Christians and the Mohammedan Turks.

In 1605, the Turks, torn by internal strife and waging a war in distant Persia, accepted as Prince of Transylvania Istvàn Bockasi who had turned against Vienna. The sultan bestowed a royal crown on his head, displacing the Catholic Bathorys who had lead Szèkelys to dazzling victories under Ottoman vassalage. But Bockasi died after a year and another Bathory reclaimed the Transylvanian crown. Enter Gàbor Bethlen.

Gàbor was the scion of a leading Protestant family of Northern Hungary, holding large estates in Transylvania . The young man was sent to the earlier Bathory court, then assisted Bocksai in attaining the crown and stayed on to support him. But Bocksai's successor, Gabriel Bathory, was another story. He was a cruel, wrathful man and Bethlen was forced to run for his life. The Turkish suzerain of the territory offered refuge, provided an army and proclaimed Bethlen Prince of Transylvania. Defeating Bathory, he was confirmed as prince by a diet of Transylvanian nobles in 1613: two years later, Mattius, King of Hungary and the Holy Roman Empire also recognized him.

Under Gàbor Bethlen, the principality of Transylvania became a marvel of religious freedom, admired throughout Europe. Caring little for spiritual matters, the Turks let well enough alone. Christian priests of various denominations functioned openly and a large Jewish community bloomed.

In 1618, while Mattius's successor, Ferdinand II, was diverted by the Bohemian revolt, Gàbor Bethlen allied himself with Protestant nations (Germans, English, Dutch, Danish), and grabbed a large chunk of northern Hungary. He accepted the title King of Hungary, but refused to wear the captured crown of Stephen; he knew the Catholic nobility would never accept a Protestant king. In 1621, for Ferdinand's guarantee of Protestant freedom to worship, Bethlen renounced his royal title and returned St. Stephen's crown.

But this prince wasn't through with Ferdinand. Not only was Bethlen undauntable, he now displayed chutzpah that would rival a New York promoter. Considering the treaty only an armistice, he secretly plotted the expulsion of Ferdinand from Hungary. In 1623, securing Turkish support and joining the German Protestant princes in their anti-

Catholic, anti-Hapsburg alliance, Bethlen entered the war against the Emperor. This time he was not successful. His allies were defeated in Germany. Unable to carry on alone, he managed to conclude a treaty which maintained Protestant freedom.

And still he was not through. Buffeted by "two pagans vying for one country," he proved himself the most brilliant of Transylvania's schizoid princes. He now turned against the Turks. Bethlen planned an Eastern alliance that would drive the Ottomans from Europe and reunite all of Hungary. To further this plan, he would marry one of Ferdinand's daughters and thus ally himself. The Emperor, "doubting his sincerity," rejected the bid. Bethlen immediately pursued Catherine, Protestant sister of the Brandenburg prince. Married, he was thus allied again with the German Protestants. Ferdinand's forces overwhelmed him in 1626, and he came to terms - - the same as those of the previous treaty.

Health fading, Bethlen retreated to Guyla-Feherevar in Transylvania where he declined an offer to ascend the Polish throne and to join the Swedish king in his continuing struggle with Ferdinand. He died in 1629, having reigned over Transylvania's most glorious generation for the arts, the humanities and the freedom of religion.

The third floor of the museum was taken up with chariots, ox carts, iron and leather tools and contraptions. There were wooden tables and chairs from the original palace, leaking upholstery and cracked wood, as well as mannequins in period costumes for harvests, fests, balls marriages, etc.

Downstairs again, Josip (familiar terms now) led us outside to a group of gates erected in a row beside the museum. They were made of polished wooden stakes about twice as high as a tall man and wide enough for several wagons at once. Their heights had been shaped into arches which were roofed by tiled trestles. I imagined gilt coaches and chariots passing through to the gaiety of the cultivated inner courts of elite manor houses.

Across a ravine, Josip pointed to a row of well-preserved white stucco bungalows with thatched roofs; peasant housing from Bethlen's time. They appeared roomy and comfortable. Our caretaker beamed with pride. I thought to ask if he regretted time's passing, but it seemed that it had not passed for him. He lived that past inside this present. It was a part of him, unlike the American past which is not a continuation for me, but distinct.

As we strolled back, I noticed a decapitated statue in another pile of junk. It leaned against the museum wall, a huge hole where the head had been torn away. One arm was bent up disjointedly like an Egyptian figure with outstretched palm. The statue had been sculpted in the gigantic style of the Soviets. I asked if it was part of the debris left in the wake of Ceausescu's execution. Yes, Josip told us. His eyes lit up. What a happy celebration it was!

"Of all the Central Europeans," I said for Matt's translation, "only Romania had to execute. Why weren't they satisfied just to overthrow Ceausescu and his wife, Elena?"

Eyes still bright, Josip shrugged and held out his hands. "Rumanians," he muttered.

As we re-entered the building, Josip was telling us of the Szèkely contribution to the revolt against the Ceausescus. They anticipated restoration of their former liberties and rights. These had been assured, he said, by the Romanian communists after World War II when they setup a Magyar autonomous region. "You know what happened . . . our hopes rose again when the Ceausescus fell, but then the tempest blew in." Incongruously, his face still wore its cherubic grin.

Passing a closed door marked "Biblioteque," Josip said he could not show it to us, and giggled. It contained the Special Roman exhibit which used to be in the central part of the museum under Ceausescu. All museums had to exhibit artifacts of the Roman past, real or manufactured. He had the key yesterday, but not today. "Will you have the key tomorrow?" I asked. No, the Biblioteque is always closed except for special visitors like those he had been expecting - - namely, Americans from the Embassy in Budapest. That is why the museum is closed.

"But they did not show up?" Matt asked.

Josip shook his head. "Istvàn the priest came." Really? Was this a joke? Would we like coffee?

Absorbed, I hadn't realized how cold it was in the castle. A cup of steaming coffee would hit the spot. We entered Josip's cubicle off the vestibule. There was room just for two stools (actually wooden chairs with backs broken off) and a plain table acting as a desk which looked out on the front lawn and Orthodox Church across the way.

I glanced about for the hot plate as Josip reached to a shelf and brought down a whiskey bottle filled with muddy liquid. Then we were each handed a cracked cup with missing ears. I was still wondering about the hot plate. Josip poured the muddy stuff directly into the cups. Drink, he directed. Matt drank. I hesitated until Josip held a fist to his mouth, and pretended to be drinking. I discovered the local coffee was less bitter when cold.

Matt asked how Josip was surviving the tempest that blew in with Ceausescu's successor, Ion Iliescu.

His face became thoughtful, circumspect. Josip shrugged. "I eat, I drink," and in English, he said, "OK." The curator-caretaker resumed his puckish grin.

7. The Citadel Overlooking Csikscereda

A bus ran up the dirt road to the village of Csabotfalva, but the sun had emerged and I wanted to walk. On the way to the dirt road, we passed a small park dominated by a huge obelisk. Sitting incongruously on top was a tiny red star. Had the officials forgotten it? Were they too impoverished to climb up and remove this totalitarian symbol? Or were they just biding time until the red star shines again? At the base were fresh funereal bouquets apparently commemorating All Soul's Day just passed. Romanian plaques were on all sides.

"Transylvania's schizophrenia rumbles on," Matt commented

"'What to make of a diminished thing?' Robert Frost"

"Answer: Patience, it'll rise again."

Only the spaced houses along the sunny dirt road distinguished it from any rural mountain path in America. But this was Transylvania, the essence and symbol of leafy strangeness and mystery. We paused for a breather at the bus stop about halfway up. Istvàn's cultural center was perched above us like a citadel over Csikszereda's meek towers. On the green slope at our side, a white steepled church counterfeited a New Hampshire postcard. The chapel, Matt said, where the hermit lives. "Want to drop in?"

I shook my head. "Does he see visitors?"

"He sees Istvàn. The villagers gave the priest a car two years ago so he could check on the hermit and fetch the sick to his hospital.

"Istvàn feeds him?

"Food prepared by the orphans. Otherwise people let him be."

An empty bus finally rumbled by, scattering dust as we reached the village plateau, dominated by St. Mary's whose miraculous healing power attracted poor and lame pilgrims from the surrounding hills. It was a grey concrete church with twin belfries. No one was about. As we entered, I felt like a trespasser eerily invading a secret sanctum.

The usual place of Jesus was occupied by a huge painted doll of the Holy Mother, crowned in gold, holding her infant god, also topped off with a gold crown. Another larger than life doll to one side depicted St. Stephen with a club, the first king, and to the other side also with club, St. Ladislus I, the only other king to be sainted in the 400-year Arpàd dynasty. Matt and I were the lone intruders in the sanctuary and I tried to imagine the commotion of sick invalids overcrowding the aisles and pews, beseeching this gigantic china doll to nurture and heal them while the sainted warrior kings swung their clubs to maintain order.

Just past St. Mary's sat the mustard-colored hospital, its red cross on a white metal panel sticking out from a corner of the second floor. Yoked oxen and empty carts rested in the lane behind. Still no people, not until we came to the children playing across the way inside a spiked iron fence. It was a narrow place with steps leading up to the orphanage, the same mustard yellow as the hospital. Several urchins were sweeping the cement walk in front, monitored by a teacher in a white frock. His face was severe and he carried a stick. Would it be too much to ask that he carry a broom instead?

The road narrowed and the gradient steepened. Matt talked about his last visit as we climbed. Istvàn had asked Matt to deliver a message to Budapest, which he had done. Istvàn had joked about the secret police, the "Keystone Kops": A parishioner was ordered to pick up a postcard from Vienna at secret police headquarters. It read "Vienna is beautiful." Keen on finding a coded message, the secret police asked,

"Why is Vienna beautiful?" The parishioner squirmed and pointed to the picture side of the card. "Look at it."

We came to wide yellow gateposts with no gate. Within, a path wound up to a whitewashed church with a steeple. It sat on the hill among trees, another scene out of puritan New England. "That's Istvàn's church," Matt said. "He just gives lip service to St. Mary's. It's showy, runs itself. This one doesn't look Catholic, probably taken over from the Calvinists."

Several unwashed young men in ragged clothes sat inside the gateposts on a collection of boxes and carts. One was throwing a knife into a tin can. They appeared deep into nefarious plotting, transplanted from a Los Angeles barrio. Our abrupt appearance startled them. I felt for my money belt. We were totally vulnerable with no one near. Matt asked if Istvàn was about. Father? The reverend? Didn't anyone extend the respect of title? There was discussion, not about us but the whereabouts of the priest. I was relieved to hear the young knife-thrower volunteer to take us to him. But I wanted to know just where before we started out.

"The orphanage," Matt interpreted.

He was a respectful young man wanting to know about our doings in Transylvania, while Matt was interested in his doings. Gèza was his name, as in King Gèza I and II. A graduate of the orphanage like the others, he was supporting himself as best he could on the streets. "Petty theft," Matt informed me in English, "purse snatching, minor burglary, but not in the village." In Hungarian, he said, "You never work in Csikscereda?" Translating, the young man's answer, Matt chuckled. "Always further away. Istvàn won't permit the operation in Csikscereda."

The children were gone from the yard, except one hustling up the stairs in oversized, unlaced shoes. A matronly woman in a white frock told us Istvàn was in a meeting and, ignoring our polite protests, took us to him. Eight staff sat about a long table, the priest in the middle in a clerical knit sweater and open shirt collar. He rose as we entered, and after an uncertain amount of awkwardness took Matt into his arms. Body and jaw were lean, cheeks handsomely chiseled; true-believer blue emanated from his deep-set eyes; a likely object for idolatry or at least romance - - or in Romania, martyrdom.

41

The meeting was recessed. Istvàn guided us to upholstered chairs side by side between lace-curtained windows on the farther wall. Pulling up a stool, he wasted little time with small talk. "So Geza brought you? Then you've been to the church up the hill? What were the boys doing?"

"Sitting about," Matt reported as if he had been a dutiful member of the crew.

"Should be clearing the yard. They're being paid."

Graduates of the orphanage were a pressing concern. He was trying to raise money from his impoverished congregations to build quarters for 25 of them. "Foreign aid provides toys and brightly covered walls for the orphans, but dos not extend to the graduates."

"Same in America," I said. "Everything for the student - - until he graduates."

"There's so much to be done," Istvàn continued, "and they don't notice. You've heard about the army maneuvers? In the fields you passed coming up here. And the helicopters? Maybe you'll see one before you leave. They hover over the church almost daily."

"What are they looking for?" I asked.

"Looking at," he corrected. "Me." He cast his eyes about.

"I thought the situation has improved," Matt offered.

"Let's take a walk."

We strolled in a field with peculiarly-shaped hay stacks, ricks with heads on them. The lowering sun kindled the houses of nearby houses.

"They've increased the police from 8 to 32," Istvàn began. "And the surveillance. Ever since we declared cultural autonomy."

"That's news," said Matt. "You mean unilaterally?"

"The Romanian Hungarian Democratic Federation," Istvàn continued, "demands right to our own language, schools, theatres, journals. . ."

I wondered if this federation was an invention of Istvàn, but Matt said he knew of it.

"That's when they expanded the vigilance," Istvàn continued, "and the murdering and raping." With a hardened face, the young priest explained that a field worker became boisterous in a tavern; a drunk policeman took him out, drove him to his home and beat him to death. The walls were splattered with blood. "We filed a complaint but were told he was no one. Their autopsy reported death by heart failure. Then a week ago, a father interrupted a drunken soldier in the act of raping his fifteen-year-old daughter. The father was thrown against a cement wall, his head cracked open. The soldier casually finished and then shot the father three times. Officially the soldier was defending himself. Nothing more was allowed to be said."

"And all you demand is cultural autonomy? Does Hungary support you?"

"Szèkely are Magyars. Once we were the mother country. Now Hungary is. It's their duty. If they do not support us, who will?"

"You view Transylvania as an extension of Hungary?"

"Historically, Hungary is the extension." Istvàn said he kept a sharp eye on Hungary's internal politics. Events in Budapest were his business as well as any Hungarian's.

Matt asked, "Are you disturbed by the Young Democrats?" They had restricted their party to those under 31. "Or is it 35?"

Istvàn laughed. "The limit rises every year."

"They were not the crowd shouting down the President," I said, referring to the recent debacle on the steps of the State Opera House in Budapest. The President, Arvad Goncz, tried to address a National Day audience commemorating the 1956 uprising against the communist regime. "Arvad had to leave the podium without giving his speech."

"Because he was pro-American," Matt explained, "and on that particular day, America was bad news."

"Almost forty years ago," I said, "Ancient history."

Istvàn shook his head and looked apologetic. "You must understand, our history is never ancient, never ages, always one piece with the present moment."

I did understand and wanted to say, "Perhaps if you were more like us, separate from your history" - - but I tended my manners.

"Americans were responsible for the uprising," Istvàn continued. "They had urged Hungarians to confront our communist leaders, promised arms, planes, all sorts of help, even tanks and troops, then stood by while the Soviet tanks rumbled in and crushed my countrymen." He allowed me a moment of repentance. I said nothing and he continued, without a trace of bitterness, "As for Arvad at the

Opera House, the Moderates are blaming the MDF (the nationalist party in power) and the MDF blames the skinheads."

Months ago, on my initial stroll down Simonyi, Debrecen's major tree-lined boulevard, I was shocked to find the pretty red benches defaced with black scrawls, "White Power Only," and "No Nigger." A Star of David surrounded by initials of the moderate party SDZ (overrun with Jews it was thought) adorned the bricks of a wall along the same avenue of this liberal Protestant town. "Seig heil" was scrawled on a gate and a number of swastikas were scattered about. Often I wondered why none had been removed in the months since my arrival. And it appeared to me that the MDF, the party in power, was not entirely blameless for the disturbance at the Opera House.

"Whoever the protesters were," said Istvàn, "they were simply reacting to a sinister side in their president. Arpàd will reveal himself in the next two years, as we shall see."

Istvàn's lean face appeared ever more finely honed as he spoke, the cheeks hollower, the eyes deeper, mouth and brows hardening to granite.

"You are determined?" I said, rather than admit to the term zealot.

"Yes, determined to reunite the Szèkelys with their people."

Matt asked if Istvàn had read the article by Istvàn Csurka, the deputy prime minister who ran the party news organ. Csurka had stridently called for a "pure Hungary" and demanded the restoration of Hungarian "living space," which included Transylvania and other territories of past empire, Ukraine, Croatia, Slovakia.

"It is the only way I can see for us."

His openness invited a response in kind. I burst out with the protest that had been accumulating in me for months. "But you can't separate 'living space' from the 'pure Hungary,'" I said. "And you know very well what Csurka means. Is there such a thing as a pure Hungarian? Who are Magyars anyway? How many tribes were combined with them? Your deputy prime minister means to exclude the Gypsies and Jews and Muslims. And the Blacks, even before you have them. Where have we heard that before?"

"The Szèkelys of Transylvania have always been known for tolerance. Our only interest is independence. So I support MDF."

44

"Even if they are nationalistic?"

"The more likely they are to intervene."

"You mean in a military way?"

"If necessary."

I offered a sympathetic close-mouthed smile, thinking, you are young, idealistic, and rash, which is dangerous for a Szèkely priest of the Catholic faith in Orthodox Romania.

"I've written another letter," he said, "to a Jerry Parker of the Catholic mission in New York who will give it to the UN, the people at the Human Rights Commission. Three men from the Embassy in Budapest were supposed to carry it for me to New York. We were to meet in the Bethlen Museum, but they failed to appear."

Glances of recognition darted between me and Matt. "Were you to meet at the Biblioteque in the museum?" I asked. Surprised, Istvàn nodded.

"We were there," Matt said. "Josip was expecting guests from Budapest."

"Their Romanian guides must have steered them away."

As we walked back through the tall grass, Istvàn talked enthusiastically about the letter. He was sure the world would respond to the plight of the Szèkelys in Transylvania, once they were aware.

"You have someone to carry it?" Matt asked, thereby committing himself.

Back on the dirt road, Istvàn detoured to show us the living quarters of his tender rogues, the graduate orphans we had encountered. They occupied a basement room in an abandoned school house. Istvàn had begged the authorities for it. The yard was an extensive untilled field, suitable for growing vegetables. Why didn't they? "Not allowed," the priest explained. "Only the basement room is theirs."

We descended a few steps to the basement door. Istvàn inserted a key but had to kick it before the door yielded. Chaos confronted us. My mind leaped for comparison to the great clay works of Stoke-on-Trent in Staffordshire, miles of dust-laden industrial hodgepodge so perfectly chaotic, Britain had declared it a national monument.

Iron-framed beds and cots fit tightly to the walls, greasy stained mattresses, quilts and pillows spilling innards were tossed so that one bed could not be distinguished from another. A hot plate glowed faintly in a corner. Had it ever been turned off? Sexy Hollywood posters of World War II vintage were glued to the walls. The bathroom was unusable. A grey crusted tub filled with old metal and wooden parts and what had once been a washing machine were corroding together with molding clothes half in, half out. More ragged clothing was strewn about with bones, relics from a rare meal consumed long ago.

Istvàn asked if we cared to see the orphanage. "Romanian orphanages have become notorious in the United States," I said.

He was aware. "With the end of Ceausescu, though, we're one to a crib."

When we reached the school building again, he turned us over to a matron wearing a lavender ski jacket over a huge bosom. She led us to the orphan quarters, down a long corridor with crayon posters between the windows. A thin balding man greeted us with an obsequious air. The children were off to assembly, but we could view the dormitories. The rooms were neat and completely filled with little iron cribs, painted white. I counted thirty crammed into one room. Apparently one child just climbed over another to reach a designated bed. But each was covered with a quilt of colorful squares. One crib was filled with stacks of fresh diapers and nighties . "No teddy bears?" I asked

The matron led us to a smaller room where shelves were lined with fuzzy animals and other toys. A Nordic-looking slip of a girl was holding a child about a year old. "I am Anna,' she announced in English, "from Stockholm." She was a student volunteer and had been there nearly six months. Anna smiled with deep satisfaction. There was affection for the Swedish volunteer in the matron's eyes. I realized people in this orphanage smiled.

"You like it here?" I said.

"Not right away, not until Liza came. She's from Denmark. Now I love it, but I cannot manage Hungarian very well. Romanian's easier but we don't try."

Matt asked, "What is it you love here?" He knew, of course; she would say the children, which she did. I perceived a spark.

Younger children ate in a long narrow room with miniature wooden tables and chairs, dark, undecorated, but not unpleasant, totally functional.

The obsequious man showed us where the older children stayed. These were smaller dormitories, less packed. About eighteen beds lined against the walls and down the middle with little study desks for each but no books. Books were too valuable; they were returned to the Biblioteque after each class. Clothes, the few each possessed, hung rigidly in shallow closets. The walls were decorated with paper streamers, posters and student drawings. The man wanted us to know that it was all army barracks "until we got rid of Ceausescu." Then the priest had cajoled the authorities to donate these buildings. The army still maneuvered in the surrounding fields, "like hornets deprived of their hives." He told us that the children were seldom spanked. They were disciplined by denying privileges.

As we re-entered the corridor, they came at us from the other end like a school of fish, running and jabbering. They grabbed our hands, our legs, matrons among them holding the youngest, apologizing for their exuberance. Matt was ecstatic.

István stood in the corridor talking to several staff from the meeting that had just broken up. They hung on his words, aging acolytes still wide-eyed.

Outside, a boy and girl were rushing to class. István patted the girl on the head as they passed. He said he hadn't quite finished the letter. His English was rough and he wanted it perfect. "I have Bible class in the town center tonight. Be there at seven. I will have it for you."

Ah, intrigue! The romance Matt implied at the outset. But the letter would certainly get waylaid passing through so many hands, or get lost in remote UN computers if ever it arrived.

People who passed on the street had to pause for hello. Some had a moment's business to discuss. An older orphan wearing an apron came by, light-skinned with neatly trimmed brown hair and intelligence etched on his narrow face. "Ion," said the priest. We shook hands and Matt engaged in Hungarian conversation that was apparently full of humor. Amid the laughing, Matt explained in English that Ion was one of István's most successful graduates. He was now the school cook and baker.

Suddenly István held out an arm; a small rundown car stopped in the dusty road. I hadn't noticed it approaching. The driver and a boy beside him greeted the priest with the same reverence everyone seemed to share. The rear door opened and Istvàn motioned for us to enter. "See you tonight," Matt called as the car began rolling.

It was five, a golden hour in Transylvania. Taken with the purplish reflections off the window panes, Matt remarked how lucky that rain had not fallen, since the air had been wet and heavy all day. The driver let us out on a wide aisled street without trees. There was time before dinner at Edit and Imrò's. We tramped through gloomy backstreets with flaking facades. A tavern sat invitingly with empty tables a few feet above street level. The sun was melting to a haze and the air was becoming chill. We heard a low buzz of Hungarian inside.

Two elderly gentlemen in withered clothes stood at a plain wooden bar. Another occupied a rickety chair beside a beer-stained table. Matt went to order at the bar while I chose a seat near the lone drinker. Several men were noising about a table in the corner, well into their beers. Some in frocks, some wore ties. The lone man at the nearby table wore filthy cotton gloves. I saw the fingers had been cut away. Both hands clutched a beer mug that was empty except for the dregs, which he dared not drink. The dregs were the ticket to his tavern seat. He looked as if someone had beaten on him, skin flushed almost blue, red eyes squeezed nearly shut, mouth sore and scratched. His grey hairs were matted solid. The pitiable wretch sat stoically, eyes unblinking.

Matt put down two glasses, a bottle of beer for himself and a liter of mineral water for me. He pointed to the table of better dressed comrades in the corner. I recognized the knit cap. Jolly Josip was in the midst of a tale, maybe about us. I shouted across the room, "OK?" His eyes sparkled.

Edit set out the salami, cheese and bread. I had been drinking too much wine for my blood sugar and refused more. She made tea. About 6:45 Matt took some of the food we'd brought and he and Imrò drove out to meet Istvàn.

Left with Edit and the kids, I was too tired to hustle my brain for symbolic gestures necessary to communicate, which did not displease her. She put the child down, turned on the TV and set about making supper. On screen a speaker of the Romanian parliament droned without pause as the smell of peppers and onions invaded the evening air. I peeked into the kitchen and spotted the pork slices. Was she really serving fresh meat? At what sacrifice? To please her English and American guests! The room was filled with the aroma and sound of sizzling pork; I was suffering anxiety pangs before they returned.

"We had to wait till István finished the Bible class," Matt said, handing me an envelope. "He wants you to go over it to make sure of the English."

Edit began bringing out the platters, honeyed potatoes, pickled beets and beans, pork cutlets. "I thought you were to carry it tomorrow. We won't have time to edit and retype."

"Imrò will take it to him and István will arrange for someone else to carry."

Overcome by appetite and annoyed by the sudden removal of romance - - our role as international messengers - - I neglected my guest manners. "Can we eat first?"

Edit giggled. She was a soft, warm creature, a natural beauty in need of a visit from the Avon lady. Her black ringlets were never quite combed and her pleasant features always prepared for makeup, in a greasy veneer like a cold cream base. In the three days we spent with her, Edit never varied from her white blouse and acrylic pants.

Looking over István's letter, I wondered whether the few telltale signs of the foreigner, such as the occasional lapse in number and lack of articles, were not more effective than a perfect document. He arranged his materials dramatically, beginning with the Catholic properties the Iliescu government had confiscated from the communists and promised to return: the churches, schools, orphanage and auxiliary buildings, but not the hospital. It was too expensive to maintain. He denounced the excess surveillance, the army maneuvers and the choppers circling overhead, and then climaxed with the rape and atrocious murders. He mentioned nothing of the declaration for cultural autonomy.

As I scratched away, Matt said, "He wants you to make it more forceful. And to write about it once you get back to America."

Imrò was skeptical. He thought the priest somewhat foolish. "The girl was raped because she was female, not because she was a Székely. And the murders were committed from brutishness, not prejudice. They happen everywhere."

Matt asked, "Romanian police are no different than other police?"

"They're all trained animals."

"But the cover up?" I protested.

Imrò took more wine, swallowed deliberately, and spurted, "Watergate."

We all laughed, even Edit understood that word.

With more wine, Imrò opened up. He thought the fuss would die. Edit said all they wanted was to be left alone by the police and soldiers, to live their lives without feeling the prejudice. Imrò said the murders had been blown out of proportion. He thought Romanian scapegoating mild compared to the Nazis. "Maybe because Romanian claims of pure descent are ambiguous."

"So were Hitler's," I said.

"Scapegoating is natural for Romanians; they need an excuse to cushion their misery. But like all people, some are extremists, some moderates. The regime takes no stand. I do not see cause for alarm. Two murders in three years?"

(One sunny afternoon, as I strolled past the Debrecen Concert Hall, there was a wild drumming in the air. I turned the corner and followed the commotion to a large open window in the basement. Looking in I was astonished to discover a huge poster on the opposite wall, a black and white Hitler in Nazi uniform. The drummer, a young man with curly hair, was so engrossed in his beat, he paid no mind to his snooper.

No big deal, my Hungarian students said. I had overreacted. They gave me none of the response I anticipated when I occasionally referred to the Nazi scourge. Only here and there did I detect a scowl of disapproval. Imrò appeared equally indifferent.)

Matt raised his glass, "To red meat." The pork cutlet on his plate had surprised him. I recalled the one pallid chicken atop the empty meat case. "Two years ago," Matt finished triumphantly, "we had only pickled cabbage and champagne."

8. Szàregy (Lazarea in Romanian)

Our train to Szàregy left at eleven the next morning, but Edit insisted we return for breakfast - - bread, sausage, more wine.

Carting our backpacks to the station - - lighter now because we had unloaded much of the sugar, coffee, and cheese - - Matt and I were oblivious to time. We strolled through the Ukraine market of parked cars, assorted wares on their hoods, extolling the generosity of Szèkelys in general and Edit's in particular.

We arrived at the station late. Then the ticket agent would not hear Matt's Hungarian request for two first class tickets. "She wants you to ask in Romanian," a bystander advised. Matt said he didn't now how, so the bystander stepped up to the window and purchased our tickets. I reached the coach door just as the train began moving. Running alongside, I threw in my backpack and grabbed the bar grips. Two amused men pulled me up. Matt had scrambled through another port.

Szàregy was only a few hours distance. We would not spend the night, having no Szèkely comrades there, but catch the evening train for the major city of Marosvasarhely where his friend Evu and her granny might put us up. Again Matt was reluctant to call ahead. The last time, Granny refused him because he hadn't written, and now he wasn't quite sure. Perhaps Granny had passed on; to Matt she looked over a hundred. In Szàregy Matt wanted me to see the statue park on the hill and visit the palace, another Gàbor Bethlen establishment. He knew nothing more about the town.

We followed the dirt road from the railroad station, past stucco houses with red tile roofs, neatly fenced with wood staves. Not an auto to be seen. Strolling toward the statue park on the hill, we encountered oxen and horses pulling carts of hay and bags of grain on pneumatic tires. One bore an exhilarated child in bright red sitting between two old men in blue workman frocks. She wielded the whip.

Climbing the hill, we came upon a school, glowing in rusty gold. The walls were scratched and peeling. In the yard, children were holding hands and dancing in a circle. "Another orphanage," said Matt. I scrambled up the embankment to the fence and leaned over it. Several children came to greet me, their hair cut squarely across their foreheads, their faces radiant. Two mentors looked up at me, then turned away. I found a roll of sugarless mints in my pocket, opened it and doled one out. In a flash, all of them were crowding the fence, stretching their hands to me. I kept doling out the treats, one to each, regretting my supply would be too quickly depleted. I showed them the empty wrapper, then threw up my hands in resignation. Accepting the situation, my new friends shrugged, giggled, and clasping hands, skipped back to resume their dancing. I rejoined Matt waiting in the dirt road.

As we climbed, the houses disappeared, white stones arose in the green fields and soon we were engrossed in a sculptured fairyland. They were spaced irregularly, some squat, some tall, some wood, mostly stone, a mountainside of wondrously whimsy cuttings, floating faces and bodies like Mark Chagall paintings, displaced arms, legs and breasts emerging outrageously from unexpected places. One statue appealed to me beyond all others. It presented a fairy tale horse or pony with two heads and a sad, sleeping maiden, a dreamer, attached where the neck should be.

All was not surreal. Diana was also there, not the classic hunter, but her descendant, the same thin limbs, slight tummy, gracious stance, one arm folded about the laurelled head, female perfection. And there were intricately carved wooden poles, some with tulip crowns.

"Szèkely cemeteries are full of them, rather than crosses," Matt said. "A tree is planted when a person is born and the pole is carved from the tree when that person dies. The tulip on the crown symbolizes a female."

The dirt road down the hill formed a huge S, ending at a wall spouting white towers and red tiled roofs. "Gàbor's palace," said Matt. We followed the S, inspecting each piece of white sculpture along the way, most of them surreal. Looking back, the sculpted hillside had the effect of a Midsummer Night's Dream in daylight.

Descending the hill, I saw the palace at the bottom was composed of discrete buildings within a wall, most in ruins but now under reconstruction. We walked around to the palace gate. The wall that contained the gate – heavy wooden doors within a red tiled arch over twice the height of Matt who stood more than six feet - - appeared like a façade on a Hollywood set. It was topped with a string of thin ornate turrets that resembled decorative shields, one after another, each with a distinctive painted design, and each topped with a miniature tower. I looked in vain for the gun ports. Matt pointed to them, scant holes in the center of the paintings, two to each turret. This dainty arrangement, I thought, truly represented the "art" of warfare.

When Matt knocked at the gate, the thud was so solid I was sure the sound had not penetrated. Examining the wall, I noticed where the plaster was chipped, exposing several thicknesses of brick. We were about to give up when a thin fellow in jeans and long leather jacket came by. "Closed," he informed us in Hungarian. "Did you want to go in?" We nodded and he left us to see what he could do.

"Who is he?" I wondered aloud as two grazing cows and their herdsmen meandered by. "And where has he gone?"

"To get the key," Matt answered my inane question. "He probably saw us trying to get in and came to help."

"Sensitive people."

Our self-appointed guide returned with a heavy iron key and an apology. We could enter the palace but not the buildings. The palace was mostly sloping grass in need of cutting. At the height of the slope was a whitewashed building which he called the gallery. It contained works that Gàbor Bethlen himself had collected. Another white washed gallery contained more recent work. It would be opened someday, when the repairs were done.

Close by, an old pile of brick rubble was being reconstituted into another structure. "For arts and crafts,' I was told, "as originally intended."

"He means 300 years ago?"

Matt translated and I was assured that Gàbor Bethlen was the people's humanist as well as the intellectual's. "Way ahead of his time." I had difficulty imagining ladies of the sixteenth century coming to this palace, kiddies in tow, to practice their needlework. For centuries, people from all parts of the principality spent weekends here with their arts and crafts. And two weeks a year the gates were thrown open for a grand arts festival.

A truncated wood tower stood in the center of the yard. The inside was filled mostly with straw, and there was a platform about halfway up. I noticed a round hole in the middle. In the ground centered below the hole was a deep pit affording just enough room for a squirming body. As I began to suspect, the structure was dedicated to discipline. "Hanging," Matt translated with a laugh. "Delicate," I said. "It hides the spectacle of black agony in the pit." Bethlen retained the sensibility of a humanist even in its horrors. I thought of our own coarse history, execution as spectator sport. Matt gave our guide a donation. Before we started for the village center, I observed his gimp leg.

As we descended the hill, we saw the grazing cows and herdsmen had moved to a field. Everything we encountered was theirs. In another part of the field, a man was sowing seed. Every now and then his head bent and his hands came to his lips in supplication. Matt thought he was praying for the seed to come up healthy. "I always took health for granted," he said.

"We all do, in childhood."

"Unless we are unfortunate."

On the village bulletin board before the post office and school, I spotted a large sheet listing the local results of the last election, won overwhelmingly by Ion Iliescu, now President. His major opponent had been Emil Constantinescu. The sheet tallied four districts:

For Jalszec: Constantinescu   965 Iliescu   2

For Kazpont: Constantinescu	779	Iliescu	4
For Alszeg: Constantinescu	847	Iliescu	3
For Guduc: Constantinescu	118	Iliescu	1
Totals: Constantinescu	2,709;	Iliescu	10

Surely a jibe at Iliescu's government, but why were they allowed to post such results, and weeks after the election? (In a replay four years later, Constantinescu was declared the winner in the close contest of 1996)

Our train for Marosvasarhely would leave at 5.00. We had about an hour and a half and the village tavern was before us, a neat Bavarian-like place. Inside, it was light and airy with wooden tables and leather-like chairs. I sat at one of the tables while Matt ordered a wine and the usual liter of mineral water for me. He passed two old men as he brought the drinks to the table. They greeted him and their brows lifted in surprise when he responded in Hungarian.

Matt said he was English; I was American. How old was I? Matt told them and again brows lifted. They could not believe such a youthful man even approached their age. They rose with much effort and joined us. Both wore curled lambskin hats. One had a brown coat over a woolen sweater and tieless shirt. His face was rough and jowled but kindly, a few days' stubble on his chin. The other had a face thinned mostly to nose and chin, clean shaven and mottled. He adorned himself with an embroidered vest and khaki leggings. He sat in a rigid military posture. Eighty years old, he told us, a veteran. "But I was a prisoner," the older man added proudly.

Of the Nazis, I assumed. Wrong. Of the Soviets? He wasn't sure. But he did know the name of his camp, Tirgu Jiu, where the Danube joins the Black Sea. It was run by the Romanian Iron Guard.

"A concentration camp?" I wanted to know.

He didn't understand. It was a POW camp. Social Democrats were detained there, and Jews and anyone suspected of helping the Allied cause. Treatment wasn't too harsh considering that Romania was formally allied with the Nazis. When the war was going well for the Nazis, his guards could be tough, but when things started going bad for the Germans and Romanians on the Russian front, they were treated more kindly. They worked on the railroad construction gang. He thought the camp was secretly run by the RCP, the Romanian Communist Party,

55

because they treated the senior communist detainee, Gheorghiu-Dej, with kid gloves. He didn't live in common barracks with the rest but had his own lodgings, and a body servant who shined his shoes and served his meals. A wide toothed grin took over the older man's face. What teeth remained were brown. He guffawed. The servant was an obedient watchdog, he said, a fellow named Nicolae Ceausescu.

Matt's astonishment showed. "The same Ceausescu? The dictator?"

The older man ordered more drinks, "To your health."

Forgetfully absorbed, I drank a wine.

His own health, he said, was not good. Suffered gasping spells, and knew that he needed an inhalator.

"None in Szàregy?" asked Matt. The old man shook his head. "Then let me have your address. I'll send it from Hungary." Matt took out a pencil and notepad. "Asthma?" he asked and the man nodded.

"I suffer dizzy spells," put in the younger one, "High blood pressure. No medicine."

"I'll send some," offered my generous companion. He wrote down the addresses. "What medicine do you take?"

"Valium."

Dutifully, Matt wrote it down. Then I wanted a photo of these antique men in their curled lambskin hats. They insisted the picture include us all and called over the waitress. Before she could snap it, both men removed their hats and smoothed their hair.

The older man would not allow us to pay. I insisted. The old man's young blue eyes were staring. They narrowed and grew piercing; my words were reduced to mumbles. His insistence was beyond honor. I sat again while he laid out the lei. Then he laughed huskily and asked if we were going to visit the priculici.

"What?" I asked.

"Vampires," Matt answered, "fairies, werewolves. Country folks believe in the evil spirits, the stafi."

Were we looking for Count Dracul, as all English did?

"Everybody is sick of Dracula," said Matt. "Even vampires. At Brasso we were within 20 kilometers of his castle and didn't bother to visit."

The older man was disappointed. He asked if we would stop at Segèsvar to see the place where Dracul was born.

Matt's translation began losing its sharpness, its confidence. It seemed to reflect the old man's sudden loss of power. His insistence on paying, the honorable thing, had drained my colleague.

I could not believe the man had uttered what Matt next translated, that Count Dracul had existed ever since the human separated himself from nature, even before 'we' Romans sacrificed enjoyment of the simple life for banal commerce, military conquest and political declamation. "Yet it is him," Matt's translation went on, "him we call evil, the immortal Dracul who mimics all of our foul complexity, our successful civilization, by drinking blood to sustain himself."

9. Marosvasarhely (Tirgu Mures in Romanian)

We traveled most of the way in blackness, except for the glimmer of a rare bulb in the night fog. Clouds shut out the moon and stars.

Evu's apartment was a long walk from the station; Matt was confident, brushing off my doubts that he knew the way in the dark. It was raining as we hoisted our backpacks and started through the city center remade of Stalin block, massive concrete structures testifying to Ceausescu's empire building dreams. We passed the darkened plaza, glimpsing some shadowy statuary and the new town hall. A many-storied hotel provided light. People went by in no particular hurry, some protected with umbrellas, raincoats or plastic sheets. We turned down a business street where the light was provided by the traffic, mostly of overstuffed buses.

"Just pray Evu's home."

"You've written this time?"

"Sent a card last Christmas." We were walking briskly in the light rain, eager to meet our fate. "Of course Granny's always there. The apartment's five stories up. Last floor. She never leaves."

We came to a walkway that gracefully curved through grass and bushes. It led to Evu's apartment house. I was exhausted by the time we reached the fifth floor. Matt conjured up courage and knocked, while I leaned against the top floor banister, catching my breath. At last we heard the lock unlatching, a chain unhooked, the door squeaking open. I was standing behind Matt and could see no one. He bent over and began talking Hungarian.

Looking over his shoulder and down, I saw a thin hand, veined and wrinkled, clinging to the doorknob. Beside it, on the same level was the top of a very old witch's head covered with a shawl. Scarce grey hairs stuck out like wires. When I glimpsed her face, I found it mostly chin, her toothless mouth having caved in.

Granny and Matt had a lengthy discussion, the dwarfed old lady still clinging to the doorknob. Finally the door opened wider. We were allowed to enter, only until Evu came home. A patterned apron was thrown over Granny's rags. Legs bowed and back humped parallel to the floor, she led us into the living room-library, a spacious chamber lined with shelves of books, LP records, magazines and professional journals, some in English. Books were everywhere - - stacked in corners, on tables, the floor.

The sofa bed and upholstered easy chairs looked comfortable. Photographs were among the books on a reception table topped with lace. Matt said he and Kauty had spent many hours reading in that room. It was a favored place in his travels.

Books in Hungarian ranged from Shakespeare to Sartre. Runs of English-language authors - - Robert Louis Stevenson, Thomas Hardy, Katherine Mansfield, Edgar Allan Poe, Emerson, Thoreau, Hawthorne, Charles Dickens, the Brontes, T.S.Eliot, Oscar Wilde, Emily Dickinson, the Brownings - - lined up in no particular order. There were also hefty volumes of history - - Austrian, German, Hungarian, Transylvanian, Romanian, English. Standing out between bookends on a carved table were three volumes of Proust - - Swann's Way, Cities of the Plain, and The Sweet Cheat Gone. Another wall contained a legal library in Hungarian.

Matt said most of these books belonged to Evu's father who now lived on the mountain with his second wife. He had been a librarian for the town and then for the whole area. Evu added to the collection as she could.

Using the evidence around me, I was speculating about Evu when I heard the door. Turning, I saw a perky freshness had entered, a spot of sunshine in the Romanian gloom; bright green eyes shining out of a pearly face. Her brown hair bobbed and fell stylishly on the hood of her wet blue raincoat. She stopped to kiss Granny, then, alight with surprise, bounded in to us.

Exhilaration took hold of me and I realized my spirits had been deflated by the bleakness of the country. I could have been in New York uplifted by the appearance of Mary Tyler Moore, but her face was rounder, cheeks fuller, rosier. She radiated an aura of even greater exuberance. When Matt promised that Transylvania would stimulate my creative juices, he must have meant Evu.

'I kiss your hand' is an honorable Romanian greeting, and I most reverently wished to as her eyes, very large and green, took me in. Her English was near perfect; she taught it at the high school. Sixty-nine and sexually flat, I was nevertheless in a stupor of enchantment as we paced through the phrases of introduction. Then, without removing her coat, she wanted to go out again, for bread, meat and wine. We'd have a dinner celebration.

Grateful that Granny allowed us to stay; I insisted we go to a restaurant. "The best in town, Evu."

Matt asked Granny, would she like that?

"She certainly would," Evu answered, "if she could negotiate the stairs. She hasn't left this apartment in three years. But don't fret over Granny." Evu opened a kitchen cupboard and pulled out a banana and the heel of a loaf of bread. In the pint-sized refrigerator, she located some leftover potatoes and what looked like greased green beans. "There's plenty to eat. Let's go."

The rain had stopped and people were clustering in the streets again. Near the bus stop gypsies were selling onion and garlic strings, red spikes of pepper, wooden yokes, urns and troughs they had whittled, metal pounded into pots, jugs, pitchers. Some were eating under a tree amid the shouting of wares, banging tambourines and shrilling reeds.

The bus carried us back over the route we had just walked from the town center. I noted the huge cement planters in the plaza were brimming with mums as Evu led us across to the multi-storied hotel.

More gypsies met us at the entrance. They besieged us, beggars everywhere, women in tattered rainbow skirts and blouses suckling infants, men with hungry eyes, heavy black beards, hair matted to their shoulders.

Within the brass and glass doors, the intended gleam of crystal and metal was just a touch tarnished, the brilliance a bit yellowed. We sat at a table beside a huge well that opened onto the dining floor below, exposing a few bejeweled patrons. In the middle of the well an enormous chandelier cast weak light through its crystals, insufficient to burn off the adorning cobwebs.

I helped Evu take off her coat and held the chair for her. Matt was overly impressed. Self-consciously he announced, "Daniel is a gentleman."

Evu had no guises. The hotel was a rare treat and she said so. "I wish to take advantage."

"I will be disappointed if you don't."

Matt reflected his own discomfort; he had sat before Evu did. He is 28 years old, I told myself. He had embarrassed me before, in Debrecen drinking with a clique of British cronies when he suddenly blurted that I was a monarchist. He based this leap to judgment, he said later, on my irreverent remark some time before that the American Revolution was perhaps unnecessary.

A wine list was brought and Matt mumbled. Evu giggled. The menu was French and Romanian. With innocent nonchalance, her translation rescued us. We all had liver pâté for appetizers. Matt followed with duck, Evu with steak and onions, saying she couldn't resist the rarity of beef, and I opted for lamb kabob.

As she lifted her fork, I noticed her hand and arm were withered. For a moment I lost track of the conversation, something about the travails of teaching Romanian and Székely kids in the same classroom. I tried to peek at her hand, and was observing that it was narrowed into three digits and thumb when she caught me.

"No bother, that way from birth. My shoulder is something else."

I looked directly and noted that the withered arm was attached to a shoulder that sloped. Actually there was no shoulder.

"My arm keeps falling out of the socket."

"You've seen experts?"

"I've had three operations. My last operation was in Budapest."

I fumbled for something to say, something cavalier, and came up with, "The imperfection of a de Milo." Matt's cackling was so sudden he spewed bits of chewed duck over himself.

She taught English language and literature to the fourth level at the secondary school. Her Hungarian class had been abolished two years before.

"Does that matter? You are teaching in English."

"Literature. To explain things in the abstract you need to compare, you need the native literature and language. For many of my students that's not Romanian."

"Your texts are in English, of course?"

"What we can get. Students tend to the American naturalists. They go for Studs Lonigan and anything by Dreiser or Jack London.

"How do they get the books?"

"Beg, borrow, and steal. Friends in Budapest send some. Often I bring them from home. I don't like Budapest anymore." She looked about; the tables around us were empty. Voice lowered (a melodious contra-alto), she continued, "Everyone's so political in Budapest, so eager to sympathize, so overbearing. 'Oh you noble Szèkelys,'" she mimicked, "'holding Transylvania for us till we - -'" She laughed at her mockery. "'For you?' I was shocked. 'For us! Transylvania is our home, it is not Hungary. We are not Hungarians. We are Szèkelys.'"

"You are under Dènis' influence," Matt told her.

I asked, "Who?"

"Dènis Fulop, the Calvinist minister who runs two English language schools. He's fabulous."

"You must visit him before you go," Evu said. "The churches are putting a lot into English teaching. Baptists especially." She launched into the offenses of one James McFarland, missionary of the American Baptists, assigned to her grade level at the Bolyai Lìceum. "A parody of the whole order. Righteously automated to say the appropriate things at

63

the appropriate time. Aims all conversation at doctrine. He's from Oklahoma City."

"I'm from Oklahoma. Tulsa, home of Oral Roberts."

"Bible belt," said Matt, "America's all bible belt."

"McFarland is overbearing," Evu continued. "Always perfect, absolutely certain, correct, and forbidding. Jesus loves, but God punishes."

"What does Denis make of him?" Matt asked.

"That he'd come to give himself and his wondrous religion to the Romanian young."

"And the Székely young?"

"McFarland is blind to any distinction. Focused only on his mission. He's determined to save us all." Evu smiled broadly, her teeth glowing in the soft light. "I've swapped classes with him for tomorrow morning. Would you like to teach it instead? They'd get a kick out of you."

"Both of us?"

"Why not? It's conversational English. Tell them about secondary school kids in America and England. They'll be so excited; you'll spend most of the time answering questions. They never ask McFarland questions."

We talked late into the night in Evu's bedroom, about literature and then our lives. Evu said she was not particularly enamored of Americans but she did relish the literature, by which she meant the classics from Cooper through Faulkner, "except for Melville." He was too "lopsided," too much the "he-man". Most current material confused or annoyed her. "This deconstruction leads to fragmented despair. Characters don't act like people." She was particularly upset with Thomas Pynchon, who didn't even try to establish characters. "He's a hot topic in Budapest. But can you tell me why he's so complicated?"

"Which book?"

"I tried to read <u>Gravity's Rainbow</u>. A friend in Budapest gave me the paperback. After his entire convolution, it comes down to a puzzle, not much more than Edgar Allan Poe or Conan Doyle in modern dress, but loaded with paranoia, the human victim of the system's disintegration. Not anything I want to read. There should be some emotional appeal in the illusions of fiction, and some aesthetic pleasure. Poe at least understood that. This is all treacherous, ugly and violent."

"Pynchon writes about system replacing love, and the waste that's left the ugly shards of our lives. Entropy and paranoia, as you say. Very fashionable."

"Why?"

"I guess it's his vision of the actual, of what is."

"Of course, but what's the point? And why is it of value to me?"

"Because your literary friends in Budapest say it is."

Again the teeth glowed in her broad, ironic smile. Granny struggled in to say goodnight. She had been watching TV in her room. Granny called herself a witch and knew she looked like one. It didn't matter, not anymore, she was waiting to die. "Already, I feel the worms creeping." Granny's chuckle split her face apart. "Can't they wait?" Evu stood and bent over to kiss the top of her head, apparently a ritual. She hobbled to the doorway.

"How old?" Matt asked Evu. Granny paused.

"You must ask her."

Painstakingly Granny turned her body to face him.

"How old?" he asked her.

She grinned, her lower jaw devouring her upper, but devils danced in her eyes. "Twenty-one."

When Granny had gone, Matt asked about her son, Evu's father. "He lives with his Romanian spouse in a fancy house on the mountain above the town. I only see him when he comes here, which is rare."

"And your stepmother?" I asked.

"Never. She's an icebox. They are thoroughly Romanian. Forget them. Matt says you write sensible criticism."

"The authorities don't remind him that he's Székely?"

"Nothing like that, not a matter of genes, but culture. The authorities just want everyone to be Romanian. My father goes along with them . . .Tell me about the books you've written."

"About ancient American authors," I said.

"But how ancient can an American writer be?"

And so we gabbed away the night on books, schools, politics, the American election being held at that very moment. "My friends like Bush," Evu said, "but what difference does it make to us? Bush or

65

Clinton, the Romanians will still act like <u>Ru</u>-manians." We ended by singing the praises of humanism, my lapsed Unitarianism, Evu's lapsed Calvinism, and Matt's lapsed Anglicanism, all feeling very much at home in Evu's bedroom.

Evu showed us the guestroom which was also the dining room. One of us or both could sleep there. It had several chairs with upholstered seats and an oak table with a lace cloth. A huge carved wardrobe occupied one wall. In a corner a box spring and mattress were cloaked in an embroidered spread with matching pillows. Family photos in wooden frames and a variety of trinkets adorned a mirrored dressing table and chest. Matt deferred to age and spread his sleeping bag on the living room floor, having suffered from the lumps of the sofa bed two years ago.

"I can see you're taken with Evu," he said, before leaving me. "I know she's impressed with you."

10 The Reverend McFarland

Defying the morning drizzle, we traipsed off to the Bolyai Liceum to share Evu's class with the notorious American Baptist preacher. McFarland was seated among his colleagues at a long table used as a mutual desk in the staff room. No one had to point him out.

The Baptist cleric was characteristically long and thin, with the thrusting ministerial chin. He was dressed in plaid sweater, checkered tie, and tweed jacket. When he stood to introduce himself, I noticed the shine of his black shoes. Steely blue eyes glinted behind metal frame glasses. He introduced himself as a "volunteer teacher."

McFarland informed us in a slow mannered monologue that he was not a pastor, having neither pastorate nor congregation; he was a preacher, though he didn't preach, not exactly. "I have the manner of a preacher, in that traditional mold." Walking to the classroom, he confided, "They are not bad boys and girls. Obedient, but they have a poor attitude."

The preacher had no curiosity, no interest in us. He was not a listener. "Class attendance is atrocious. They are irresponsible and

67

careless. Sometimes they come and then decide to leave if a particular chum is not there." Neither of us responded; he continued, "I try to impress upon them that the Christian week begins on Sunday and class begins on Monday." Then he confided, "I want them also to be informed about their bodies. As I say, they are good boys and girls, but they must know about the AIDS epidemic emanating from the Black Sea port of Castanta . . . I pray we have a decent showing for you."

We were talking at the door in front of the classroom; two students had trickled in, cast inquiring glances and, without greeting, took seats. Guiltily, I bent my head to acknowledge the next to appear, a rather busty girl in tight, torn jeans and a black tanktop. Her pale face was burdened with too much lipstick and mascara. She swished by us with self-conscious sensuality. Abruptly, McFarland looked away.

At fifteen minutes after the hour, he said we had waited long enough. "You see what I mean? No discipline. Evu has eighteen pupils and only three are present." He asked us to introduce ourselves by writing our names on the blackboard. Then McFarland began taking the roll, requiring those present to answer with their given name. Four more students trooped in, apparently hearing that an American and Englishman were class visitors. Disdain oozed from the preacher as he lectured on the evils of non-attendance to those obviously present.

The hour was a quarter spent with his beating about when he asked what they were prepared to discuss. I felt embarrassment for this dictatorial hog who had taken the classroom for his pulpit but had no sermon.

He was rolling in vituperative nonsense, actually trying to find a topic. I felt obligated to get something going and raised my hand. "May I ask a question?" I desired to know whether these students followed the American election; maybe they even knew how it turned out.

"Go on," McFarland said.

Without any reference or identification, I asked bluntly, "Who won?"

The responses were like cheers, "Clinton." "Clinton." "It was on TV."

Apparently news to McFarland; gloom engulfed his hawkish face. He asked the student who mentioned the TV, a dark, mature looking fellow in jeans and tee shirt, "Did you wish Clinton to win? Or Bush?"

The student had no time to answer; McFarland jumped in and took control. "The debt will soar, the economy will plummet, the country will suffer - -"

"You mean the wealthy," Matt interrupted. "They may get higher taxes, but suffer?" He guffawed.

McFarland realized his position and tried to turn our display into a lesson on democracy, but Pollyanna and national drum- beating fogged his vision. "You see we disagree. But we are Americans . . .and Englishmen. We can hold differing views without striking each other." I cringed. Was this textbook Baptist their only model of an American?

One of the students said she wanted Clinton to win, and I sensed the others agreed. McFarland, attempting fairness, asked "Why?"

"He gives us hope that change is possible."

McFarland struck quickly, "Change indeed, but not what we want, a ruinous public health policy, taxes, troops to Somalia and Bosnia, if he can get away with it. What interest does America have in Bosnia?"

"No oil there," Matt said.

"Precisely. America has no interest there. Nor in Somalia. Of what value would a national health service be to famished Somalians?"

I didn't get the connection but I was upset by the demolition job McFarland was doing on America, to the point of bopping him in front of the students; I was also disturbed by Matt's smarting off.

Looking at me, McFarland said, "I see your young colleague's a liberal?"

"Worse," Matt offered. "I'm a socialist."

McFarland fell right in. Indignantly, he said, "Perhaps a communist!"

The class roared.

McFarland continued defensively, "That's what they'd call him in Oklahoma City."

Now our presence was making him uneasy. After a few incoherent moments, he happened upon a topic. He was annoyed by the jeans two of the three girls wore. The third was dressed primly in a skirt, blouse and jacket. Her brown hair was cut to flow neatly about her ivory bright face. "You can see Miss - - " he looked over the roll " - - Miss Carzkèc, is it? She's properly prepared for class. Her dress makes her even prettier than she is." The girl's head tilted toward the floor. "Just the opposite of this one," he said pointing to the enticing figure in the tanktop. Miss Carzkèc said that she had to dress for work after class. Her face reddened. "You see," he was talking directly to us, "she doesn't wear those filthy overalls or dungarees or whatever they are, and she takes responsibility." Then he asked, "Where do you work?" She mumbled inaudibly. I may have heard the word 'bank.' The girls in the jeans were also looking at the floor as if their embarrassment were otherwise unbearable.

McFarland's supply of moral nonsense dribbled out and he dismissed the class early. Walking back to the faculty office, he told us that he was actually retired, and took strength from his volunteer field work at the Bolyai Lìceum, reinforcing Christ's message in Romanian youth. He was indifferent to the ethnic differences in Transylvania - - it was all Romania to him. That was the official view; that was his view. He came every fall for a few months, then returned not to Oklahoma but South Carolina, where he was born and where he had retired. His wife lived there all year. She didn't care for Romania. "Evelyn wants a more normal existence. But this is my life's work. And it's a good deal, a few months a year salving my soul in Romania."

"No doubt financed by somebody somewhere," said Matt.

McFarland squeezed out a laugh. "I even have a ministry of sorts among the Romanian Baptists. I intend to continue indefinitely." Talking about the ease and pleasure of his current arrangement, McFarland's voice became more natural and sincere, childlike, almost pleasant.

It was raining again as we crossed the barren yard between the buildings to the coffee stand. Students milled about, snacking from small paper packages and drinking tea. I recognized two young men and the busty miss from Evu's class. Her meek smile contradicted the siren body language. She followed the young men in shaking our hands. They apologized for Mr. McFarland. He had embarrassed them. He didn't understand that most of the class are Szèkelys when he made insulting remarks. "He is not aware," said the overdone young lady. I asked if they preferred their regular teacher. They nodded almost in unison. "Not because she's Szèkely," the young woman said.

"Because she's real?" I asked. Again nods all around.

"She's neat," offered one young man. "Went wild when Michael Jackson came to Bucharest." I mentioned the signs we had seen, even on the Black church in Brasso.

11. Gypsies

We found a restaurant set up in a downtown store with a dirty window front. It was like a cafeteria except that only two or three dishes were offered, plus salami. It was a crude, unfinished place. Large red and yellow signs painted high on the wall illustrated sausage, salami, hamburgers, cokes and French fries. A woman with straggly grey hair interrupted her sweeping to take our orders. Matt spotted a pot of simmering soup and asked for a cup, plus a hamburger. None. He could have sausage. I ordered the same.

Another woman with a veil lifted above her mouth sat with an unshaven man eating silently at one of the plain wooden tables. Behind a barrier, the lackadaisical cook got up and shuffled to the grill to fix our lunch. We joined their silence, waiting till the grey-haired woman called us to the counter to claim our food and collect our lei.

The rain had stopped and the wet streets were crowded. Matt spotted a Hungarian newspaper as we passed a busy kiosk. It was published in Budapest, he said, then pointed to a fascist sheet that came from Koloszvar and several Romanian party papers. At the corner we encountered Romulus and Remus suckling the wolf. This one was mounted on a tall pole like the Roman original. It was recently sculpted, or recently painted. Below it oxcarts passed among the trucks and buses, carrying sacks of grain from countryside mills, the waggoners shouting directions to their oxen. "Strana," they shouted.

"Means 'right' in Hungarian." Matt said. "Szèkelys from the villages."

A woman dressed like a gypsy in a skirt striped with brilliant colors heard us and put out her hand. As Matt filled it with lei, I wondered how they manage to retain the bright colors when all the other parts of her were so dusty. Her face crunched together. She looked like a witch, like Granny. Her dirty bare feet stood in the film of rainwater on the sidewalk. I stared and she began reciting metrical spells through gums which held one dark tooth: "Woe to anyone," she warned in Hungarian, "man or beast, who drinks rainwater from the wolf's footprint."

Translating, Matt suddenly cackled. "She's making it up, all she can offer in payment. She uses the wolf's paw print because we're at the statue. The folk myth really calls for something larger, a bear's paw print. Her spirit's still in the forest, hiding from werewolves who lurk everywhere." Pitching his voice to mimic an incantation, he continued, "At dusk, when the moon is right, the wolves change shapes for the night."

The crowd swallowed the witch and we strolled on to the Palace of Culture, passing several uniforms bearing the ubiquitous machine guns. The Palace was on 'high' street as Matt called every town's major thoroughfare. To get there we had to pass through the market near the plaza, a sea of wooden booths with canvas canopies. Merchandise overflowed onto side streets. Amid acrid odors of vinegar, garlic, charcoal, and dill, the merchant haggling merged into a devilish chorus.

Away from the few food stalls, mostly cabbage, pickled and fresh, we entered a world of cutlery; knives, sickles, scythes. These gave way to sheep bells, brass and iron. Then the holy tables; many plaster angels and tinsel-framed icons for the Orthodox, a few bundles of rosary beads for the Catholics. Down one row, we swam in leather, cotton and woolens; purses, studded belts, jackets conical fleece hats, blouses, coats, sweaters. Down another aisle, carpets. And yet another, carved

74

wood, instruments, strings and flutes, tobacco pipes, copper and brass pots, clay plates, statuary.

There were tables of lace and inordinate space was given to floral glories. Flowers when they are so poor? In Hungary as well, where the flower kiosk is all that's open on Sundays. Must be a necessity, I concluded. Women hawkers in print sashes and padded feet dawdled at the tobacco counters, where I learned the name for Turkish water pipes - - <u>nargileys</u>.

We came out on the "high" street and I was at once stunned by utterly corrupt beauty, the sight of a gypsy Madonna and babe. The mother was a dark and sooty teen with a full-cheeked face of unadorned but soiled simplicity, set in determination. She couldn't have been more than fourteen. Her black dress was grayed by ingrained dust. The dress clung to the nubile curves of her breasts and thin waist, drawn in tight. She bore a huge sack on her back and an unblemished blonde baby in the crook of an arm.

Perhaps it was the lightness of the baby's skin or the blonde hair that arrested us as she lowered the tot onto the filthy sidewalk, where it became absorbed with the detritus of cardboard, paper and glass. It was a pretty, golden creature, obviously fathered by a western European or American, a girl we observed when she fell back, kicking up her legs and exposing her unprotected genitalia, which appeared extraordinarily large and raw. She plumped down again, her naked bottom on the bare, filth-laden sidewalk. The mother meanwhile had put down her huge sack and was pulling out clothes, stuffing them into two more manageable packs. They must have contained everything she owned on earth.

Finishing, she nonchalantly hoisted the packs, picked up the baby, then continued down the street, maybe walking to the end of town where the gypsies made their camp. But a bus passed and immediately she broke into a run. Clutching a pole of the moving vehicle, my beauty swung her huge burden and baby aboard. Never have I observed anyone so alone, so burdened, so vulnerable, as that juvenile cavewoman brazenly confronting a bus with child and belongings.

We heard a strain of music, wooden instruments in a swirling tempo, and followed it. Suddenly we encountered great circular wreathes of long skirted and ornamented dancers, a kaleidoscope of color - - a gypsy wedding. They danced, hands upon shoulders, stopping, stomping, stepping again, raising dust in endless gyrations. The groom danced with the wedding nymphs who feigned abduction with staccato cries. Then the bride was taken from a window and hoisted aloft amid shouts of acclaim and display of a stained sheet, a maiden no more.

Instead of rousing my spirits from the dismal scene I'd just witnessed of the nubile matron and blonde babe, this wedding depressed them. I recalled years back in Madrid, when a British Counsel named Walter Starkie had taken me to a Gypsy fest. He had written a book on Gypsies and was accepted like an honorary chief. My enjoyment was marred by the same thought it was now. Gypsies are for color, for entertainment. They have no existence beyond the show, except to serve. Later, in Macedonia, I did have a Gypsy servant. Whatever my domestic need, I called the Gypsy, as the old Southern gent called the Black, or as the medieval Szèkely might have called the Vlatch.

12 Palace of Culture

The most ornate building in the town center was labeled with large letters, PALATUL CULTUR II, the Romanian name for the Palace of Culture.

"Hungarian built," Matt informed me.

The second floor was trimmed with huge bay windows sitting atop bronze panels that illustrated select moments of the past, actually the Magyar past, as it turned out, in spite of the Romanian name. Above were smaller Romanesque windows and a long painted panel in the center, depicting what appeared a coronation, or perhaps just a royal wedding. The whole effused a gaudy kind of grandeur. A relaxing feature was the roof of checkered tiles, black and white. On the street in front was a giant bronze soldier, done in the heroic style, machine gun at the ready. On the wall behind, sculpted reliefs of Hungary's literary luminaries stared out in stony silence. Matt identified Arany Jànos, Vorosmarty, Csòkonai.

Inside, the grandeur darkened, in spite of the gilt mirrors at either end of a long exhibition corridor running the palace length. The exhibit

77

in this corridor consisted of stained glass images inserted across the bay windows. As we entered, Matt pointed to a wall plaque. It commemorated Marosvasarhely's beloved Hungarian mayor of 1915, Dr. Bersènyi, also the town pharmacist. "I'm surprised they haven't removed it," Matt said, "You'll see his shop's cupboard in Denis' study."

We were the only guests in the hall. An arched ceiling of plaster and wooden beams failed the attempt at loftiness. But it may have been responsible for the sudden emptiness that overcame me, a feeling that all was still, that I was out of time. I heard nothing but the ticking of the clock. It assured me that time still passed.

A profound bass voice that might have been haunting had it not been garbled on the English tape, directed us to the far end for a recorded tour. We strolled on a faded oriental rug to reach the beginning, past the Hungarian legends stained in the windows. A smiling sun Mandela woven into the center of the rug added feeble cheer.

Because the sky was overcast, the light through the colors in the glass was dark and shadowy, befitting the tale. I took my time before each window, forcing the scene to fire my imagination. I was soon envisioning the legends and history I barely grasped: The separation of the Magyars from the Turkic hordes roaming Southeastern Europe, the Khazars, Huns, Avars; the vicious Pechenegs chasing them into the Carpathians, some pressing on to besiege the Romans and drive them out of their forts and settlements in Pannonia on the Danube, then barbarizing the land that is now Western Hungary.

Magyars quickly gained a reputation for ruthlessness, and were feared wherever they appeared. They were also attractive warriors, tall handsome, great horsemen, affluent, in fact conspicuously rich. Their clothes were brocaded and their weapons encased in silver, inlaid with pearls. Jewels of precious metals adorned their necks, wrists, and fingers. The ornaments worn by their horses were even more ostentatious. One panel showed a Magyar burial where the hide of the horse, still containing the head and hoofs, was placed beside the slain warrior in the grave. The meat was eaten at the funeral feast.

A saber of exquisite craftsmanship appeared in another window panel; I imagined it was "Attila's sword," appropriate for the Hun. Today many think the name Hungary derives from Attila's cruel horsemen; actually it derives from "on-ogur," an ancient Turkish word meaning "ten tribes," though it was seven tribes that Arpàd, the great Magyar leader, unified when he opened the veins in the arms of his seven chieftains and let the blood spurt into a common vessel.

Inhabitants trembled in fear as Arpàd reached the Verecke pass through the Carpathians, but according to legend, it was deception that conquered. Arpàd sent a beautiful white stallion to the prince of the domain, asking in return for samples of soil, water, and grass. Finding the soil black and sandy, the water sweet, and the grass abundant, Arpàd declared that by offering the gifts, the prince had ceded the land.

One window seemed to be illustrating Magyar origins. A glass bird with white prickly plumage and black crow's eyes brought to mind the great golden bird on Castle Hill overlooking the Danube in Budapest. It sits atop a huge column with wings spread to protect the nation. Neither hawk nor eagle, it is a turul which impregnated some ancestral mother (a la Leda and the Swan) who gave birth to the first Magyar. To this day in Mongolia such birds are inviolable.

Another myth suggests Persian and Turkish origin. The stained glass shows two young princes in a violent struggle. In the myth, one prince is Hunan (for Hun) and the other is Magor (for Magyar). According to the myth, they have been on the hunt for grazing land and come upon the two beautiful women tending cattle, as shown in the glass. The myth tells us their men are away at war. So Hunan and Magor stop their violent struggle, rustle the cattle and make off with the women. This is the marauding version while the first is the bird of prey version.

The most recent version was formulated in 1768 by two Hungarian linguists while studying the Lapp language. Discovering similarities with their own tongue, they placed Hungarians with the Finno-Ugrian family of mankind which includes Finns and Estonians. It was an embarrassing discovery. At the time, bronze turuls were perched atop state buildings and bridges all over Buda and Pest.

As the afternoon wore on, the light through the stained glass grew even feebler; red, green, yellow, never bright, now melded into shades of grey and brown, and I realized that for some time I had been reading my own thoughts into the panels.

79

Walking back to Evu's, I enjoyed the cleared sky and drank in the refreshed air - - not cleansed as after a country downpour, merely renewed as if it were ancient metal just burnished.

13. Walk Along the Maros

Granny insisted on making dinner, and Evu had gone shopping for it while we were at the school. We ate in the kitchen, a galley less than ten feet wide. A waist high refrigerator, and iron woodstove refitted for gas and an old sink filled most of it. The small dining table was pushed against a wall at the far end. We could look out of a window they had decked with plants and seedlings to a waste of back porches filled with mops, brooms, buckets and such. These utensils also stuffed most WC's (in Hungary as well) whether people had porches or not.

The table had room for only three. Evu told me I had the honor seat her father usually took on his rare appearances. Matt sat at the other end, Evu in the middle opposite the window. She had purchased a Romanian red wine which tasted sweet. I put the glass down after one sip. Again guilt rose in me as Granny placed a platter of bread before us, cut from the gigantic loaf Evu had just bought. Next, she set down the customary slices of salami and cheese, then the main event: pork cutlets with sliced potatoes and beans. Granny sat on a little stool hunched over her plate (cabbage replacing the pork) on a low shelf beside the stove.

The brightness had drained from Evu's face. "I stopped by the Liceum," she said. "You made a bad impression on McFarland. He said your performance was disgraceful, Matt. He didn't like you at all."

"He was the only one that performed," said Matt. "Really boiled over Clinton's election. He gave your students his anti-public health view and managed to associate it with aid for the Somalian famine. Then he defended Bush's non-intervention in Bosnia with the fact that there's no oil there."

Evu smiled and sighed. "I told you he was goofy." Satisfied the preacher had confirmed her judgment, she asked, "What did you do this afternoon?" And in the midst of my Palace impressions, she suggested we walk along the Maros.

It was the great river of Transylvania, although I had not heard of it, not even under the Romanian rubric, Mures. Its tributaries vein the western slope of the Carpathians, rushing downhill through steep wooded canyons, gathering in a major artery that flows southwest through mountain meadows, finally reaching the Hungarian great plain, the Alfold, to join the Tiza which dips deep into Serbia and loses itself in the Danube.

A moon just beginning to wane laid a metal gleam on the water and a line of silver wire along the poplar spears on the hills. The constellations showed vaguely in the faint purple still fading in the early November sky, now emptied of its vapor.

We were quiet until Evu broke the silence. "This is the moment I love most," she said, "when time fades and the Maros opens up." She pretended to listen for the river's faint purl. "It's telling stories."

Were they the stories I had read in Hungarian history, of the Magyars returning to this valley where they reunited with Hungarian-speaking kinsmen who had settled on the Maros in the ninth century? We remained quiet as time disintegrated . . .

From the banks of the Maros rose a renowned general of 15th Century Europe, Janos Hunyadi, said to be son of the Magyarized Vlach, Vajk, but also rumored a natural son of Sigismund of Luxemburg, later the Holy Roman Emperor.

In spite of his uncertain and unpromising birth, Hunyadi became the most celebrated hero in Magyar history, the champion of all Christendom. He supported the Polish king, Wladslaw III, against the partisans of the Austrian Làzlò V, and when Wladslaw was crowned King of Hungary (Ulàszlo I), Hunyadi was made viovode (governor) of Transylvania. Fighting like resurgent crusaders, his army broke the power of the ever-invading Sultan in Herzegovina, Bosnia, Serbia, Bulgaria, and Albania. Three years later, after King Wladslaw fell in battle, Hunyadi was elected regent for all Hungary.

His greatest achievement was the rout of Mohammed II before the walls of Belgrade in 1456. The victory chilled the Ottoman threat to Europe for seventy year, until the resurgent Turkish scourge triumphed at Mohàcs in 1526. Hunyadi's deliverance was celebrated daily by the tolling of church bells at noon throughout the Catholic world. The bells are still ringing. A few weeks after the battle, the knell was for Jànos Hunyadi as well, a victim of the plague that raged through his encampment.

In the struggle for his successor the following year, Hunyadi's eldest son, Làzlò, was beheaded by the king, the Hapsburg Ladislas V. The public execution was horrific. Three times the executioner struck the young Làslò's neck, and he still lived. Custom dictated that he therefore had the right to amnesty. But Ladislas V, already a debauched psychotic at seventeen, gave the signal for a fourth blow. Làslò's head tumbled to the ground. The king then fled to Vienna, taking with him Hunyadi's younger son, Mattias, as hostage.

Romanians celebrate Hunyadi as their own, proudly claiming his father was a Vlach, a Wallachian from a distinct part of what became Romania. But Szèkelys insist on his identification with the Catholic Church which cast him beyond the Orthodox orbit. Evu observed, "How sad to see this Magyar superman dragged into ethnic bitterness." She suggested we visit the Hunyadi castle at Vajdahunyad further down on the Maros. "The wall plaques brag about their purely Romanian hero. They think the Treaty of Trianon awarded them Magyar history along with the territory."

The castle's magnificence is so reputed that Budapest built a replica at City Park in 1896, which now houses the Museum of Agriculture. As I toured the replica's towers clustered and embedded in the walls at different heights - - some round, some square - - I believed what I was told, that it is unmatched in all of Central and Eastern Europe.

83

A flourishing network of Gothic tracery links the jutting towers with flamboyance worthy of a French cathedral. The towers are topped with steep cones and faceted pyramids, some rectangular, some octagonal, all roofed in tiles of intricate pattern. The inner courtyard is tiered, a hodgepodge of balconies, balustrades, Romanesque arches, and spiral staircases. Inside, leafy capitals of rose-colored marble pillars support the vaults over a hall of knights. It is so fanciful, so theatrical, so Disney.

But Vajdahunyad was a modest castle when Hunyadi's father, Vajk the Vlach, took possession from the king. Jànos built the great fortifications and fabulous towers which were burned or destroyed several times. The current structure, Evu informed us, is an expert restoration completed near the end of the 19th Century, closely followed by the duplication in Budapest.

The flourishes may have been the work of Jànos' younger son, Mattias, who enlarged the castle. The former hostage, escaping from the Hapsburgs, became known as Mattias Corvinas (or Corvin, from the raven on the Hunyadi shield). Upon Wladslaw' death, he was elected king of Hungary by the lesser nobility of Pest then encamped on the frozen Danube below the Buda Castle. Again the country had a national king, unbeholden to an empire.

Mattias raised a mercenary force, the Black Army, and resumed his father's struggles against the Turks. He also fought and beat armies of the Emperor and the Poles; the Czechs elected him King of Bohemia. But his reputation is not for military gifts (he lost as many battles against the Turks as he won), rather for his learning and compassion. He established a brilliant renaissance court and the fabulous Corvinus Bibliotheca, among the first of the new European libraries. He was a scholar, who sat up half the night reading, and a host to leading humanists.

After death, the folk elevated him to a legend, Mattias the Just, who walked the land in disguise, condemning fraudulent judges, shaming the greedy rich, succoring the poor. He also took the opportunity to seduce full-bodied shepherdesses and wily maidens. Perhaps that is why Beatrice of Naples, his last wife, is suspected of murdering him with a poisoned fig. The great Gothic gingerbread church on Castle Hill in Budapest where he was coronated is known as Mattias Church (officially Church of Our Lady).

I was looking at the tapering poplars and the sleeping willows and aspens along the river when I realized my academic mindset had stolen attention from the lovely moment with Evu in the rain-burnished air on the Maros embankment. What had the river murmured to her? In me the stream had evoked no sweet melody or romantic tale, only bloody history. Facetiously, I said, "The Maros tells me horror stories. What does it tell you?"

"It says I am a mortal who must find some reason to exist, like its wild flowers and lush weeds."

"Life is its own reason," Matt insisted.

"That's just fuzz, Matt, for those who already have a reason."

"Matt means the essentials, the enjoyments of eating and copulating."

"And what your senses provide," he added, "beauty, intellect, architecture, music, like that."

"Those are the pleasures of living, not motives."

"What difference?"

"How about survival as a motive?" I asked. "Or power, an excess of survival at least in business execs and kings?"

Evu's lip curled. She giggled and said, "If vampires exist as we know they do in Transylvania, why? I mean, what for? They exist to exist, which means to drink blood, which means to kill. Why exist to kill?"

"Your vampires," I explained much too seriously, "are the evils of our nature." It escaped from me without thought, as though straight from the mouth of the old soldier in Száregy. We were talking about the basics, the ultimate, the purpose of life and nature, not human concepts like evil. I tried to amend with a touch of trite humor, adding, "The root of it all," which only increased my error.

Her green eyes flashed but then her face drew into a pout. After a thoughtful moment, Evu exclaimed, "People don't think about that! About motives for living, or its horrors."

"They must," I answered. "But not for long. We hardly ever confess to such thoughts. We push them back into the unconscious, and then go on eating our hamburgers and decorating our parlors."

"And besting our buddies," Matt put in.

"Most of us embrace existing illusions," Evu offered, "myths to satisfy our needs - - console our fears."

"Still, some people yearn to stretch beyond the answers we've invented for ourselves."

"Mental gymnastics, delusions of scholars, heroics."

"As in the heroics of conquest?"

She stiffened. I had offended her history. "As in your American gang murders." Satisfied, she softened. "And love?"

"Of your fellow beings?" Matt asked roguishly.

"Romance?" Yes, romance, you old fool.

She admitted to a sometime boyfriend, though she was old enough to be married and remarried. Michael was Romanian, "Dacian," she confessed, "and Wallachian."

"A Vlatch?" Surprised by my own outburst of sudden prejudice, I tried to recoup by plunging into a story of two Macedonian colleagues at the University of Skopje. One, who looked like a Turk with thick black hair and dark skin, angrily called his somewhat lighter colleague a Vlatch. "How can you tell?" I had asked, more to diffuse the situation than to make a discovery.

"'By the way he walks,' answered my dark colleague, 'He walks like a Vlatch.'"

Evu giggled briefly to acknowledge the humor then let me know that from St.Stephen's conquest of Guyla in the eleventh century to the Treaty of Trianon in this century, Hungarians in Transylvania have merely tolerated the Romanians. Even before they were Romanian, when they were simply Wallachians and Morovians. "So isn't it natural they do to us what for all those centuries we did to them?" Again, she giggled, this time more sincerely. "But Michael doesn't give a hoot. He has no interest in history. He doesn't read, except for puzzle books and comics. He's a math teacher at the Bolyai Liceum, and a cop before that, but a beautiful savage like our barbaric ancestors."

"Is that the attraction?" I asked.

"The want of love attracts me, and candor. Most men I've found are not honest, whether in Budapest or Bucharest."

"Don't leave women out of this. Societies are built on deception. To be sophisticated is to be deceptive."

"Michael is uncorrupted by society. He is innocent."

"Naïve?"

"No, innocent. He is not easily fooled. He needs none of society's illusions to justify his natural - - what? Behavior? Evil? Michael lacks the need for illusion. And the beauty is that he doesn't know it. Students cling to him. Beneath his thick black brows, his eyes gleam with childlike intelligence."

"That's precisely the intelligence we're demonstrating now," I said, again self-conscious, "with this sophomoric blather."

"But most adults do not tolerate him," she went on, "at least not his colleagues at the Liceum."

"Because he is innocent? Or evil?"

"Michael refuses to respect his colleagues' illusions."

"He doesn't participate in prayer?" She shook her head. "How about crime?"

"He was a cop. He obeys the laws. But if crime wasn't illegal, he might . . . well; Michael says he obeys the law for self-protection, because he's not naïve in his honesty."

"Is he macho? Like those American authors you don't like?"

"That would be the opposite of honesty."

Honesty! All the years I had been professing literature, I knew honesty was easily said but difficult to achieve, a mighty act of intelligence, in fact. Honesty requires the tearing through of society's illusions, the accepted realities and truths. To my students, I had often quoted E.B. White's "go to the scene of the accident without your galoshes on," but my work, I realized for some time, never followed the admonition. Instead, I had imposed new illusions upon those I was taught or inherited, until the illusions dimmed. I was tramping through Transylvania like a vagabond because Matt convinced me this legendary land might rekindle them, but I never believed him. It was only an illusory fire, lacking the honesty that illuminates all brilliant literature.

"What would you say is the first step to honesty" I asked Evu.

"Godlessness. To lose your sense of sin, guilt, and subordination. They are empty boxes, false griefs."

"False griefs for broken illusions?"

She nodded. How did this happen, this reversal? I had become the inquiring pupil and Evu the dispensing master. We fell quiet. I wondered if she were listening to the purling of the Maros. Her eyes sparked. Suddenly she said, "We're at the end of an era. Like the Romans when worn out faiths were still practiced." I did not want to interrupt her with a response. She continued, "Oh those people still believed in their magic and superstitions, their ritual ceremonies, but not the budding intellects, the deeper minds of that world. They were the skeptics. I don't mean Jesus and all that. They just switched gears, exchanged gods so to speak, and drove on. I mean minds like Ovid, Cicero, Lucretius . . .I think we are into another skeptical time. We've stopped anticipating our gods."

I picked up on Lucretius, and thoughtlessly sputtered, "<u>De Rurum Natura</u>," the old Greek's interminable poem, about natural things.

"Precisely," Evu laughed. "In the nature of things. And illusion is in the nature of human things."

"Except for your Michael, your romance?" I could never swallow contradiction.

"Not illusion, very physical. Michael is the magic of creation, the miracle of being. His face - -" abruptly she stopped, wonder in her eyes.

"Aren't we all?" Her excess astounded me.

"For the artist, a face is the essential data," Matt said.

"The most conspicuous," I offered.

"We are always aware of our own," he plunged on, "though it is invisible to us. But we endlessly contemplate the faces of others, the light and shadow, looking for mood and meaning, like studying a cathedral of the flesh."

A line of Shakespeare floated in. I worked to grasp it, then quoted, "'To find the mind's construction in a face.'"

"It's a cathedral," Matt repeated, "never fully lit, the shadows subtly suggesting the unknown, even of ourselves."

I was enjoying the mental play and ventured T.S.Eliot's "face to meet the faces that you meet," then threw out, "This social cohesion that faces make is only external, forms of convention."

Our art student was inspired. "Impersonal, like the geometry of spaces and vectors structured into stiff, balanced composition."

"But the composition," Evu objected, "is a veneer of vicious politeness, freezing the interior lives and isolating them, no matter how close we stand together."

"And that's how the witches enter," I mumbled. "Cold and frosty." I turned to the river.

It seemed to shimmer and I no longer listened. The night felt numinous, as if light from another world were bleeding through, augmenting the moon's. I smelled a faint charcoal smoke like the dust of centuries. The river breeze carried a musky dampness from the night forest. Evu expanded into it. For a moment she appeared sublime, fecund nurturer of a speechless being outside myth and logic. . .tantalizing, the paradox of the sensual and the transcendent. She moved toward the water's edge where the moon's reflection silvered her face. It shadowed her cheeks and shone on her chin. She became a budding version of Granny, an apparition, a witch. The Granny specter broke the power of her spell.

"This is crazy," I blurted in sudden rebellion. "Lucretius' nature hides a world of inhuman horrors."

"Human horrors are worse." Evu began to list the more recent - - tortures of the innocent, deliberate starvations, violent burnings, mass slaughters, gassings, appalling butcheries - - from the current Somalia and Bosnia to Adolph Hitler and Nicolae Ceausescu.

Facetiously I said, "At least the old Transylvanian atrocities had divine purpose." I was thinking of the Christian Saint Stephen. After slaying the Vlach and securing the nation, the sainted king went roaming about central Europe, extracting tribute and earning the ironical title, 'scourge of God.' Early Hungarian chronicles are contradictory and anachronistic, being recorded by lettered slaves and probably falsified for spite. But it's obvious that Stephen and his followers in the house of Arpàd killed rather than argued to sustain God's power.

But Sainthood notwithstanding, Stephen was a cruel murderer. Vasezely, a potential rival, had his eyes gouged out, a favorite means of suppression. Hot lead also poured into his ears. Such operations became standard procedure for the Catholic rulers who followed. Newborns not in the line of succession were disqualified through blinding. But that play didn't always work, as in the case of Blind King Bela II, whose predecessor, Bela I, was mirthfully dethroned when the royal seat

89

toppled over him. Later they took to beheadings as with Hunyadi's son, Làslò.

Evu was inspired to tell the story of a God-fearing gentleman, Gyorgy Dosza, who led a peasant revolt against intolerable taxation in 1514. A zealous St. Franciscan, Dosza mobilized the peasantry under the Sign of the Cross. In the midst of the bloodbath, the viovode (regent or governor) of Transylvania, John Szapolyai, captured the peasant leader and suppressed the revolt. Gyorgy Dosza was punished with grisly humor; an iron throne was heated to glowing red and he was seated as "King of the Peasants," with a burning iron crown upon his head. Then his lieutenants were forced to partake of his roasted flesh before they were broken on the wheel. "Horrified?" asked Evu.

"Naturally."

"No, unnaturally! You are horrified because you really do believe in your illusions. Our culture has always been self-devouring. What happened to Dosza is not some fiendish aberration but as natural as wheat and apples. And so are the decimations of the Ceausescus, and their own executions; the same horrors through all these centuries since Apràd. Well, perhaps not exactly the same - - more sophisticated, efficient. We've made progress." She giggled, "For me, living with it, the horror is natural, but for you it's unnatural. It violates your illusions, not ours."

"Transylvania does not have a corner on the atrocity market. Our horrors are no more natural than yours."

They are caused by nature, by our illusions."

"By the grandiose dreams of your Hitlers and Ceausescus? I'll agree with that."

"And of our barbaric Chieftain, Arpàd. I think of myself sometimes as his daughter however removed. I might be, or not." Her eyes danced. "Remember, my skin is light, my hair is red, my eyes green, and there was an Irishman, General Karl Graf O'Donnell, who governed Transylvania for a time inthe18th century."

Both Matt and I laughed. He said, "I've read that O'Donnell was a caring ruler. And you are caring."

I offered. "That should discourage your notion of a nature that results in horror."

"Oh there are other results," she confessed.

"You've already admitted your need for romance. Won't you one day marry your Michael?" I asked, although I suspected he was illusory.

She thought for a moment, then hesitantly said, "I believe marriage is for a lifetime. . .why should I want a guy. . .forever. . . who'll probably drive me nuts?"

Matt stirred again. "You did say we are entering a skeptical age."

"I suppose the cycles will churn back to optimism some day."

"If the race lasts that long?"

"Oh, it will," conceded my enchantress. "Our illusory worlds will prevail."

Daniel Marder

14. Dènis Fulop's Study

If Matt lauded the civic and Messianic virtues of Father Istvàn, he worshipped the Calvinist Minister of Marosvasarhely. For Evu, Dènis Fulop was quite simply the Szèkely guru.

We were to see him that afternoon, though Matt had arranged nothing, as usual. "Hard to find him in," Matt alibied, "Too many commitments." All the more reason for an appointment, but I knew the futility of suggesting it.

Granny was sleeping. Evu fixed our breakfast: coffee, toast and oats. Then we browsed among her books.

"Wait till you see Dènis's library," Matt said.

"Actually," Evu told us before heading off for school, "Dènis' collection is part of the library given to Transylvania by Count Samuel Teleki (Transylvanian chancellor in the 19th century). He collected so many books and manuscripts they built a special biblioteque for them."

Talking of libraries and books, we passed a shop along the way, dimly lit and sparsely stocked. Matt pointed to a thin volume displayed alone in the window. "By Romania's World War II leader," he announced. "General Ion Antonescu. Communists shot him as a Nazi collaborator."

The parsonage was appended to the back of the Calvinist church which stood just off a corner of holy places dominated by the bulbous Orthodox, which Evu had called "Greek oriental." It was constructed after the Treaty of Trianon to serve the newly-installed military and government functionaries. The Catholic church occupied a less conspicuous structure in the shadows of this grey monster. The Unitarian church sat opposite. "It's the second to be built here," Matt told me. "The Calvinist is the first, constructed when baroque architecture was still emerging from the medieval."

"Now you can see us from the square only by standing below the Orthodox fortifications and crooking your neck," said Ilona Fulop. She led us through the kitchen and a corridor thickly lined with books to the study, a long high-ceiling chamber housing the main part of Dènis's library.

The minister's wife was a frumpy woman in her forties. She had answered our knocking in a house frock, but her brown hair was neatly coiffed and her unpainted face was full and rosy.

Dènis had gone to market. He'd not be gone long. Ilona continued with half a laugh, "Our Ru-manianization did not stop with the building of their church. Michael the Great arrived next, in the form of countless tons of bronze. Then came the fête to celebrate Romanian liberation from the fascists. You saw the soldier sculptured in front of the Palace of Culture, the block-headed monster menacing pedestrians with his machine gun?"

"Ironic," Matt said, "About half a block from your granite liberator is a bookshop that stocks a volume praising your wartime traitor, Antonescu."

"He was just confused," Ilona Fulop said, "First we were on the Nazi side, then the Soviet. What's a body to do?" See a therapist, I thought, for your hereditary schizophrenia. "Did you notice our new Romulus and Remus and mama wolf? And Trajan's face in relief on the pedestal below it?"

"And your great writers in the stones of the Palace wall."

I surveyed the study as Ilona inquired after Matt's family. A library table was stacked with newspapers and books spilling onto

94

leather-upholstered chairs. A pile of penciled notes, periodicals, and opened books crowded an oddly-shaped desk occupied by a computer. There was a decanter of wine amid bottles and glasses, figurines on stands, an aged globe, framed maps, alabaster jars covered with Egyptian hieroglyphs, exotic shells and fossils strewn at random. A sofa faced the tiled fireplace. Embroidered footstools squatted before the leather chairs. The study radiated warmth and intimacy, long hours of comfortable messiness, lots of wine.

When Ilona offered tea, Matt insisted we wait for Dènis. "He makes the greatest cup of coffee in Eastern Europe."

My survey was dominated by the black-lacquered bookshelves lining the long wall of the study. They were inscribed in gold with Biblical quotations, highlighted in Hungarian, leather-bound, including the ubiquitous Tacitus and "Shakspear." There were first editions; a Guy de Maupassant, a Paul de Kock, and a Colette were scattered through the French and German editions. One shelf contained at least half a dozen historical novels by the popular Maurus Jòkai (1825-1904). I had read a number in translation, tales of the flaming rebellion of 1848 and of wars with Turks - - soaring castles, yawning chasms, wolves, pashas with six horsetails, janissaries, magnates, sieges and last stands - - Scott and Dumas transplanted to the Carpathians. An ebony bookcase against the room's shorter wall was inscribed with the reminder that it was actually the cupboard from Mayor Bersèny Ghyorgy's pharmacy in the town's Hungarian heyday. Opposite the bookshelves by a door to the bedroom stood macquets of Dènis Fulops heroes: Rakoczi II, Szèchènyi, Kossuth, Bem.

Ilona explained that full-sized sculptures developed from these models once dominated the squares and parks of fin-de-siècle Marosvàsàrhely. "They met their fates in two bouts of iconoclasm, first the fascists in the 1930s, then the communists in 1945."

Her husband considered them the most creative, humane, magnanimous fighters for Hungarian rights.

I had read that Rakoczi II was an overconfident pleasure-seeking aristocrat; the ruling prince of the early 1700s, hardly a humanitarian's choice for glory of the realm. Perhaps Dènis admired him because he was asked to lead the peasants in their uprising of 1697. But the prince was so terrified by the appeal that he rushed straight to Vienna, where brutal reprisals against his rebelling countrymen allayed his fears. And by 1701, the Hapsburgs were so suspicious of his changed attitude that they imprisoned him under threat of execution. He escaped through a romantic ruse (and at the sacrifice of his rescuer's life), then reluctantly joined the leaders of the popular revolt, and turned on Vienna. His peasant army struck blow after blow, scattering imperial forces before the Ràkòczi banner. But it was the banner that lead, not the prince. Even at the peak of the independence movement, he devoted only a day or two each week to affairs of the state and war. A religious zealot, inquisitive intellectual, and relentless romantic, he spent most of his time at prayer, study, and the hunt, which was a pretext for trysts with his paramour.

Perhaps Dènis was overly impressed with his mature writings, though Ràkòczi's zealotry peeps through. His Christian meditations are actually sensible, and his analysis of class relations are astute, sometimes profound, especially in perceiving the way social backwardness and the country's inadequate development contribute to its struggles.

Unfortunately his rebel infantry armed with scythes and axes was insufficient. Ràkòczi needed the lords and nobles. He was their prince also, though their interests dictated something else. Ràkòczi was forced into exile, accused of selling out the peasantry, whom he never much championed. In 1717, burdened with the curse of traitor, he went to Turkey and, failing to gain the Sultan's support, became an ascetic in Rodosto, alleviating his agonized mind by immersing it in theological analysis. A son joined him for a few years and his estranged wife looked him up but stayed only a short time.

The glory of Dènis's other heroes was far more sterling. Like Ràkòczi, they too were enlisted in the cause of independence. Otherwise, I reasoned, they could not have qualified. But I was more dubious of Transylvania's claim to them. Count Istvàn Szèchenyi, in fact, was not Transylvanian nor was he a true champion of the people's independence. His entanglement with the revolts of 1848 was inadvertent.

Szèchenyi was an aristocrat of nineteenth century Hungary, as the sharp features on his sculpted face demonstrate. His noblest battles were fought against the destructive elements of nature, cultural ignorance, and economic backwardness of the Hungarian people. He was a generous civic benefactor and engineer, perceiving practical problems and devising solutions that would carry his country into the twentieth century.

István Szèchenyi inherited a philanthropic strain from his parents. His father founded the National Museum and the National Library. He gave a huge sum to establish the Hungarian Academy of Sciences. He also fathered steamboat navigation on the inland waterways and construction of stone streets, among other innovations. But internally, he suffered; his journal is crowded with Hamlet-like doubts, terrors, death-thoughts. For years Szèchenyi surreptitiously pursued his brother's wife, finally winning her after his brother's death, then failing miserably in marriage.

In 1848, when the Hapsburg Empire was flaring in disorder and its undistinguished monarch lay ill, councilors assented to the formation of a separate Hungarian government. István Szèchenyi was appointed Minister of Public Works and Transportation while Lajos Kossuth became Minister of Finance. Szèchenyi was contemplative, Kossuth fiery, the mixture explosive. Although Szèchenyi considered the flames of revolt unquenchable, he worked to cool them with patient argument, while Kossuth poured on the fuel with inspirational rhetoric. As Thomas Paine appealed to farmers in the American Revolution, Lagos Kossuth stirred the workers. The fight for independence became a peasant revolt.

When the ill and incompetent Ferdinand V resigned, his sixteen year-old nephew, Francis Joseph, took his place. The Imperial forces launched attacks that drove the rebels beyond Buda and Pest to Debrecen on the Alfold; they set up a provisional government and the Szèchenyi-Kossuth feud became irrelevant. For a while the Hungarian army succeeded almost everywhere; in Transylvania, General Bem, the Polish itinerant soldier of Central European revolutions provided brilliant leadership. Encouraged, the Debrecen government announced dethronement of the Hapsburgs and declared Kossuth its regent.

Within a few weeks the Russian Czar rushed to the Empire's aid. Kossuth resigned and fled to the east. A particularly vicious and senseless atrocity occurred soon after. On October 6, in Arad, Transylvania, Austrian Field Marshall Haynau, known as the "Hyena of Brescia" for earlier cruelties, executed thirteen captured generals, then celebrated by clinking beer mugs through the night. The "Martyrs of Arad" are commemorated on October 6 throughout Hungary and

Transylvania; clinking of beer mugs is taken as an offensive breach of manners. Haynau has become a Dracula-like vampire in the legends of Arad.

General Bem closed his life as a Turkish pasha, a Mohammedan convert in Aleppo. Kossuth took tours of England and America, speaking passionately of the "1848 state of mind," and inspiring a cult of American immigrants to emulation. He finally settled in Turin, Italy, a European idol. A tall statue in New York City memorializes him, and the University in Debrecen bears his name, as do many streets and institutions in major Hungarian towns. Istvàn Szèchenyi came to an opposite end. Broken in body and spirit, a recluse, he committed suicide in a Viennese mental clinic. Of all these heroes, only Kossuth retained his illusions to the end.

Ilona was showing us a print of the old town square with its neo-classic band stand when Dènis strolled in without a word of greeting, leaned over and pointed at the print. "Famous landmark had to be torn down for the Greek Oriental church. Now we're all in its shadows."

His English was better than his wife's. "I must go dress for my women's auxiliary," she said, excusing herself. "Do American churches still have auxiliaries?"

She left us with a benign smile.

Apparently Dènis was a man who expected anything at any time. Without the least hint of surprise, he hugged Matt, kissing both cheeks, and shook my hand. Though Matt introduced me with full pedigree, American professor, etc., I was just another bird landing in his study, no more or less deserving than an emperor or servant who flew in through the window. Casually he asked after Matt's parents and sister. Dènis was the epitome of informality, a man as comfortable in his world as Bob Hope.

But there was also an aura of unworldliness about Dènis Fulop. (Was I still under the spell of the numen on the Maros river?) He moved slowly and grandly, as a monarch might. His gestures were excessive. He seemed a primitive medicine man, possessed of immense wisdom; no, of immense conviction, though unstructured and unspoken. His face was remotely Asiatic, amused, slightly ugly, heavily cheeked and jowled, possessing a small chin and mouth. His eyes were dark behind thick, gold-rimmed spectacles, the ring of hair about his bare head nearly white. A neat grey suit, with a vest over his tender paunch, enclosed him, a mildly spreading man.

"I'll make coffee," he said. Before going to the kitchen, Dènis showed us his recent finds, facsimiles of the earliest printed Bible in Romanian, made for Ràkòczi Ference II, and the first printed Bible in Hungarian.

We sat on the sofa before the tiled fireplace, Matt with the facsimile Bibles, and I with a selection from the shelves, a history of Koloszvar, Transylvania's capital city, next in our travels. The history was in Hungarian, but illustrated.

Dènis was soon back, bearing a tray with a glass carafe of coffee and simple china cups. "You'll never taste any better," Matt announced, as if the coffee were a personal triumph.

Not knowing how to appraise coffee, I took a sip and remembering TV ads, "Full bodied, flavorful."

Dènis spotted the book in my hands and said we shouldn't miss Koloszvar.

"It's directly in our path back to Debrecen," Matt told him.

"You'll call on Irina and Miklós? They'll want to see you."

"They're the poets who run the review," Matt reminded me. Turning back to Dènis, he said, "Miklós had a play produced in Miami, Florida. They're the reason we're going. I don't really care for Koloszvar. Too Byzantine." Matt turned again to me. "Besides, it's the town that stands for all of Transylvania to Reka."

"Reka?" asked Dènis, "How is she . . .and her American professor, what's his name?"

"Ruark," I said, cutting off any snide remark Matt might offer. "David Ruark. They're doing very well." I switched subjects. "We've met the Baptist Reverend McFarland."

"Gods and devils," said Matt.

Dènis chuckled. "A man cannot live without some philosophy. McFarland has been a thorn, I won't deny it."

"That's Evu's observation."

"To my school as well as hers." Dènis explained that he ran the English language school. Time to time, Evu taught there in addition to the state institution. "She's doing too much, but isn't her attitude on life refreshing?" Without waiting for our response, he continued, "Evu questions why American churches put such great efforts into English teaching in our schools. The danger comes from agencies like the American Baptists. They contribute money, and then assume they can dictate terms. They also contribute preachers like McFarland. Their mission deals directly with the Romanian government." Dènis paused, and then chuckling, said, "Whenever one of their uppity missionaries gets frustrated with the realities in Transylvania, he complains to Bucharest."

Ilona came back, trussed in a knit suit, her face lightly painted and adorned with silver earrings. A tall, muscular man entered with her, wearing a fedora. "Ah, Lazar!" Dènis called, as his wife kissed Matt and took her leave. Dènis then introduced us with a hearty laugh, "Lazar the Khazar, meet my English speaking friends. Matt and Daniel are teaching at Debrecen. Lazar is our <u>reb</u>."

He was a man of some fifty years. His graying hair and his complexion were reddish. Except for his high-cheeked face, he appeared a hulking Irishman, possibly another genetic result of General O'Donnell's Transylvanian tenure. "Khazar?" I blurted.

"A few Khazarum here." His accent was heavy. The plural suffix transformed "Khazarum" into a Yiddish word. "You are surprised?"

"Is this possible? Khazars are supposed to be extinct."

"The tribe, yes," said Dènis. "After the Russians chased them all over Eastern Europe. They are undistinguishable from Ashkenazi's."

"Don't know who we are," said the rabbi, "so all right, Ashkenazi."

Dènis gave a short discourse on this puzzling tribe of rovers from the 7th Century. "Some say they are derived from the Huns, or from a Persian tribe the Turks call Sabirs. Too confusing. How does anyone know who he is? Ancestry, heraldry, how foolish. Between 610 and 640, the record says they fought the Persians alongside the Byzantine Emperor Heraclius. To reward their victory, Heraclius gave his daughter's hand to Kaghan, the Khazar king.

"The next we hear they are ruling Transcaucasia, after defeating repeated Arab invasions. In 722, the Khazars sent their enemy reeling out of Armenia, which became the Arabs' northern barrier. And during the 8th Century, the Khazar Empire reached its glory, exercising sovereignty from the Black Sea to the Volga, the recognized overlords of the Magyars, Slavs, Goths, Bulgars. But they were no match for the Russians, who rose in the next century to devour everything on the horizon. By 1030, they were finished."

"But three centuries before," Lazar continued, "maybe 740, they say 'no' to Charlemagne and 'no' to Mohamed. 'No,' they will not be Christian and not Moslem." He shrugged. "So what is left? They become Jews."

"But what did they know about Judaism?" I asked with a chuckle. "They could hardly claim a line of descent from Abraham. What can they claim? The Old Testament? The Torah? Moses? These are what define the Jews."

Now Dènis and Lazar were chuckling. "Many hours we spend with this puzzle, much wine," the rabbi said.

"What do the other Khazars think about it?" I asked Lazar, "You aren't the only one in this town?"

"Some are Christian." He looked at Dènis, held out his hands and shrugged at the accomplished fact. "So?"

Dènis explained that the town had no active synagogue. The rabbi nodded with another shrug. "Yes, some Khazarum are Jewish Christians."

Dènis anticipated my surprise. "We do have them here too. Proselytizers know no bounds and never rest." Lazar grinned broadly. Dènis continued, "Our Jews are not religious. Peace loving, in spite of this violent planet, like most Szèkelys. Maybe that's what cost the Khazars their empire. They till the soil, plant gardens, vineyards, make clothes."

"Don't forget trade."

"The cause of their fall, the Russians seized their trading routes."

Inevitably the subject turned to anti-Semitism. Matt observed, "Ceausescu hated all Jews."

"Yes, he would not allow any Jew around him, ever. Romanian peasants have always hated Jews."

"I've heard atrocities by the carload," Matt said.

The rabbi was reluctant. "What you hear is so, and more, much more. But not like the Nazis, not until Ceausescu. Before him, we have Gheorghiu-Dej, his secretary was Jewish, a woman, and Ana Paulker, his rival, Jewish woman."

"But it's in the people," said Matt. Dark-complected, heavy-bearded, and curly headed, the Englishman described how he was taken for a Jew two years ago. "Right here in Marosvàsàrhely. I was asking a lady for directions on the street, and she stared at me with hard eyes, then spit out, 'Jude!' and turned away."

Lazar examined Matt more intently. "True?" You Jewish?"

"I was born to the high church in Sussex. But let me say, your Magyars in Hungary are not much better. On a tram in Debrecen, two punk skinheads came near assaulting me for the same reason."

"That prejudice has a long history," Dènis said, "but Maria Teresa, you know, was kind to them. She drove all the non-Catholics from her realm, but then relented against the Jews, though she forced them to take German names."

Lazar inclined his head toward Matt. "You right. In Budapest, during war, Jews wear yellow badge. So Christian women put on badge to protest when Jews sent away - - to camp in Poland. Admiral Horthy [regent of Hungary before the war] arrest them. For centuries, we settle here in Transylvania; then Romanians say, 'You alien.'"

Between Dènis and Lazar, I learned more of anti-Semitism in Romania and Hungary that afternoon than I could use. Hungarian Jews were overtly accepted without distinction before World War I. But then came the early communist revolt in 1919, which was unfortunately led by a Jew, Bèla Kun. He inspired animosity which produced the "White Terror," popular anti-Semite vigilantes. Hungary did not have to wait for Adolph Hitler. In the thirties, under Admiral Horthy, it competed with Poland and Romania for anti-Semitic leader of Europe. And after World War II, it was the first country to have Jewish quotas; five percent of university enrollments. The practice of Jewish doctors and lawyers was also restricted and Jewish properties were often confiscated. In 1956, when the Hungarian revolt against the communists failed, 35,000 inhabitants of Budapest were shipped to Soviet slave camps, 14,000 of them Jewish.

In Romania, there was Octavian Goga, the poet laureate, virulent anti-Semite and darling of the Iron Guard, a rogue fascist organization that rampaged through ghettoes. In1937, King Carol actually appointed Goga as Prime Minister though his fringe party had only nine percent of the vote. Goga posed what he called the "Jewish problem," then despaired of any outsider ever understanding it. The "problem" was simply that Jews had become too significant. They constituted over fourteen percent of the urban population, half of all doctors, a quarter of the journalists, and three-quarters of the bank clerks. They controlled over half the country's capital. Goga suppressed Jewish-owned newspapers and suspended free railroad passes to Jewish journalists. The Iron Guard pitched in, sharing with Nazi thugs the enormity of crimes against Jews during the war.

When Ceausescu came to power, he proclaimed all Jews Zionists. They were loyal to Israel and therefore state enemies. He suppressed Jewish cultural activity, just as Iliescu is doing to Székely culture.

Lazar revealed that he met Dènis at his father's funeral several years ago. His parents and Dènis had become friends in prison where Ceausescu held them for four years.

Astonished, I asked Dènis, "You were in prison for four years?"

"Cutting reeds in the Danube delta." He began removing his coat, vest and shirt. Lazar continued, "My mother buried in prison cemetery. Went mad from hunger. They shoot her. They beat soles of my father's feet, forced him to stand on one leg to beg for bread, hands raised to 'Lord.'"

"Will evil ever end?" asked Matt.

"Evil," responded Dènis, naked from his belt up, "is a positional and relative term. Whatever hurts is evil." He displayed red welts on his sides and back, "Fourteen. Too bloody to count. Should have been fifteen. They still owe me one."

I could not laugh. Lazar sighed, "Life just along for ride; God does what it does."

"The universe," Matt corrected. "The universe does what it does. Which is to reproduce, to expand." Then pointedly to me, he said, "And it's no illusion you can make philosophy out of."

Dènis was putting on his shirt. "Why did they take you to prison?" I asked.

He exchanged glances with Lazar, questioning my naïve sincerity. I felt the fool.

Finally, Dènis said, "The charge was neglect. I refused to praise the dictator from my pulpit, as fellow pastors suggested." His voice was a grave baritone, but suddenly shifted to a high falsetto as he recited, "'Morning flowers spread their petals / whispering Ceausescu to the new day's sun.'" Lazar's chuckle was loudest. "And maybe I was too critical. I used my pulpit to object when I heard Romanian officers were forcing prisoners to admit crimes they did not commit by beating on their testicles and jamming feces down their throats."

"Worse thing," Lazar offered, "no bucket. More necessary than light or food when stomach growls. Or they make you eat. You allow to go to toilet at five in morning, three in afternoon, ten at night."

Dènis was forced to stand hours in a damp, dark cell. "Hell is to stand in darkness remembering past sins."

15. Szèkelys Are Romanians?

When the coffee ran out, Lazar left. I thought we should do the same, but Dènis asked us to stay. He went to make another pot. Before he could even pour the new brew, Matt announced that he had brought coffee for Dènis but had left it at Evu's. Then he pressed Dènis for an opinion on autonomy.

"The Hungarian Romanian Federation has declared itself. They are making a mistake."

My colleague was taken aback. "Why?"

"What could happen? What could be gained? The Romanians have always hated us, you know. Since they are the majority . . .Have we learned nothing from history? Better to leave it as is, avoid the bloody horrors, go along, be citizens."

"Of Romania?" Matt was incredulous.

"Szèkelys are Romanians. If we live in this country we should be citizens and act like it, as Hungarians do in America. If that Federation fancies a Hungarian reannexation of Transylvania, God forbid! A greater Hungary inhabited by seven million ethnic Romanians! It could lead to the end of Hungarian culture altogether. Romulus and Remuses popping up all over Pannania." He sipped his coffee in silence for a moment. "I see reversals again and again, Romania, then Hungary, then Romania again. Back and forth, and always prejudice and violence. We must recognize what's in our face, or we'll all be bloodied through the centuries to come, like Bosnians. We've had enough heroes. Maybe if we stop annoying them, stop protesting, act like citizens - - who knows? They still allow us to teach Hungarian, even if our classrooms are diminished. You can buy a Hungarian newspaper on the street."

He refilled our coffee cups, sighed, and went on. "This howl for autonomy is loudest in Budapest. The reactionary party in power, the MDF, never accepted the Treaty of Trianon. They suffer the myth that Transylvania is still Hungary's and demand it back. Hitler returned it, you know, most of it, and when the Soviets conquered the Nazis, they gave it back again. They kicked out King Michael and installed their National Democratic Front which gave way to the Romanian Communist Party of Gheorghiu-Dej. He bested Moscow's monkey, Ana Paulker."

Matt's face was a squelched moan. His idol was crumbling. I watched as he screwed up courage to ask, "The Iliescu government has not returned the church property, have they?"

"One grievance at a time. The property was taken by the communists and Iliescu has promised to return it. Romanians are easily confused; accepting government promises may seem naive, or even cowardly." He chuckled into his hand. "You think this is betrayal? Who has been betrayed may I ask?"

"The Martyrs of Arad, for one." Matt was suddenly resolute. "It's a matter of simple justice."

"And morality!" Dènis added. "I know," he continued with more gravity. "The Szèkelys endured years of misery under Ceausescu and helped overthrow him. They believing in the promise of the new government. All chimera. Iliescu continues the old ways."

What would Evu say? That Iliescu is merely following Romanian nature? Matt's face was glum. Must the world of romantics be forever black and white, my friend?

Dènis continued, "At least Iliescu wears a face of tolerance. Perhaps our condition will improve; perhaps world opinion will make it improve. We have no other power. Maybe you will help inform the world. Remember the past, but do not repeat it . . .and who will break the pattern of hate and vengeance? Surely not the martyrs you hold sacred. They exist on both sides, always have, and always they ensure bloodshed. Look at General Antonescu. We see him now as the evil one, the Nazi collaborator, the 'betrayer.' The Soviets encouraged that view. Before King Michael was deposed he turned Antonescu over to them. They returned him to Bucharest for trial and he showed a martyr's courage before the court, laying out Romania's inherent ambiguities through history. The court was impressed.

"Because he had been so admired, the government worried the army might refuse to provide a firing squad. So-called 'shock troops' in Romanian uniforms were brought in. After their first volley, he rose on his knees and shouted, 'Can't you people even shoot straight?' The second volley was not lethal either. 'Long live Romania,' he muttered before the <u>coup de grâce</u> finished him. Now Matt, if our 'betrayer,' Antonescu, does not qualify as a martyr, who does? Please, no Jesus!"

Not once had this loquacious Calvinist pastor seriously mentioned a God. I suspected he was among that group of religious advocates who had lost belief along the way but held fast to the pulpit because of the good they might yet do, or because they knew no other way to live.

With Matt somewhat mollified, Dènis tried to lighten the air. He introduced God in a popular tale about Romanian confusion: "God was distributing the natural wealth of Central Europe among the nations. For Hungary, a flat, dry plain, for Bulgaria, a bare, rocky mountain, for Croatia and Serbia, dry, impoverished soil, but for Romania, fertile plains, grand rivers, magnificent mountains, and vast quantities of coal, oil and iron. The other countries cried out. 'Why does Romania get all the riches when we are so poor? She will be greater than all of us and come to rule us.' They pleaded for God to restore the balance. So God created the Romanians."

Actually, I did question Romanians' innate capabilities after observing from my railcar window field after field of harvested wheat shocks and hill after hill crowded with sheep and poultry, then arriving in Brasso to see people lined up for blocks awaiting the bread truck or the opening of a window for a dressed chicken. How can the most fecund real estate in Central Europe house such impoverished people?

The Roman province of Dacia (Transylvania) was legendary not only for its deposits of gold and silver, but for its granary, the most plentiful in Europe. Romania was a prosperous country right through the Second World War. I remember our fierce air raids on her rich Ploiesti oil fields. What happened?

Dènis had an answer. "Ceausescu was a monomaniac, but his cult of personality was not enough to ruin his country. I regret to say it was her communist economics. I've been something of a sympathizer myself in Marxism as in Christianity. Both require too much of us, beyond our capacity. What's required? Love - - I mean for each other, for society. Simple? Too simple. And impossible." His eyes closed and he paused for a second, and then snapped back. "But you're not here for a sermon. Most scholars realize Marxism is a Christian ideal; as you know, ideals are illusions. And like Christianity, communist organization is easily corrupted once people are beyond the tribe and into the marketplace. Soviets were market creatures, also thieves."

"What's the distinction?" Matt asked.

Dènis grinned and went on without a laugh, "When they took over, they stole everything in sight. And they did it the way capitalists do. They set up Soviet-Romanian companies – maybe you've heard of the notorious 'Sov-Roms?' They were pipelines for transferring raw material to the Soviet Union: grain, coal, iron, oil. No other Central European country, not even Hungary, was so victimized by the Soviet capital imperialism.

"By the mid-fifties this country was destitute. With Stalin dead, the Soviets saw they had nearly strangled Romania and would soon have a corpse on their hands. They dissolved the 'Sov-Roms.' With Gheorghui-Dej and Ceausescu, his henchman, in control, the Romanian economy suddenly spurted.

"How did this miraculous reversal come about? The government relentlessly pursued industrial expansion. They meant to drag our backward country into the twentieth century whatever the human cost in ruthless schedules and slavish labor. No one was to be excluded from the harsh conditions imposed for our salvation. Farm lands became oil fields and strip mines. Hundreds of thousands of acres were converted to industrial crops for export: oil, seed, sugar beets, hemp, flax, cotton. Enormous fields were devoted to wheat or maize; special fields for tomatoes, peas, potatoes, cabbage. Collectivization smothered peasants trying to live off their small plots. To market the produce, roads and trucks were necessary. But in a country of regional self-sufficiency, trucks were scarce, roads terrible. For the first time in history, we had to depend on bureaucrats to schedule and organize our supply of food.

"By the late seventies, there were shortages and rumors of rioting, and of Ceausescu exporting our food for hard currency while he flaunted his lavish living and nepotism - - his children and nephews in the highest government ranks. By the 1980s, our black market was so common that Marlboros were accepted as a medium of exchange. Then came bread rationing and austerity measures. Hoarders faced up to five years in jail. We were ordered to cut back on energy consumption. Commodity prices tripled. Your Mr. Reagan rejected Ceausescu's plea for another 65 million because we already owed 91 million for grain imports."

"How did Romania get that first 91 million?" asked Matt.

"Ceausescu hoodwinked Reagan. He made noises that we were independent of the Soviets, that we were establishing private enterprise, even though Ceausescu didn't understand it. But he had Reagan salivating, he was so eager to win the Cold war."

I vaguely recalled some joint venture with Romania that we proposed long before Reagan was on the scene. It involved William Randolph Hearst, and stuck in mind because I had met Hearst in 1953 when I was reporting in Spain. He had stopped in Madrid on his way to the Soviet Union, seeking an interview with Stalin. I asked Dènis, "Didn't Ceausescu invite William Randolph Hearst to discuss a joint venture with America, something like the Sov-Rom setup?"

"Ceausescu dangled cheap labor before Hearst's nose like a carrot," Dènis replied. "He guaranteed no labor troubles. The Americans took that as a break with the communist countries, a step toward Western capitalism. They were blind to Ceausescu's scheming. Romanian workers would be farmed out like Mexican peons to toil for American capitalists. They had already been terrorized to collectivize the land. Unknown numbers were still being executed at drumhead trials. While Hungary was decreasing shortages with decentralization, Romania was outlawing them. Ceausescu said he was encouraging private enterprise while he undermined it with quotas, strict control, and corruption. And he soothed the public with ostentation. Look what he's done to our beautiful old cities. Monstrous parks of concrete tower across Romania, mazes of pathways slice through buildings, dying grass and junk trapped between the pavements, too small for children's play. And a grand plaza in every city so all the people can hear and worship their leader. Ach!"

I perceived that Evu's guru was, after all, a Calvinists minister. His spirit retained myths of moral and political correctness, though he was rational and open-minded, nothing doctrinaire like his puritan forebears. Obviously he held himself to be of the elect. It was a satisfying observation.

At supper that night, our last, I asked Evu, "Do you suppose Dènis is without illusions?"

"That would be unnatural."

"Is Dènis a man of faith?"

We've never discussed it, but he is a minister."

"I've concluded that he's really a Calvinist, deep down. In the oldest sense, the elect."

"Oh, not Dènis."

Matt offered, "Dènis believes in social equality. How can he hold himself elect?"

I answered, "Quite simply, Matt. He may promote equality with his natural intelligence which in itself elevates him. But the equality he promotes tends to restrict the use of that intelligence. It's a conundrum.'

Evu said, "The more equality, the less freedom."

And Matt responded, "The more freedom, the more corruption."

"Because humans can't handle freedom," Evu said. "That's what Ceausescu thought."

Matt continued, "People may preach freedom but can't manage it and don't want anyone else to. They become patriots, rednecks, hunters, rah-rah royalists, fascists, capitalists, Cossacks, Baptist preachers - - "

"Is that your critique of America?" I asked.

Evu was laughing. "Matt's illusions."

I turned to her. "Does anyone in Romania question that corruption is natural? The natural result of illusions?"

"Not a Romanian question. We're too busy getting on. What is natural and what is not? That's a fruitless abstraction."

"But Romanians are Europeans, and share some illusions. Don't they assume people are corrupt and therefore perceive them that way?"

"Americans have the same perceptions," Matt interjected, "but pretend they are not corrupt and maintain the farce of their innocence."

Evu slapped her withered hand in applause. "Good for Matt."

"Corruption is what destroyed the Soviet Union," he continued, "even though Americans claim Ronald Reagan did it. Because of corruption, which too much freedom guarantees, European societies make provisions to protect the people. Less is left to chance. Europeans are prone to provide social support systems."

"Just their habit of <u>noblesse obligè</u>," I responded.

16. Granny

"Ironical that the idea of social equality has rooted in Europe which still clings to its aristocratic illusions - - ."

Granny interrupted me. She came into the living room with a kettle of steaming tea, held just above her head, bent parallel to the floor. Fearing she would bump into something, I rescued the kettle. She wobbled back to the kitchen for cups and saucers. When finally tea was safely in our grasp, Matt was eager to include Granny. He asked did she think Dènis Fulop was truly a minister of God? She cackled, her creased skin folding upon itself like twisted dough.

"Dènis went to school with Granny," Evu said. They were sitting together on the couch and Evu was patting her grandmother's arm. Hearing herself, Evu joined Granny's mirth. "I mean she taught him."

"And kept quiet about him," Granny added in Hungarian. Then cackling and coughing up, she launched into a story which Evu translated. In 1952, when Dènis was a fledgling minister in his foolish twenties, Moscow displayed incredible ignorance of Romanians and Hungarians; they promoted "Danubian Unity," which meant cooperation

113

between the two vassal countries. A Magyar Autonomous Region was established within Transylvania; Szèkelys were overjoyed. Dènis celebrated from his pulpit with sermons on the Magyar's Transylvanian roots. The party of Gheorghui-Dej and his underling, Ceausescu, gained massive popular support, opposed by the Moscow-trained monkeys, Vasile Luca and Ana Pauker. It was said that Pauker was sent back from Moscow to run Romania for Stalin. The communists were too embroiled for the moment to give Dènis much attention.

Hoping to annex the rich soil of Moldavia, Moscow fostered the notion that Moldavians, like the Wallachians, were not Romanians but separate peoples, and they provided "evidence" that even the ancient Dacians were actually Slavs and their language was derived from Slavic, not Latin. Dènis ate it up. His sermons harangued Romanian pretenses to Roman grandeur. But then Luca and Paulker were purged. Moscow lost its dominance of the Romanian Communist Party and the hounds of Gheorghui-Dej and Ceausescu came after Dènis.

On a hot day late in August, six blue-uniforms took Granny away for a "statement." Her body was still straight then, and her face was clear and colorful as Evu's. A bull-necked soldier who never stopped shouting was in command. Immediately, before she learned what they came for, his underlings were opening cupboards and emptying drawers. Then they clamped smoked goggles on her eyes, blinding her. They drove and dragged her to a barren place crowded with women sitting on benches and the floor. A steel door was continually being unlocked to admit more. She recognized a well-dressed woman of means and another prominent one in a light dress with low-cut bodice. Another had been seen with a Soviet official and had been suspected of spying. Her satin evening dress had been torn and hung in shreds. She had used strips of the dress for handkerchiefs and other needs. Before night, over a hundred of them, "the socially rotten," were huddled in that long, naked room sweating under a light bulb without food or drink, each shut in fear. The one toilet overflowed, stinking mightily.

Before morning, the woman of means was screaming, "I've done nothing. I've done nothing." Intermittently she assured the others, "You'll see, they'll release me."

Translating Granny's compassion, Evu said, "Poor thing thought innocence would save her. All were there to give statements." Granny interrupted her story with more cackling. Evu translated, "Some statements took ten years."

At last she was taken to a fat, mustached major all full of himself behind an ink-stained desk. He informed her she was being retained by the Secret Police. "I already know that," Granny said, and received a frightening stare. She was given pen and paper and told, "Write a detailed statement about your offense." "What offense?" she asked. "What shall I write?"

She was shifted to another barren room, this one smaller, with desks and fewer women. What to write? The problem was familiar. She'd faced interrogators before, in Nazi days, and mislead them. Lying was better than denial or silence. The statement they wanted was surely about Dènis' improper preaching. She wrote that yes, she had been the minister's teacher, but knew nothing about him now, having been a non-religious person. She never met with him and saw him only in the street, in passing.

Again standing before the Major, Granny was told that her statement would not do. "We have methods of eliciting better. Don't be clever. It wastes our time and maybe your life." Now he wanted her to name anyone who she knew talked against the regime. He repeated his questions, insisting she give him names. His voice echoed in the corridor as she was finally returned to her sour smelling cell.

After weeks of such resisting, she won. What she won was classification as an "administrative," one of thousands who went into forced labor camps without benefit of trial.

"We were an essential part of the economy," said Granny. For nearly two years in "camp" she endured "re-education" along with the "Saboteurs" who failed their "work norms" - - gypsies, Jews, criminals, priests, prostitutes, wealthy merchants - - all misfits in the communist scheme.

The news media carried no word of trials or sentences and the regime was congratulated. Prominent writers in the West praised Romania as a rare progressive country in the communist block who had solved its post-war unemployment problem.

Matt made comparisons with current Hungary, bringing up the recent row in Budapest between governing MDF and the president who was of another party. "The West knows nothing of that either. They see Budapest as the shining jewel of new capitalism."

Before Granny retired, she let us know we were all wrong. The Hungarian President, Gònc Arpa, was shouted down not before the Opera House, as we believed, but on the square before the House of Parliament. And it was Gònc himself, not the Young Democrats, who said the government intended to embarrass him, though it was the skinheads who prevented his speech. The government wanted Gònc to look foolish because he had approved the sacking of fascist officials from Magyar TV. Granny thought the Hungarian government was riddled with nationalist's forces that encouraged neo-fascists by not opposing them.

Silently and somberly, I wondered about essential differences between the governing Hungarians who hated Romanians and the governing Romanians who hated Hungarians.

17. The Illusion of Koloszvar (Romanian Cluj Napoca)

Invading Slavs called it Balgrad, one of the many "white" towns they settled. In the middle of the tenth century, the Magyar prince Guyla honored the Slavs by renaming it Gyulafhervàr, "Guyla's white city." The Saxons first translated the white town into Weissenburg, and then changed it to Karlburg, after their Emperor Charles VI built the great eighteenth century fort.

Ferdinand and his Marie were crowned King and Queen of Hungary in Koloszvar's old Romanesque cathedral after it had been rebuilt in Gothic style by John Hunyadi. The city became the stronghold of John Szapolyai in his battles with the Hapsburgs. Szapolyai's son, John Sigismund, the last Hungarian king-elect, was content to occupy the throne of Transylvania and rule from Kolozsvar. And when that young king died, Transylvania once more fended off the Hapsburgs by accepting a shadowy vasseldom as a "Principality of the Ottoman Empire. Koloszvar served as capital of a succession of Transylvanian princes until the reconquest in 1711, when it was recombined with Hungary into the Hapsburg kingdom.

In the tombs under the vaults of the old cathedral lay the Catholic bones of Emperor Sigismund, his mother Queen Isabella, the first prince Ràkòczi, John Hunyadi and his headless son, Lazlo.

"During the Thirty Years War," Evu said, "Gàbor Bethlen founded his academy in Koloszvar; the city became a religious refuge for the Calvinists and Lutherans, all of them, Unitarians too, against the Jesuit Hapsburgs. In the 18th Century, when Count Batthyàny became bishop, he gave the town a magnificent library; they built him a palace."

"Mattias Corvinus was born in a Kolozsvar palace," Matt added.

"And don't miss the Bànffy palace," said Evu. "I think that's where the leaders of the uprising in 1784 were broken on the wheel. Anyway, Liszt gave recitals there. Or St. Michael's church. Enormous! The vaulting and shadows." She asked Matt to extend her regards to Irina and Miklós then cursed her homebound fate.

Evu especially loved to sit in the ruins of the old citadel at sunset with all of Koloszvar spread below, looking over the misshapen roofs and bridges spanning the river bend as the evening light sparkled against windows, cupolas, and steeples. She enjoyed the chiming belfries. "First, one strikes the hour, then another picks up the challenge, and another. Soon all the bells in town are knelling their medieval rivalries in the purple light."

We sat silently sharing her fancied scene till Evu broke the charm. "You must stop at Torda too. The first place in Europe to declare religious toleration."

"We don't know anyone in Torda," said Matt.

I found it on the map, some thirty kilometers south of Koloszvar.

She told us of the wonder not to be missed in Torda. "Old Roman salt mines still worked by convicts who zigzag tunnels into the mountains, their echoes resounding through the walls until they die in the distance . . .and limestone clefts and huge caverns carved with arches, arcades, natural windows." Evu described soaring old castles and villages once sacked by the Mongols, still crumbling in the gloomy forests. "Cobblers and potters line the main street, Socinians, mostly."

Matt knew them as a sect of Unitarians, "named after Faust Sossini from a family of theologians. He wandered into Transylvania from the Medici court and settled in Koloszvar long enough to establish his creed, then strolled on to Cracow."

"Do Irina and Miklós know we're coming?" I asked Matt.

"We're always welcome."

"I think we should call."

Evu found the number in her black book and went to the phone. When finally the call went through, no one answered. She turned on Matt. "Why must you always surprise people?"

I had been wondering the same thing. His want of etiquette seemed deliberate, like his unshaven face and unkempt clothes. "Negligence signals carefree," I said. Of course after seven days of trampling Transylvania in the rain, I was not the sparkling image of a country gent, but I did shave every day and had a change of pants.

He answered a bit facetiously, "Maybe I want to be loved without trying, or maybe I'm just indifferent to unimportant things. Or maybe I'm lazy. Anyway," he said, changing the subject, "Reka boasts about Irina 's poetry. She and David were responsible for having Miklós' play produced in Florida. I especially wanted you to meet them, but if they're not home, what's the point in Koloszvar?"

"What's his play about?" I asked.

Matt collected his thoughts a moment. "The anguish of the Szèkelys . . .their ambiguous position as Romanians. Its about emigrating to Hungary, the political conniving and bribery to get permission, the tearing apart of an established family."

Evu went to the phone again. After a brief exchange, she hung up. "That was an aunt. They're in Budapest. Won't be back until tomorrow or the next day."

We discussed alternatives and I could see that Matt was quite satisfied to skip Koloszvar. "Reka would be appalled," he gloated.

Evu knew a family in Segisvar, directly south, less than half a day away. "It's a Saxon fairyland." The Gorgey's were part of the Szèkely network. "One's Unitarian, the other's Calvinist. I can never remember which is which. Lagos, their eighteen year old is neither. Both teachers, but he's actually a lawyer."

Evu put in the call. If her English and American friends could share the pull-out in the living room, they were welcome.

"I can sleep on the floor," Matt offered, "On my bedroll."

"They'll be home after seven. You can call Irina and Miklós from there."

Before bedding down, Matt unloaded his pack: a five-kilo sack of sugar, another of flour, several tins of meat, packs of cheese, coffee, candies, old magazines and paperbacks. Evu was overwhelmed. "Save some for the Gorgeys."

In the morning it rained again as we rode with Evu to her school. The bus was crowded but two seats were suddenly vacated. Matt insisted I share them with Evu and our lightened backpacks. A group of gypsy women, toting their ever present baggage, apparently resented the space we took. Their long skirts were so brilliant I could not keep my eyes away. One of them bumped me as she passed. Instead of excusing herself she glared, hatred in her dark eyes. She was jeweled to her fat jowls. Evu told her, "Move on," not intending to be understood.

The gypsy woman answered Evu in surprisingly clear English, "Can't you stand looking at us?" She addressed me. "Too cheap for a taxi?" Then she struggled up the aisle.

Fortunately the bus allowed no time for sentiments. At the school stop I quickly promised to send my last book (through Matt, not the spy-pocked Romanian post). We hugged goodbye and I waved as the bus pulled away. Disappearing in the crowd, her blue all-weather coat under the umbrella, Evu was still the vulnerable and the brave, but not quite the same Mary Tyler Moore I had first envisioned, wielding her weapon of confidence as she stepped out to melt the cruel world. That vision assumed a world of myth and hope receptive to her charm, but blind to the dark side, not true to Evu's nature.

18 Segisvar (Romanian Sighisoara)

What a contrast! The train ride to Marosvasarhely had been lightless, a river flowing through black ocean depths, drowned in the odors of garlic, onion and alcohol. We rumbled toward Segisvar in a clear morning's brightness, just the two of us in an empty compartment, observing the sheaths and hayricks in the fields, and the brunt-browed workers. I enjoyed the peaceful sheep on the hillsides, the cattle taking breakfast in the stubby pastures.

Matt could distinguish between the Hungarian and Romanian field workers. Both were shod in rawhide. They wore low-crowned hats of felt and white linen tunics. But the Romanian shirts were open at the throat and gathered at the waist, then flared over the trousers, while the Hungarians' were buttoned, their trousers shorter, pleated and almost wide enough to be skirts.

The country side was better groomed as we approached Segisvar. Tiles replaced thatched roofs and more farmhouses were gabled. Arched gateways allowed carts and trucks through the stone yard enclosures.

121

Then as the train ran along the Maros, we were treated to a fantasy of steep roofs, towers, spires on a grand knoll rising from treetops.

"Schassburg," said Matt. "That's what the Saxons called their city."

According to Hungarian chronicles, King Gèza II found the region deserted and welcomed Saxon settlers from the Rhine and Flanders. They tilled the soil and established villages, amiably dovetailing with the Szèkelys. A century later, crusading Teutonic knights were invited to join them in resisting the Cuman invaders from the East. They were rewarded with fiefs in the Brasso and Segisvar regions. But when the Knights tried to make their fiefs independent, the Hungarian King drove them out. They moved northward and founded the warlike state of East Prussia. Enough Saxons remained to cultivate the fertile land around their walled farmhouses. They practiced their crafts and built their Gothic burghs with soaring steeples and towers. Segisvar is now home to a mere 800 Saxons.

Evu claims their character is quite opposite the Szèkelys. "No notion of friendly intercourse with strangers. No personal extension." She had difficulty explaining their ungracious reserve; they were learned and intelligent. But even those informed in sciences and arts, on intimate terms with Geothe, Schiller, Mozart, and Beethoven, lacked outward polish and appeared ignorant of the simplest rules of social exchange. They might stare in answer to your question or turn away in the midst of an introduction. Harry Cloos was certainly an example. And they were snobbish, speaking seldom but offensively: "'Transylvania is a fine country dreadfully contaminated by too many Romanians.' They breach etiquette," Evu thought, "because of a tactless nature, not intention."

But Hungarians also looked upon the Romanian as vermin. "The term," Evu said, "comes from the Wallachian <u>rumani</u>. Just means peasant. Saxons also see us Szèkleys as Magyar barbarians. We consider them boors. 'God grant me enlightenment' says the Saxon, 'which Romanians always get too late.' Frankness is a Saxon virtue and for Hungarians a duty, but Romanians consider a person a fool who injures himself by speaking the truth."

Still, like all Transylvanians, the Saxons retain a strong sense of myth and legend. "Dr. Faustus," she informed us, "is believed to have resided in the Saxon city of Hermannstadt (Sibiu). Wondrous tales about the great doctor still circulate. He rolled around great stones that turned out to be human heads until they stopped rolling, then became stones again. Once Dr. Faust assumed the shape of the town parson and stood on his head at the tip of the steeple until the genuine person came by, then jumped down and became a black cat with fiery eyes. At a large cattle fair he attended, military music suddenly sounded. The sheep, calves, oxen, and horses turned into a regiment of soldiers marching in robust color behind the band. When the bandmaster gave a signal, the music turned to bleating and bellowing and the animals stood as before. At last he was carried off to hell, though the Lord would have saved him because of his kind heart. He was good to the poor. But Dr. Faustus had sold himself by contract to the devil."

For centuries, the Saxon settlements were comprised of massive buildings surrounded by formidable stone walls, while the Székelys built dwellings of formal simplicity and the Romanians settled for wretched earthen hovels. Building and repairing their homesteads was a favorite Saxon pastime. When the Saxon has nothing better to do, says the Székely, he pulls down his house and builds it up again.

The Romanian hovel symbolized the peasant condition and may of itself have contributed to his mere toleration through the centuries. Romanians did not possess the rights of citizenship in the Principality either under Ottoman or Hapsburg rule until Michael the Brave in 1600. In many Saxon and Székely minds, the Romanian is a veneer of arrogance; behind it crouches a servile peasant.

In 1848, when Tsar Nickolas sent an army to dampen Kòssuth's threat to Franz-Josef's Imperial troops, one of the final battles was at Segisvar. But Segisvar is best known for the castle where Vlad III was born. He was destined for the synonym Dracula, when his father, Vlad II, was honored by Emperor Sigismund hanging the Order of the Dragon around his neck. As a boy, Vlad III was taken hostage by the Sultan. Later, as Transylvanian prince, he captured a Turkish division, whereupon, the Sultan, Mehmet II, marched a punitive army to annihilate him. Approaching Segisvar, the Sultan's army suddenly halted. In the wide valley before them, they beheld unspeakable horror: a forest of Turkish corpses from Vlad's recent triumph spindled on sharpened pikes, rotting in the air, faces frozen in agony. Among them was the Sultan's general, mockingly spiked in a ceremonial robe.

The Sultan recoiled in hysterics. Vlad III, son of Dracul, became infamous as Vlad Tsepesh, the Impaler. The practice became his lifelong obsession. Woodcuts show him feasting in the groves of his skewered enemies.

Packs in place, we hiked over a utilitarian bridge on a plateau of industrialized land, then began a mild climb up a stone road through the old gold buildings roofed in red tiles, to a stone stairway leading to a toyland of shingled spires, towers, yellow brick walls and shops. The structures were punctuated with clocks, some in ornate Gothic décor, one high on a tower topped with an onion dome that spouted a spire. This clock dominated our approach. Surely, some German tourist had arranged the scene to resemble the old home burgh on the Rhine. We had arrived before one o'clock and within the hour stood before a square golden structure, a marble plaque on its well-kept walls. The Romanian script read,

> In this house and location
> Between the years 1431 – 1435
> Lived the Romanian Prince
> VLAD DRACUL

Was the reference to Vlad II or Vlad III, The Impaler transformed into Bram Stoker's Dracula, in silk cape, white tie and fangs for his bloodthirsty excursions through the midnight castles and forests of Transylvania?

An English-speaking waiter within did not know. We were told the plaque was hung just a few years ago, but we were indeed standing on the floor of the tourist mecca, Dracula's Castle. The floor was polished grey marble. A bar and high leather stools were at one end of what appeared a modern pub. Chairs and tables lined the thick, whitened walls. The waiter directed us upstairs where lunch was served.

Dracula's Castle was as good looking a restaurant as any we'd encountered, but as a castle it was bland, just another pile of plastered stones. The walls bulged in age. Though the interior was white, the trim was deeply varnished. The rooms were dark, as everything in Transylvania. Gruff workers in high spirits were drinking beer at a table opposite, elbows jostling one another. Returning from the WC, Matt reported it clean and neat.

We ordered sausage and kraut with our beer. Matt asked the waiter if he could store our packs while we toured. We'd return for dinner before looking up the Gorgeys.

Ascending the street of stairs again, we passed an ancient watering trough, beside it a stone slab with a bronze engraving of the Roman conqueror Trajan who colonized the place in 107 A.D. Behind in forlorn neglect sat a tourist office. Faded cardboard signs of faraway scenes stood in the greasy windows along with a framed train schedule. A train for Koloszvar was listed: 3:40 AM daily.

"Awful," I said.

"Let's skip it and head for Debrecen. I'm getting long in the tube." I just stared until he explained, "I really miss Kauty."

"O-ho!"

Debrecen was not listed on the schedule framed in the window, nor any train to the border crossing at Artand. I opened the door and we entered an empty, poorly lit office-store with well-grooved wooden benches. The floor boards creaked as we approached a barred window in the wall. Another gloomy establishment of Transylvania. Far back beyond the window and behind a table covered with lace, sat the attendant in an old upholstered chair. She put aside her knitting and approached, a fair-complected woman no more than forty. Her light hair was braided and her face had none of the glumness that greeted us in most of the public places we'd experienced. She seemed an aging milk maid, smiling as Matt asked in Hungarian, "Can billets be purchased here?" "Yes," she responded in accented English. "Where to?"

Matt looked to me, appeal in his eyes. He had assumed responsibility, had deferred to my choices of beds, of restaurants and sights. He was my tour director, in charge of my satisfactions and comfort. Now his Kauty beckoned and he wanted to go back. Besides, he had determined to make the trip on 8000 forints. In Koloszvar we'd have to pay for a room, as we did in Brasso, which was not his idea of visiting Székely friends in Transylvania. Buying a room rubbed the wrong way, not in a proper spirit, it was meretricious. After all, wasn't Koloszvar just another precious pile of stones? Only an ingrate could ignore Matt's appeal.

"We're going to Debrecen," I said.

"I can billet you to Artand on the border." She scanned her schedule.

"Border check still two hours?" Matt asked.

"Yes . . .then the train for Budapest." She consulted her tables. "Get off at Puspokladàny, and catch the local to Debrecen."

"You take lei?" Matt asked.

"For tickets to the border."

"And beyond?"

"Hard."

Matt pulled me aside. We sat on a worn bench and he explained that we could follow the same scheme we planned at the start, buy our tickets to the border in lei, then walk across to the Hungarian stations, buy tickets to Debrecen with forints, and reboard the same train when it arrives on the Hungarian side. Never pay hard currency.

"How far would we have to walk?"

"We'll need a taxi to the border, then walk across - - a hundred meters, two hundred at the most."

I felt as silly as I did going into the country. We returned to the window. "Two first class tickets for Artand," said Matt. "What time?"

"Leaves at 3:40 in the morning."

"But that's the train to Koloszvar."

Her smile broadened. "Same train."

"Impossible," I said.

She agreed. "A sacrifice of sleep. There's an afternoon to Koloszvar, at 4:30. But to reach the border you'll have to wait until 7 in the morning for the train that leaves here at 3:40."

We settled on the lesser evil. "I admire your English," I said, "Where did you learn it?"

"Bonn."

Surprised, Matt asked, "Schooled there?"

"Born there."

"You don't speak Hungarian?"

"Not at work."

We had exchanged our last 1500 forints with Granny for 7500 lei (about $20). The agent wanted 2200 lei for two first class tickets with seat reservations. As she prepared the tickets, Matt prepared our money, and my curiosity was itching. I was about to ask what brought her to

126

Transylvania when Matt handed the money over and she began punching the date on a decrepit machine. It failed. She opened the cover and removed the paper, replaced it, then tinkered with adjustments till she got the old gadget working. We laughed and she joined in, explaining, "The last time I sold a ticket was two days ago."

Politely she waited till we were outside the tourist office before she turned back to her knitting. "Guess she doesn't expect any more business today," Matt said. I still didn't know how and why she came to Transylvania.

The ornate clock tower that dominated our ascent proved to be a museum twelve stories high. My legs began to wobble as we climbed the ever-narrowing casement. Halfway up I stopped to catch my breath. Matt continued up to the observation deck just below the soaring spire. The deck was enclosed and ran around the entire top floor, giving a circular overview of the old walled city. Surveying Segisvar from that height, I became a Transylvanian prince inspecting his domain. A higher mountain rose behind us. "The old church and Saxon cemetery are up there," said Matt.

Outside the town walls, I could see the railroad station, the industrial flatland, the utilitarian bridge crossing the river, the ubiquitous apartment houses Ceausescu built. Intrusions. According to our directions the Gorgeys lived in one of those buildings.

The floor below was devoted to the clock and its works, an ordered jumble of innards in a lighted glass coffin. Shiny gears, rods, pendulums and flying panels intricately connected - - a Rube Goldberg contraption of the 16th century - - moved the great hands and rotated the hip-high dolls that made hourly appearances. Ornate robes were painted on the rotating figures to represent royalty. Each doll had three revolving faces, a different face showing itself every three hours - - lofty nobles with changing faces! Ah, what crafty satirists these Saxon clockmakers. The 'working' works were surrounded by retired mechanisms that had worn themselves out through the centuries.

The first floor was essentially a gift shop. As we came down, I heard the blaring of heavy metal music. A demure young counter attendant paid no attention to us. We left.

Rain again. We approached the covered stairway that climbed to the summit. Matt had taken his notepad, prepared to spend time in the

127

old church on the grassy mountain top. But I was not sure I could make it. The stairway was like a long railroad tunnel bored through a mountain base, but worse, it ascended steeply. I was discouraged at the start by the distance; the opening at the upper end emitted a pinpoint of light.

I determined to pause every 15 steps and not before no matter how heavy my legs. As we climbed, my eyes fixed on the dilating pinpoint of light.

During the last segment, frivolous students came bouncing down, notebooks abreast, giggling, poking and punching each other. Their frivolity seemed out of place, nymphs and fairies among the ghouls. At the top, we joined a classful huddled under the trees, out of the rain. Immediately, Matt began a conversation in Hungarian. Two students on a bench under a tree rose and offered me the seat.

The rain was letting up but the sky was still iron grey, casting gloom on the old stone structures crumbling about us, apparently a school and monastery. When it stopped we climbed again, up a muddy path to the old Gothic church sitting on the grassy summit. Brick battlement walls several feet thick surrounded it. An arched passageway had been cut through one wall. It framed the valley and farther mountain.

The roof of the church was steep; its tile scales had lost all color. The stone walls were eroding; large chips lay crushed on the ground. "Saxon church?" I asked.

"Lutheran."

"Looks Catholic to me."

"Because it's not as bleak as the Calvinist's and Unitarian's?"

"Because it's built like a Cathedral."

A rusty chain and lock secured the tall carved doors. We tried a side entrance, then walked around and found a makeshift door, also locked. A small cottage sat to the side of the church, guarding the gates of the cemetery beyond. Matt knocked and was greeted by the caretaker and his wife. Again he employed Hungarian charm to entice the old lady (a younger version of Granny, as were most aged women on Transylvania). She found the key, which was also rusty.

Inside at last, we could barely see. The air was cobwebby, musty. No bats flew; I imagined their radar was scanning us from upside down perches in the medieval vaulting. Evidence of abandoned repairs lay about - - displaced stones, piles of wooden beams, carpenter horses, mortar trays, a ladder. The monotony of the stone walls was alleviated with a brick and plaster trace of a fresco, mostly flaked away. There were pointed arches, scalloped openings, lancet windows. But the church definitely was not Catholic - - no sanctuary lamps, no icons, or Stations of the Cross.

Outside, gaping holes punctuated the remnant battlement about the cemetery. Headstones and obelisks, cracked, chipped, and worn beyond recognition lay or leaned at odd angles. They bore names of clergymen, tradesmen, craftsmen in middle German spellings. The grass was green as Ireland's in spring. Matt put my question to the caretaker, "Have you chosen to maintain the grass and let the graves decay?"

He was stout and heavy jowled, smeared with the substances of his work. He laughed. "The church as well."

It was after five when we reported to Vlad Dracul's Castle, now appearing taller, more rectangular, an urban manor house or monastery. We had been expected and were the lone guests in the formal dining room, an ornate surprise. The tables were set with linen, crystal, and silver, and centered with vases of dried field flowers. A pretty waitress attended in uniformed propriety. The menu was plentiful, but whatever we ordered was not available. We settled for roast corn cobs, mountain trout, melon and apricots. The trout was served in a scarlet blaze of paprika, usually a mild spice. This was fierce as gunpowder.

"Dragon's fire," Matt called out.

"Evermore," I choked.

19 A Family Debate

We got lost in the maze of inhuman apartment buildings near the railroad. I imagined wandering all night, like Romanians trapped within their bureaucratic walls. Asking directions in English and Hungarian, we finally found block 12, a massive square of identical Stalin-block buildings. A dim wall bulb revealed Stairwell F, and we groped upwards in the dark until a descending flashlight met us. Then a vague glow diffused the hallway and the flashlight went off. A young man materialized, his face angled and strong. "Lagos?" I asked.

He guided us to the fifth floor where we entered a second hand makeshift 18th century salon. A baroque framed mirror reached to the ceiling, chests were painted and carved with curlicues, a dark landscape graced the living room wall. But in typical Székely fashion, the apartment was compromised by overdone, bulky upholstery, tables, and lamps probably from a furniture bazaar. A blockish sleeping sofa, already pulled out, filled a corner.

Lagos was just graduating and looking forward to college. "Here?" I asked.

"Oh no, Hungary, maybe Budapest."

"There's a good university in Debrecen. A lot closer."

"Kossuth? I know. Mom says you teach there."

"Can't you get a good education in Romania?"

"Possible," Lagos answered, "but not for me."

His father had graduated from Brasso. That was before the government relocated Romanians to harmonize Transylvania's population. His father was lucky, he had his position for twenty years and they let him alone. "But my persecution began in school because of my Hungarian name, Lagos." If he remained in Romania, he'd not be as fortunate as his father. "Hungarian offspring are allowed street cleaning positions."

"You expect better in Budapest?"

"At least everything will be in Hungarian. And no trained hounds."

"There are malignant police in Hungary too," said Matt.

"Romanian police aren't really malignant, just cowardly."

Maria came in with two market sacks dangling from her arms. She is plain and petite, a touch unnerved by our presence. "Zsolt is at a meeting with his minister," she began, then proudly rattled off the information that Zsolt's church was heavy into the Pro-Democracy Association, local chapter, while she was in charge of its Women in Public Life program. It was a while before I had an opportunity to say how much Matt and I appreciated her generosity

"It's rare," I said, "to meet strangers who take you in so selflessly."

"But for Szèkelys," Matt offered as a matter of fact, "it's natural."

She asked us into the kitchen while she prepared dinner. "We're having chicken."

"We've already eaten," Matt told her.

"You'll have something, even if it's only an apple." She waved a hand. "Under communism, women's role in public life was a masquerade. Their Great National Assembly allowed maybe ten percent to be 'elected,' to prove they had a hand in governing the country - - "

"The American Congress," I interrupted, "has less, and you have more women doctors than we do. Wasn't Elena Ceausescu a Ph.D. chemist?"

"A charlatan chemist. Did nothing but ruin the image of all women participating in government. We've had our dissidents - - you might have heard of Doina Cornea and Ana Blandiana? They fought and died with the men. But since the Revolution, men have held nearly every leadership position. Very few women are listed as candidates for election, even though they're active in the parties, thirty-five percent to be exact. Yet none of the governments since the Revolution have included women ministers. The Parliament has ten women deputies out of 328, three senators out of 143. We have forty-four women's organizations in Romania but no one knows. We get no media coverage. Women are still kitchen persons, cutting string beans into a pot of boiling water." She laughed at herself, but the recitation pressed on. "The trouble is women don't recognize their role, don't believe they have any. Our organizations hardly know each other. No coordination, no communication." She might have gone on forever had Zsolt not come home.

He appeared a reserved man in suit and tie which he did not remove in spite of our disheveled appearance. If ever he felt joy it had long been drained. A brief smile cracked his dark face as we shook hands. He ignored Lagos and nodded acknowledgement of Maria's presence. This appearance proved deceptive. Zsolt was no more reticent than his spouse. Soon I was stifled by his dull recitation of Pro-Democracy's struggle on the local level, "democracy's incubator."

It seemed they had been waiting for an opportunity to unburden themselves and along came a young Englishman, even better, an older American. Could a sympathetic ear be the price of their hospitality?

We listed as Zsolt vented himself: first the local elections in five years took place last February. The newly elected were still learning their duties and responsibilities. "On-the-job-training." But oh, the barriers to hurdle! No dialogue between citizens and their officials. Mayors do nothing to assess citizen needs. And the citizens have no idea of their powers. They still tread in the old servile grooves, ignorant of rights, insinuating rather than demanding. They use cunning to seek favors, or beg them. Council meetings are legally open, except when the councilors vote to close them. Dates of open budget meetings are never published, nor are the agendas.

Zsolt searched in his briefcase and came up with two stapled sheets. "Our program. Seminars. Americans will join other panelists from western countries."

"Who are the participants?"

"We hope to attract local office holders."

"You have money for all this?"

"Precisely what we're working on now, with the UN. We're planning ten seminars across Romania, and town meetings to create a dialogue between citizens and local administrators."

Dialogue. Zsolt already knew the jargon.

Lagos left the room with showy displeasure.

"You have your finger on the crux - -" I was saying when Marie called from the kitchen. We sat at the table with tea and apples as the three Gorgeys ate. Dinner debate seemed a performance for our benefit, sparked by Lagos.

Maria: If Lagos will submit the forms, he has a chance at a Romanian University. But then I worry he'll be swept up in Romanianizing of the country. Decisions are so difficult."

Lagos: My mother can't make up her mind - - the result of living so long under communism, carried along in the current like a serf.

Zsolt: (Directly) I object to that, young man! (To us) He doesn't respect her independent work for women.

Maria: I don't want him in Budapest. People there are too busy chasing forints and deceiving each other. If he must suffer for being Hungarian, why can't he suffer in Erdèly, in the bosom of his family?

Lagos: (Mimicking) Erdèly, ah, where the sweet air rolls down the mountains bringing its tingling scents.

Maria: Where at least he has an Aunt Zena who lives in the next block and holds tea at 4:30 every afternoon. And when Simon, the butcher, receives a carcass he saves a few cuts for us. Cut your roots, Lagos, and you'll wither away.

Lagos: And if I stay in Segisvar, I'll not wither? I'll be giving up expectations every day of my life, settle for less and less, until I won't even think about deciding. I'll become Romanian in every way.

Maria: You must never sink into such vulgarity.

Lagos: It's the only road open . . . And I'll wait in line for an egg, or a few ounces of coffee that come once in six months.

Matt left the table. I could see him through the doorway unloading the food remaining in his pack. He also brought out a bottle of Hungarian apricot brandy and bars of Austrian soap. "For you," he called. Maria and Zsolt thanked him, perfunctorily, it seemed, as though gifts were expected, and the family debate ran on:

Zsolt: Not all that terrible. Pro-democracy will make a difference. It will change everyone's life.

Lagos: Better do it soon. That drunken spy is in the cafes again.

Zsolt: (Directly to me) From Secu, secret police.

Lagos: I think he's eyeing Nagy. (To me) The barkeep. Because he plays tapes of Bartok and Kodayl. Even Liszt is blacklisted, you know. The Secu detained a group of us for doing the Chardas when there was no wedding. One spy ordered vodka and was given white wine.

Zsolt: We're all treated the same. Wine is all Nagy stocks. Everyone's paranoid in this country. (To Lagos) You sure it was the music that disturbed them or the exchanges? (To Matt and me) Our economic network. One trades a sugar connection for a gasoline connection, beets for potatoes, a kilogram of powdered milk, a pig, a carton of cigarettes for admission to the pharmacy college. All hush-hush, under the table, as you say.

Lagos: That's the Szèkely life, in each other's pockets, swallowed words, choked thoughts, like tamed animals among predators.

Maria: Not just Szèkely. When have Hungarians lived without fear? How many of those greedy sybarites in Budapest are not afraid?

Zsolt: What do they fear? We have the Secu.

Maria: They have the capitalists.

Zsolt: Decadence is what they have. Is that to fear?

Maria: You can smell it over the city. The rancid vacuum replacing the soul.

Lagos: Hospitals in Budapest still allow operations when you reach sixty. Romania can't spare the anesthetic, unless you're somebody.

Zsolt: I am proud of him for wanting to be Hungarian, but it's futile. The regime pressures young Székelys to ignore their roots. Those who do, qualify for an education and a decent job.

Lagos: And self-hatred.

Zsolt: He can't see that Hungary has written us off.

Lagos: Do you expect them to come here and make war over us?

Maria: So he should learn to live in Romania as his family does.

Lagos: And suffer! A Székely who does not suffer must be a traitor!

Maria: Their poisons cannot penetrate the family if we stay together.

Lagos: How can I? The only position I'm offered is in a forsaken place called Malaia. Do you know where that is?

Zsolt: It's on the map. Somewhere in the provinces.

Lagos: They start by shipping out the youngest family members and work their way up. It's happened to my friends. Mother will follow. She'll be transferred next to the Ukraine border. Then my father. He's the one they want.

Maria: It's that Pro-Democracy they're after.

Zsolt: No. They want loyalty, and I'm always careful to show that. If Lagos did the same, the university might be open to him.

Lagos: Why bother? When they've changed Beke, the street I grew up on, to Bakau. When stores have impossible lines and only radishes and champagne to sell, except when visitors show, then butter and meat turn up with them.

Maria: Even in Debrecen, if you don't like one butcher you can go to another. Say, 'two kilos of chops' and he'll ask, 'Rib or loin?'

Lagos: We're all participating in our own annihilation because we're hiding the facts from ourselves.

Zsolt: A popular thing to say, but not so. Our lives are not so hopeless. The Secu hasn't stopped our Pro-Democracy Association. And because one drunken Székely and one flirtatious <u>vengerka</u> were murdered in Csikscereda doesn't mean the police are conducting a terror campaign. Those were isolated acts. Covered up, true, but remember we're just working on our democracy. We don't have it, not yet.

Lagos: A <u>vengerka</u> is a loose woman; the girl in Csikscereda was fifteen, hardly a woman, and she was raped, not killed. It was her father

136

they murdered when he tried to stop them. So please begin with the facts.

Maria: Lagos is set on becoming a handsome Hungarian in Budapest. Sometimes I think he's right.

Zsolt: When was running away ever right? So he can forget his Székely parents who live across the mountain? Does he have any idea of our progress toward a better life, toward democracy?

Lagos: That's rot! All you're doing is stirring hatred for yourself and the rest of us. The best thing your Pro-Democrats can do is shut up.

Zsolt: Everything in their young eyes is bloodstained, repugnant. Romanians are determined to annihilate us because we are in the way of their greater Romania. So why resist them? True, they give us little room but we can work in it.

Lagos: It is impossible to survive through accommodation, by putting pretty faces on the horrors, offering to build bridges while they plot to destroy us.

Zsolt: Run away and your gut will dissolve like bread in milk.

Lagos: Do I stay and end up like you? Your process of building democracy is already eating you. They will act more and more atrociously and you will also, in retaliation. And you'll end up embittered, a gloomy, defeated man. Or you'll finally turn about and fight, when it's senseless.

Maria: Hungarians always begin to fight when it becomes senseless.

Zsolt: When is it not senseless to fight?

And there it was - - the insoluble Székely dilemma.

Zsolt had arranged to spend the night at his minister's, insisting it was not to make room for us. But why else?

I was too tired to pursue it. When he was gone, Lagos and his mother relaxed. They wanted to know all about us. But I was drooping, and as Matt carried on, I dozed off on the green pull-out. I was aware when she covered me and set an alarm clock nearby. He must have told her of our early departure. I undressed, thinking that again I had hogged the best bed. Matt stretched out in his sleeping bag on the floor.

Toting our packs - - Maria had deftly inserted salami sandwiches and apples - - we trooped across the flatland to the railroad station. I

137

paused to snap a photo of the sky breaking purple and pink over the old city on the knoll, penetrated by one soaring steeple.

20. At the Border

Eating our salami breakfast on the train, Matt expressed appreciation. "All part of the Szèkely network." At seven we pulled into the Koloszvar station, having chugged through the urban backside, much the same as any industrial city's. From the train's windows I glimpsed bits of the stone grandeur and wondered if I'd ever come back. For the moment I regretted succumbing to Matt's appeal. But then I noted the police roving about the station platform in twos and threes and on the street leading away. Koloszvar was out of my mind hours later when we reached the border town of Artand and set our scheme in motion.

It went smoothly. A taxi was waiting at the ready and we drove past at least a mile of cars lined up to cross into Hungary. At the head of the line drivers wore heavy beards and crumpled clothes. Matt guessed they'd been in line since the night before. Our driver delivered us to the border gate where a knot of machine-gun toting guards directed us to wait.

I looked about for the 'Fat Woman,' the border guard who had bedeviled Reka and David. I had forgotten Reka's warning upon entering the country, and might have forgotten now but for the long wait.

One guard was female, dour enough but not fat enough. We showed our passports and walked to the next set of guards, Hungarian. We thought we were through, but came onto another barrier, once more Romanian. At last we were free and began up the road to Hungary with easier breath. Behold in the middle of the road on the very line separating the countries, machine gun on his back, stood a final Romanian guard. One more time we had to whip out our passports.

"English," Matt volunteered.

"American."

He handed back the passports with a nod but when we moved on, he removed the machine gun, aimed, and commanded us to stop.

"What is this?" I saw the cunning in his eye. "The Romanian way of requesting a bribe?"

Matt spoke with him, then informed me, "We cannot walk across the border.'

"How so?"

"He says it's a new regulation."

"Baloney! Since when?"

Matt smiled.

"Are you sure he's not adept at the ways of the world? See how much he wants."

"I've already tried. He insists we must ride across the border."

At the side of the road I noticed a hitchhiker with backpack. At least the guard was not partial. In English the hiker said he was suffering from the same regulation.

"You expect to get a ride?" I asked incredulously.

Matt meanwhile had put out a thumb, which actually stopped a car. I ran for it. The hiker stood still, baffling me.

But when we drove off and I had profusely thanked the driver, I understood. We were in a private taxi without a meter and out of service. The driver was delivering his daughter to school in Budapest. She sat next to him and translated. They were not Székely; in Romania she preferred English to Hungarian. They would only accept hard currency;

the fare to the Hungarian station was ten dollars. The Romanians' final touch. Our train was waiting when we arrived.

"Are the juices flowing?" asked Matt as we rolled through the flat Alfold on our way to Debrecen.

I had spoken of scholarship draining me; he proposed the Transylvania journey to restore my spirit. But those creative juices were of youth, and like most, were misspent in a variety of corruptions. To again stimulate that energy would be like returning Transylvania to the Magyar chieftain's fresh conquest in the new forest. I am as far removed from that creativity as nations are from their remote origins. In Transylvania I attempted to see the trees but could not resist the compulsion to look beyond the forest.

Evu clarified it all; across the forest, past the woods, all is illusion, except for the pain illusions may cause, the horrors.

"De Rurum Natura," I replied.

Sturdy wives pouring hot oil on Turkish heads breaching the wall (Eger, 1552).

A bread truck unloading loaves (Brasso).

Chinese Restaurant; next to it, "The Palace." Peekless Támpa Mountain hovers

The mall gives onto a picture postcard of a German burgh, circa 1700 (Brasso).

The dog paused to stare at the cow (Brasso).

Sheer movement, energy, two aluminum hockey players racing for the puck (Csikszereda).

**Salamis behind empty counters, a single scrawny chicken on a tray
(Csikszereda).**

**City Hall balcony where Ceausescu reportedly gave his last speech.
(Csikszereda).**

Orthodox "Greek Oriental." (Csikszereda).

Cherubic face — Josip, caretaker of the museum. (Csikszereda)

147

Old Szèkely estate gates assembled outside museum . (Csiszereda).

**Cover. Debris of communist sculpture against the museum wall, in wake of
Ceeausescu"s execution. (Csikszereda)**

Red, yellow and blue homemade Romanian flag atop Tampa Mountain (Csabotfalva).

Three purple peaks. Bruzenland – terrain of old German district the Saxons tilled for nearly 8 centuries.

Orphans sweeping walk, monitored by teacher. (Csabotfalva).

Huge painted doll of the Holy Mother crowned in gold, holding her infant god, also topped in gold. (Csabotfalva).

Black scrawls deface a red bench along a tree-lined boulevard.

(Debrecen).

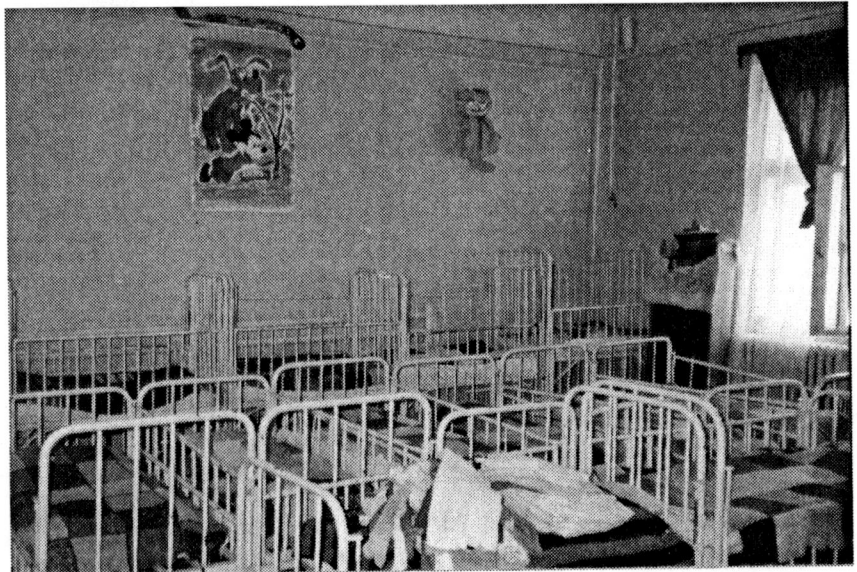

Orphan quarters were neat and completely filled with little iron cribs.

(Csabotfalva).

Ion, successful graduate, now orphanage cook and baker, with Father Istvàn (left) and Matt (Csabotfalva).

Dancing orphans came to greet me, faces radiant (Szàregy).

**Whimsy cuttings, floating faces and bodies like Mark Chagall paintings
(Szàregy).**

The dirt road formed a huge S ending at a wall spouting white towers and red-tiled roofs (Szàregy).

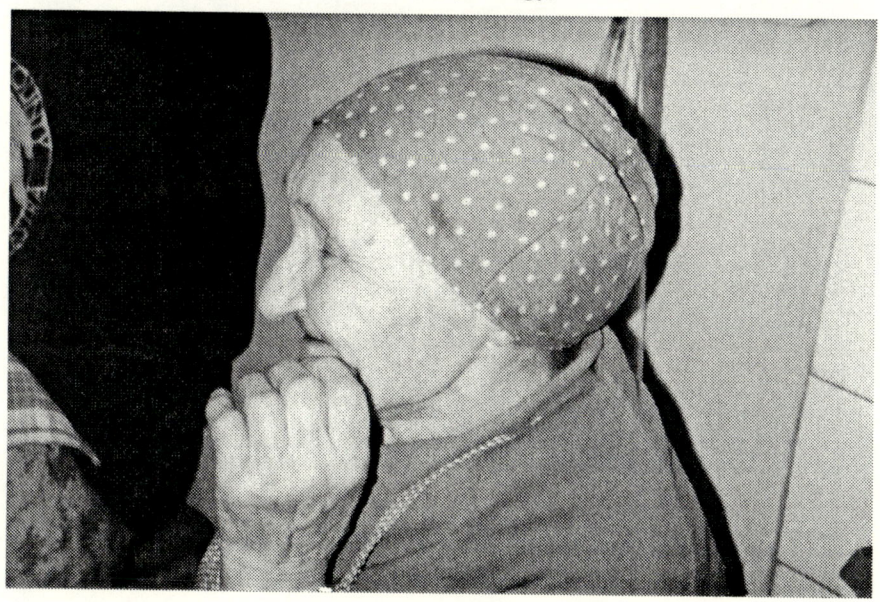

Granny

Daniel Marder

Evu; at kitchen table with Granny and friend

Author with self-appointed guide inside Palace (Szàregy).

A Gàbor Bethlen palace with "Hollywood" turrets (Szàregy).

Replication of statue in Rome depicting Romulus and Remus suckling the wolf (Marosvasarhely).

Old vets of Szàregy: Matt on left; author on right.(Szàregy).

Ornate exterior of the Palace of Culture (Marosvasarhely).

The clock tower topped with an onion dome sprouted a spire (Segisvar).

The square golden structure was Dracula's birthplace (Segisvar).

"…in this house lived the Romanian prince, Vlad Dracul between the years 1431-1435" (Segisvar).

Ruined citadel walls and old fortress next to alpine club house.

The sky broke pink and purple over the old city on the knoll, penetrated by one soaring steeple. (Segisvar).

Hungary Map

163

Eastern Hungary Map (Debrecen)

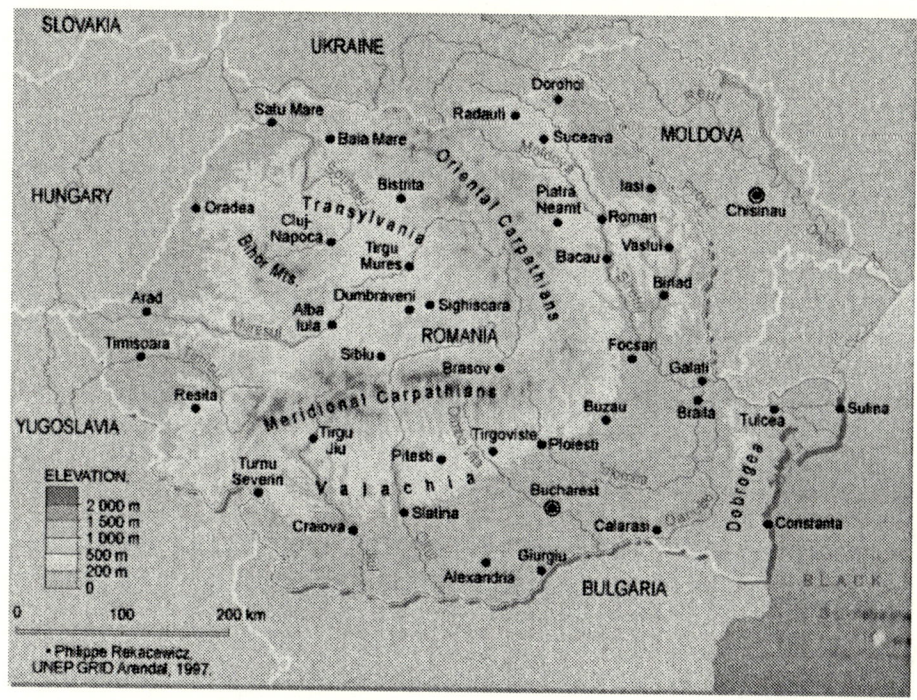

Transylvania Map

Hungary: Men, Beasts, and Stars

HUNGARY : Men, Beasts, and Stars

Contents

1. The Nagyerdei Forest

Wednesday, September 2.

Reva Milany had written:

> You will have no problem catching a train from the Western Station (Nyugati Pàlyaudar) in Budapest. There is one at every hour starting from 2:00 p.m. Unless someone meets you, show this to the ticket clerk:

> Kèrek egy elsò osztàlyù jegyet gyorsvonastra,ha expressz, helyjegyet is, Debreening. (It requests a first class ticket and seat reservation for the express to Debrecen.)

> If no one meets you, I suggest you take the minibus from the airport. Avoid taxis. During your stay you will understand why. Someone will meet you in Debrecen and hand over the keys to your apartment.

Clearing customs, I pushed through the swinging doors; a paper sign stood out in the crowd: DR. MARDER. It was held by a tall,

173

unpainted golden girl who guided me to the minibus. As we rode to Nyugati, she spoke of her professors at the university. She was studying with the American Fulbrighter, Steve Ruark, but was especially fond of his Hungarian wife, Reka, Professor of English Studies. Next year Anna would try for a scholarship to America. The traffic was thick. As the minibus approached the station, Anna asked, "You know the Eiffel tower in Paris? The same Eiffel designed Nyugati." The graceful squat structure of glass and steel seemed afloat in the city's bustle.

No porters at the station. I had three huge bags, weighed down with books, notes, and a year's clothing. The concourse was a huge chamber with ticket windows at the far end. Passageways on either side led to the tracks. Anna asked me to wait with my bags; she crossed the floor and purchased a ticket for the four o'clock. Then she disappeared in the passageway. I did not have long to wait and wonder. She came riding back atop an electric baggage cart with two husky workmen. We rode up to the very portal of the first class car. The workmen threw my bags aboard and I tipped a hundred forints to each. "You are too generous," she scolded. "That's nearly half a day's wage." I had given each the equivalent of a dollar and a quarter.

For two and a half hours in the late autumn sun, the train rattled through Hungarian flatland, the "Alfold," duller than Oklahoma's grasslands. The Alfold is the home of splendid horses and their csikòs, their cowboy riders. Villages of one-story houses, grain towers, and an occasional factory sprawl broke the plainness of the prairie. It stretched east to an ever-vanishing horizon. A few goats and stray cattle, never a cowboy.

Dumped at the end of the platform in Debrecen, I sat atop my baggage, perplexed. Should I leave my entire property in Hungary unattended while I walked to the station for a porter? Why would Debrecen have a porter when the cosmopolitan Budapest had none? Finally, when I was the only passenger remaining, I slung the duffle over my shoulder, grasped the suitcase handles, and stooping, began inching along.

A small figure emerged from the underground at the far end. My savior? She walked briskly and soon I could determine a face smiling from embarrassment, high cheeked, colorfully rouged and framed with straight black hair. Jeans and a red sweater clung to her thin frame. She saw me and started running. I dropped my load. We had only corresponded but I felt an urge to hug her.

Reva said she had been waiting in the station when two arrivals described a foreigner struggling with baggage. Instantly she discarded her sign and ran down the stairway, under the tracks, and up again to platform 4. Again I sat atop my luggage while she rounded up some help, again an electric cart with workers arrived, and again I was berated for over tipping.

In the taxi, she wondered whether I'd like the flat that Imrè-Bali had arranged. Bali was the institute head, "It's near the university, just fifteen minutes through the Nagyerdei. That's our forest. You'll scream when you see the furniture, upholstered black and red, like the House of Usher." My ear was too insensitive to pick up her accent in her impeccable English.

The taxi rolled down Simonyi Ut, a broad boulevard with grand sidewalks, neat red benches, the city's only tramway. Estate-like homes and a variety of institutional buildings sat far back on fenced lawns. We turned into a narrow, leafy lane, lined with smaller homes, trees vaulting overhead, and stopped before a spiked iron gate.

Depositing me in a roomy second floor apartment, Reva apologized. She had to leave me. "My Scottish pen pal is here. He visits every year. There's an ABC - - food market - - a few blocks down Simonyi on the corner where Nagyerdei begins." But I'd have to hurry. It closed at eight. "A restaurant's on the corner, another just a few steps into the forest across the way."

She opened a liquor cabinet. "Have yourself a toast. Your predecessors were last year's Fulbrighters. High lifers. They left everything."

The cabinet contained at least a dozen half empty bottles. She turned on a lamp and pointed to the bookshelves. In the feeble light I saw abandoned anthologies, travel books and maps lying atop Hungarian doilies. Funereal rubber plants occupied most of the corners amid clay pots with overgrown leaves. Reva showed me the kitchen galley, abundantly furnished, utensils, dishes, glasses, but only four mugs. Linens were on the beds in both sleeping rooms, more in the closets. Then the blue-tiled bath. I was delighted to see the long English tub. There was also an obsolete washing machine and a turbo for drying.

175

"Your landlord left instructions, in English." Reva pointed to a note atop the washer. Then she was gone.

The apartment was suddenly deserted. It was depressingly dark and I was lonely, spoiled after too much attention. I tested the Poesque sofa and armchairs (one of the red and black chairs swiveled). I summoned a laugh at my encasement in this desolate apartment, at my instantaneous estrangement. And the irony of its size. A few years ago, when my wife and child accompanied me on a Fulbright to Osijek in the now redeemed Republic of Croatia, we found comfort enough in a one and half-room apartment on the tenth floor of a high rise.

The apartment was dark, shuttered, though it had large windows and glass doors leading to balconies, front and rear. Hoping to dispel the gloom, I rushed to open the blinds. It was late in the day; I should not have expected sunshine. A faint light made little difference. Switching on a lamp, I saw that I was standing on a rich red carpet with blue and yellow designs. The fake oriental claimed most of the living room floor.

The kitchen galley had an opening into the dining room for passing dishes. A rickety dining set, table and chairs, was positioned below it on a worn brown rug. I returned to the tiled bathroom, relishing the pleasure of extended baths in the English tub. I tinkered for a moment with the obsolete washing machine trying to unlock its secrets of operation and gave up.

The heartening sight of the TV on a living room table was usurped by a huge mural of trees and leaf-strewn paths covering the far wall. For a second I fancied it as authentic, the view through an enormous window, then I was offended, it was gauche, a monster photograph. Later I recognized it; my living room was decorated with an immense blowup of the Nagyerdei forest. The more I studied the mural the more I was intrigued. The huge photograph caught the textures of tree barks and tamed underbrush; its tranquil perspective drew me and fascinated me.

It became spiritual, exuding the feel of the Macedonian forests when I was teaching in Skopje twenty-five years before. I recalled the forest deities; our first idols. The Macedonian inhabitants believed they had sprung from the trees. One of my colleagues in Skopje insisted that higher beings still resided in forest oaks where they determined human fortunes, good and ill. The oak, he reminded me, was the oracle of Zeus.

And didn't I notice that classical Greek temples were architectural replicas of the forest? The pillars were trunks holding up the tree crowns.

All the time I spent in that room, I never tired of the mural, and when my time was over, I regretted leaving that apartment, mostly because of that enormous, gratifying photograph on the wall.

The ABC was just closing as I reached it. I strolled across the street and, guided by a string of Christmas lights, followed an asphalt path into the forest, past a small hotel and a tall granite statue with four figures depicting Magyar warriors from the 18th to the 20th Centuries. The Christmas lights led to a garden restaurant with crude picnic tables and chairs. Young couples, one with child, were quietly drinking beer in the soft autumn light.

The waitress, there was only one, stood patiently while I whipped out my lexicon and matched names with those on the menu. I grasped halat (fish), pronounced it unsuccessfully, and finally pointed to the lexicon listing. She marked it down. "Kenyer?" (Bread.) Yes. "Salata?" Yes "Leves?" Yes. She was close to laughter when she set the levas before me, a thick soup with cabbage and meat, all reddened with paprika, enough for a full meal. The salata was more cabbage, with cucumber and onion. The fish was fried crispy and so bony I had to concentrate on it.

2. Kossuth University

Thursday, September 3

Mrs. Dinya, the landlord's wife, came in the morning with her son as interpreter. She showed me how to use the washing machine. First we had to pour in water from the tap, then a hose had to be connected, then - - we couldn't find the hose - - I asked if there was a laundry nearby. The son laughed, "On Egyetem, only a few blocks."

Before they left, I received incomprehensible instructions about paying gas and electric bills and something about the gas stove, which proved to be leaky. Within the month the authorities shut off two of the four burners. Leaving, Mrs.Dinya inspected her funereal flora but said nothing about my husbandry.

When I hunted for the laundry, I was directed to another broad tree-lined boulevard with a Soviet name on the street sign, Tanacskoztarsasag. "Egyetem?" I asked a person who spoke no English. He nodded. Only a few street signs reflected changes since the communist ouster. Directions in Debrecen were problematic. But this avenue had a beautiful ending a few miles away, a view of a magnificent fountain spewing water arcs.

Reva brought over my teaching schedule. In Hungarian. Impossible to figure out without an interpreter. I perceived that she was designated to provide that office, in fact that she was in charge of me. The schedule, as finally understood, had me teaching only two courses; I had agreed to three and had prepared three.

"I sent Imrè Bali outlines for an American lit., and two culture courses.

"If less than five sign up, they drop the course. Your American lit is in and your American Reformation. What's that?"

"A title I invented - - reforms, political, economic, social, not religious, not like the European reformation. Sweat shops, labor movement, agrarian movements, the Grangers, Progressives, Teddy Roosevelt, New Deal, like that. The dawning of American social consciousness, of Social Security. They must have dropped my racism course."

"It was given last year, and someone else is offering racism in America this term, or feminism."

"Who? Another American here?"

She nodded, "Tom Riedel." The name displeased her. She smirked. "Does Indian dances."

"Anthropologist?

"We don't have that. Teaches history and makes trouble."

I let that go. "Isn't Steve Ruark your Fulbrighter?"

"Kossuth rates two."

Reva guided me through the forest to the university. We strolled along a row of old gabled mansions in disrepair (wash hanging on a line), past the new structures housing the mineral baths, four huge octagon pools connected by an immense bathhouse and outdoor bathing facility. The path led to a pavilion. Benches were strategically placed in tree shadows. Then we crossed a wooden bridge between two massive reflecting ponds bounded by willows, water lilies on the surface. A dinghy rested on the shore, framed for romance. The Simonyi tram looped through the forest and formed the boundary where the university began. We crossed the tramway and beheld a mammoth building.

The structure had the configuration of Chicago's Merchandise Mart but graced with empire trim; beige sandstone carved in grand fashion. Beside this tribute to Hapsburg glory stands a sleek square-columned building with a tall flight of granite steps leading to its entrance and a thin square bell tower reaching beyond the tall trees, once a proud edifice of the Calvinist faith, now a university reference library. I would visit its reading room daily and soak up news from the "Herald Tribune" and "London Times."

Fronting these magnificent structures is a huge pool with greening nymphs and other bronze fantasies, one diving in. Waters spray from either side and meet overhead. It took me a moment to realize I was viewing another prospect of the fountain I had admired from the laundry on Egyetem Ut.

A formal garden with tan gravel paths leads to the beginnings of Egyetem. Great Hungarians on tall pedestals line the paths. The vista from the university to the centrum past the pool with its arcing fountain resembles a Champs Elysees or Pennsylvania Avenue from the Capital to the White House.

Professional colleges, dormitories, and a student union occupy the tree'd campus behind. The lawns are dotted with bronze tributes to great professors past in academic garb and severe Calvinistic poses. Beyond are botanical gardens and a medical park with hospitals and clinics along separate avenues arranged by specialty.

"Shall we take the elevator?" Reva asked. We stood among the marbled pillars on the black and cream tiles of the huge concourse in the main university building. She pointed to the magna-scale stairway, also marble. "Institute's on the 4th floor." I preferred the stairs.

We stopped at the liberal arts library on the second floor, entering through rows of card catalogue in old wooden cabinets. In the periodical room, a librarian took down a volume of the "Dictionary of Literary Biography" and proudly turned to my entry on C. Day Lewis. "You can get everything here," Reva said, "from 'Critical Inquiry' to 'Time.'"

On the third floor, Reva ushered me into a huge chamber paneled in light, shining wood. It seemed an empty ball room. In a large glass case on the wall was a gold crown with a crooked cross. "A replica of the crown of St. Stephen." She promised to explain it when time permitted. In another case hung the shield of Hungary. Perhaps she'd also explain the three crosses interwoven upon it? Green and white flags were standing about.

On the fourth floor, I was delivered to the impressive double doors of Imrè-Bali. Inside, his office was empty. An oriental rug lay on the polished wood floor. I waited on a long couch below a pennant of Oklahoma University. Erika, the Institute secretary, told me Imrè-Bali spent two years as a Fulbrighter. He was excited that a "Sooner" was chosen for the Soros professorship; however, he was unable to meet me. "Lunch at 11:30 tomorrow?"

"I meet my American lit class tomorrow. It goes from 10:30 to 12."

"Imre knows," she responded.

Steve Ruark was also unavailable. "He should be back from Budapest tomorrow. Goes often since he's become Chair of the Fulbright Commission." She told me he also chaired English.

Steve wrote about his Fulbright arrangement when he nominated me to the Soros professorship. Strange enough, it was a Hungarian commission; but chairing English in a foreign university! How very ambitious. Unlike my university, English and American were separate endeavors at Kossuth under cover of an "Institute." Linguistics was the third program, also called a department. How very grand! I met their famed linguist, the owlish Dr. Isaac Ferenc.

Reva explained that both Steve's positions were temporary, as he was. She took me to the Zerox room, converted from class use, actually the Institute's reading room and overflow library. It was so disheveled I could not get to the glass enclosed shelves along the wall. A library table and desk sat cockeyed atop a rolled carpet down the center. Against the other wall were a leather couch and chair. Cartons overflowing with books were stacked everywhere, over furniture and atop each other. The cartons blocked access to the bookshelves marked "American Studies." They may have contained the volumes I'd ordered. A magazine rack was overhead. There were also mail slots, and I was surprised to find mine already prepared and a slip in it, invitation to a private party. Only the Zerox machine was unencumbered. It was in constant use, reproducing big chunks of texts and periodicals. As we entered, the tall fellow at the machine abruptly stopped and stared, then continued. Reva turned about and left. He introduced himself as Tom Riedel.

A ruggedly handsome man in his early fifties, Riedel was clean shaven and amiable; his blue eyes sparked with intelligence. The tall, thin body had a slight bent as if poised to spring into one of his Indian dances.

"How many in your American racism?" he asked.

"Cancelled. How many in yours?"

"Cancelled."

"When Imrè-Bali accepted my course proposal, I had no idea there'd be another."

"Bali never saw your proposal, the committee accepted it."

"You were on the committee?"

Tom nodded. "They thought mine different. 'American Prejudice.' I included feminism and emphasized Indians, as I did last year."

"It's been offered before?"

"Every year I've been here, three out of the last five. Administration is not their strong point." We laughed.

He finished with a stack of copies half a foot high; we decided to go for a drink. I found Reva and asked if she'd come along. "Not with him. Anyway, Terry's waiting for me." She invited me to dinner with them the following night.

3. Hoosier Indian Dancer

Friday morning, September 4.

Not a Native American, Tom Riedel was a Hoosier. His crippled wife held a French professorship in Bloomington, "with medical benefits for the spouse," he emphasized. We sat at the outdoor café across from the ABC at the bottom of Nagyerdei forest. Though he had published articles and a book on myth and Indian lore, Tom had not landed a professorship in America and so had been bumming about European universities.

He had started at Kossuth as a Fulbrighter, and was granted the Soros to stay a second year. He hooked up with a university in Berlin, followed by a year in Finland, took a fellowship at the Smithsonian in Washington, and had just returned to Debrecen for a third tour, again as a Fulbrighter. During my time at Kossuth, Tom had speaking invitations to France, Denmark, Finland, and Germany, and wrote articles for European as well as American periodicals. He was a scholar to the bone, but engaged less in dull tautologies than exciting explorations.

Tom was concerned with living arrangements. He was cramped in an apartment complex shared with a friend; no space to spread out books and research materials. "I've got extra room," I offered.

He knew my apartment. "Just missed it. I was too hesitant." I surmised the friend was female, an entanglement. Casually he asked, "Reva treating you well?" Surprised, I started to answer, but he continued, "She's sizzling."

Yes, I heard it right. They had been lovers. Tom brought her to Washington during his Smithsonian. The malls and shops had blazed in her eyes. "And God, she was petty!" He lost a day dawdling after as she taxi'd mall to mall seeking just the right t-shirt for her nephew in Budapest. Still, before she returned to Hungary, Tom vowed he would get divorced and marry Reva.

But when he finally made it back to Debrecen, she had taken up with his replacement, the new Fulbrighter, David Schwartzman from Iowa. Colleagues shunned David. His criticism, like his personality, was arrogant and convoluted. (Later, Tom showed me a copy of David's perfunctory lecture to the Institute, and I had to agree, though Reva considered it intellectually elegant.)

"Schwartzman left before his time was up though he was paid for it. And Reva lost good will she could not afford." Without a word I refused to accept Reva as so heartless a femme fatale or Tom as so romantic a boob. "I hope you won't tell that poule tart we talked."

I suffered the guilt of complicity.

4. The Harried Head

Friday noon, September 4

Imrè-Bali wore a red turtleneck beneath a crisp, grey suit coat. He was still thin, and springy. His face was sharp as his manner and showed creases of middle age. The head was triangular, a grand forehead, curly blackish hair beyond. Erika, the secretary, worshipped him.

We were headed for a restaurant in the forest, a short walk, but he insisted on driving in his new Fiat. Rather than the straight path, his auto had to follow the tramline around the forest, then cut in near the bathing pools. He was restless. "I'm squeezing you in between appointments." I replied that because of our lunch, I cut my opening American lit. session. I dismissed them after an hour, too much of it spent scurrying for extra chairs. Then sixteen of us pressed around a table in a seminar room designed for twelve. He was immune to my implied criticism.

The room was half filled with diners. Cut flowers were on the tables, waiters in white coats, walls trimmed with carved wood, and a strolling violin. My favorite here is gypsy steak," he said as I scanned an incomprehensible menu. "And they have wonderful leves, ham hock soup."

"Not gulyas?"

"Always that, if you want." He ordered the gulyas for me and the steaks for both, then immediately asked for the check.

I was the third Soros Professor at the Institute, he informed me, "Steve Ruark was the first, followed by Tom Riedel, both originally Fulbrighters. And now again." He whipped out my contract, all in Hungarian except for the letterhead, which read, "The Central European University, Budapest Centre, Uri Utca 49 and Prague Centre, 130 87 Prague 3." Seeing my consternation, he explained, "Kossuth is part of the new system. The Soros Foundation, your sponsor, conceived of the Central University. George Soros plans to include major institutions from every Balkan and Central European country, including Russia."

"So ambitious! I am grateful to George Soros, but who is he?"

Now, my ignorance twisted my host's face. "He is the young Hungarian in New York who has shaken up the financial world, who has made billions, not millions, by shrewdly outguessing the money markets. And he's devoted great chunks of it to philanthropy. His foundation offers fellowships and professorships to leading Czech and Hungarian universities, which he hopes to unify."

"Is amalgamation good for Kossuth?"

He shrugged. The gypsy steak was fatty paprika pork, but the gulyas was divine. I excused myself from the wine. Diabetes, I explained. Imre wanted to hear about the University of Oklahoma, not its English, its football. He had also been a Fulbrighter at Duke University. The only business I could force him to discuss concerned the weekly lectures in 19th Century American literature which might replicate my offering. Imrè said, "Professor Kiras' lectures are intended to compliment your discussion course. He may be rusty. Just returned from two years on Fulbright at the University of Minnesota and he's taking over the institute."

This news was a shock. "You are leaving?"

"To become Dean of Liberal Arts. I'll still teach two courses."

I congratulated him on moving up the university ladder, and determined not to mention the confusion I found in his institute. He regretted my racism course did not hold, but promised me another chance next semester. Imrè tried to explain the institute's complicated system of course offerings. Third year students had "required options" and the fourth year students had "optional options," which I understood as limited and free electives. "You are staying the year?" he asked suddenly. Already I missed Roberta and Danya.

"I intend to." An obvious lie.

"Good. You can help us design our Ph.D. We plan to start next year.

I was not quite done with the pork steak when he looked at his watch. "Shall I leave you to finish?"

I gulped the last bite, wiped my mouth and stood without another word. On the way back he discussed his career; he was in line to be rector of the university. Imrè interrupted himself to put my mind at ease about my salary. It was to be paid monthly, not in a lump sum as his letter had stated. I should be pleased to know that Soros also provided three-quarters of my monthly rent of 21,000 forints (approximately $375).

5. Reva and Her Pen Pal

Sunday, September 6

Steve has returned. We had a moment together, just before I went to Reva's. An old acquaintance from professional conventions, I hadn't seen him in four years when we met by chance at a conference in Lake Bled, Slovenia (then Yugoslavia). Reka was along, his graceful new Hungarian wife who had been instructor of English at the Reformed Teachers college in Eger. Steve had just finished his first Fulbright and was determined to remain in Hungary with his bride.

He had asked in correspondence whether I would undertake leadership of the Poetry Club and now pressed me. "I did it last year. It'll get you started with the students and faculty. All you need to provide is a few drinks, for ten people at the most, and a poet for discussion."

"What do you mean a poet?"

"I mean the poetry; you'll lead the discussion of some poet's work."

"Established?"

He nodded. The Poetry Club had been fallow for years. Steve had resurrected it. With amusement I reflected that he was still driven by ambition while I was comfortably retired. I accepted nevertheless.

When I stood to leave, he asked, "Aren't you bringing her flowers? In Hungary you can't go to dinner empty handed." He wrapped a bottle of wine for Reva. Steve made sure I was aware it was not just gulping wine. "You can replace it."

Terry was a slightly-built Scot from Liverpool, an obsequious fellow with a heavy brogue. I had difficulty with his tongue. Eva said they'd been pals for many years. For appearances, I suspected nothing more. He worked with leather in Liverpool. Every word he uttered was a mundane observation or silly acquiescence. Reva spent little time with him. He read potboilers and walked about, discovering the town. That they had anything to write each other puzzled me. But the relationship deepened my interest in Reva. According to Tom, she did have needs. Terry? Maybe she continued out of sentiment, for tradition's sake? Terry was going next to visit Reva's friend at the university in Pecs, also his pen pal.

A grand piano dominated her living room. Rare is the Hungarian home that does not include music. Reva played only for herself. Books everywhere. An inoperable TV was stuffed among them on the dining room table.

Judit arrived, the institute's expert in Canadian literature and apparently Reva's close friend. Judit shook my hand with surprising strength; her appearance was on the frail side. Her dark hair was bound in a braid like a milkmaid's, but her complexion seemed dipped in wine.

We ate at a crowded table in the kitchen; the sink close behind was stuffed with dirty pots. "Cooking is not among my pleasures," said Reva, serving noodles and diced beef smothered in paprika.

I made a pretense of enthusiasm, "Paprikas!"

"Standard," said Judit.

"My mother used to make it."

"Your parents are Hungarian?" asked Judit

"Just my mother."

"You look Magyar." Enthusiasm lit her dark face.

Terry could not take the paprika. Reva served him a colorless plate of beef and noodles. He picked at it. "Stomach," he offered. He contributed nothing to the conversation which whirled about Judit's Catholic readings of Margaret Atwood, the only Canadian woman I had read. Before long, my sensibility was accused of being skewed by skepticism. I could not resist saying that I found her reason blurred by superstition.

6. Centrum

Tuesday morning, September 8

Brilliant warm sun. I watered the plants on the balconies and at the foot of the gigantic wall mural of Nagyerdei forest, then bounded out for Debrecen's centrum, my first tour. The blue and yellow trams hummed by frequently as I strolled beneath the trees and beside the bright red benches and plots of late flowers down Simony Ut.

One red bench was marked with black paint which formed ciphers, graffiti. The ciphers were English, an attempt at the language: POWER WHITE ONLY read the horizontal slats, and on the seat, NO NIGGER. How could this be? The only blacks I had seen were medical students from Ethiopia. I spent a moment examining the people along the walk, mostly older men and women with shopping bags on the way to market, some rather neat in slacks, blouses, suits and ties. A few in jeans, no tank tops. Later, I was to come upon a metal gate in my own neighborhood, chalked in white, SEIG HEIL, and in a centrum doorway, a swastika scrawled in red.

The plaza is shaped like an enormous coffin several blocks long. It's filled with cement benches and grand old elms. At its head stands the Great Calvinist Church, painted that Empire yellow found all over the former Austrian-Hungarian realm. The church's square towers are not outstanding, nor its neo-classical columns nor its plain white interior. The church is impressive only for its history, its size, and its raised position overlooking the plaza.

The site has been inhabited since the Stone Age. Debrecen was already sizable by the end of the 12th Century; by the 14th, it was a privileged market town. Called "the Calvinist Rome," the city played a hefty role in the Reformation and has been a stronghold of European Protestantism ever since. The present church, build in the 19th Century, is the largest house of Protestant worship in Europe. Here in 1849, Lajos Kossuth proclaimed Hungarian independence from the Catholic Hapsburgs, and established his government. And here in 1944, the anti-Nazi resistance government met, sustaining the hope of freedom for the war-ravaged country.

I decided the hefty alpine building behind it was city hall, but the second story engraving - - TANITOKEVZO FOISTOLA - - indicated something else (tanitani - - to teach, and tanito - - school teacher).

Actually it was a teacher's college, where some of my new colleagues were moonlighting. As I passed, a conference was ending; people in Sunday best were streaming out and seeking taxis. (The city hall, I discovered, was just another neo classic structure of no distinction except that Kossuth resided there in his brief tenure as regent of Hungary.)

On one side of the square, a new shopping mall had been erected, extensive in depth and breadth, still unfinished. But business was already thriving. It was also in the alpine motif. In my neighborhood all the new structures were of like design, which puzzled me since Debrecen was in the Alfold, Hungary's city on the plain. What I called alpine I was to discover was a native Hungarian style, unrelated to mountains.

Inside the mall, shops surrounded cemented space decorated with ultra-modern fountains, sans water at the moment. I was attracted to a projectile-like structure attached to a building like a rocket mounted on its gantry, poised for the cosmos.

Behind the 'alpine mall' as I call it, stretches the original market, a grand shed enclosing acres of fruits, vegetables, cheeses, chickens, sausages, pork, cut flowers. At one end, barrels of kraut were tended by huge women with rubber aprons over their vinegary sweaters and jackets. I bought bread, tomatoes, and hot dogs.

The art nouveau Arany Bika, the Golden Bull, occupies a block on the other side of the plaza. Its cuisine is reputed to be unmatched in Hungary. I preferred the gulyas in the crude forest restaurant. Behind the hotel is a complex of theatres and night clubs with all the markings of strip joints. The posters outside were alive with bared flesh in erotic poses. Just beyond were the old synagogue and ghetto.

Simonyi Ut becomes Peterefia just before the shops. Crowds urbanize it utterly. Then, for the decrepit stretch to the railroad station, the avenue becomes Voros Hadsereg. And so that was my first glimpse of the town. I saved the two major museums for later, along with a third college, which was devoted to converting former teachers of Russian to teachers of English, another source of moonlighting for our faculty. And behind the church was yet another college, established by Calvinists, and still unwavering in its religiosity.

Saturday, September 12

Yesterday, Terry invited me to lunch with Reva. She led us to her favorite rathskeller in the centrum. It served thick, spicy levas. Again he was picky, eating only unseasoned meat, and no vegetables. Certainly no levas. But he downed the beer steadily. Reva marveled at his capacity, he was so slight. Though he had grown up in Liverpool, the Scotsman's English was as difficult for me as Hungarian. Reva translated. He intended the luncheon to be his leave-taking celebration.

"When are you going?" Sunday. So I invited him to a more extravagant celebration for tonight, that is, if Reva had no plans. Would I have to go through with it if she did?

I asked her to choose the best restaurant in Debrecen, anticipating an evening at the swank Ariny Bika Hotel. She chose the green house of the alpine mall and I discovered the function of the rocket on its gantry. It encased a circular stairway to the glass-roofed greenery and crystal of the Centrum Restaurant. At night, the gleaming

197

mall resembled an old German village newly constructed; from outside, the soft orange lights cast an antique glow over the greenery in the restaurant windows. Inside, the glass ceiling and sides of reckless modern angles were softened by a jungle of broadleaved plants, just emerging and creeping.

Reva wanted us to notice the new air conditioning. "They'll probably turn it off if it gets hot again. It was off during our heat wave this summer. But now that the evenings are so comfortable, we're allowed to enjoy it."

In deference to Terry, we spoke of other things besides literature. He was a big-hearted goof but tough looking with a red-complected face, hair the same. His Scottish lingo came in spurts, followed by private guffaws at his unintelligible wit. He made strange faces and did tricks with his tongue. I wondered if Terry possessed a suit. Apparently, jeans and a change of plaid shirt comprised his wardrobe. Occasionally, Terry hummed and tapped fingers on the table. He had brought Reva several old Beatle tapes, but she had no working tape deck

The young lady he would be visiting in Pecs tomorrow was only "coincidentally" Reva's friend. When Reva had first entered the university, she was assigned a bunk bed in a ten-person dormitory. During pillow talk, the girl in the lower bunk revealed she was from Pecs. She also let it drop that she had corresponded with a man from Liverpool, which brought Reva upright in her bed. She bent over to examine her bunk partner. "For how long?"

"Ten years."

"Is the man's name Terry Donaldson?"

Both were stunned at the coincidence - - two Hungarian girls from different towns corresponding with the same man from Liverpool for ten years.

We talked of the communist "retreat" as Reva put it. Not a downfall in her eyes, in fact, that party was merely taking respite from power and must be enjoying the country's fumbling efforts at democracy. When these clumsy democrats turned belly up, the communists would roar back.

"By the people's vote?"

"Of course, that's the democratic way."

Terry made a mocking face. I asked her about the party in power, the Democratic Forum (MDF), having heard they were nationalist. Their deputy prime minister and editor of the party news organ had stridently called for a "pure Hungary" and demanded the restoration of the nation's "living space," which included Transylvania and other territories of past empire - - Ukraine, Croatia, Slovakia. "And who would they be, pure Hungarians? Does he mean Magyars? How many tribes combined to become Magyars?"

Reva said, "He means to exclude Gypsies, Jews and Muslims."

Terry was getting a rise from our discussion. He tittered.

"The Free Democrats are no better," Reva continued, "Liberty means excess for them," She smirked, "Among their liberties is the pursuit of hatred. You've noticed the graffiti along Simonyi?"

"Those are skinheads, not communists." Terry put in.

Reva said there was little difference, both were nationalists. "It's the political fashion these days; Communists pretend to democracy and call themselves 'Socialist.'"

Needing a touch of levity, I mentioned the Fidesz, Young Democrats, who confined party membership to under thirty-five but found they'd painted themselves into a corner and so increased the age each year. We speculated on the causes of such aberrations as skinheads and fascists - - I had discovered an old black face on a wall with the inscription, "where is Uncle Remus?" Terry concluded that Hungarian democracy was dewy-eyed. But it was still possible to teach Hungarian youth that freedom requires responsibilities. Otherwise this country would go the way of England and America. "Amen," I mocked.

"Crime is increasing in Debrecen," said Reva. "Since the Communists lost control, more rapes and robberies. I won't go into the streets alone after eight, not any more, even if it takes half my salary for taxis." Casually she referred to a murder.

"Here? In Debrecen?" Terry asked.

"You read Hungarian?"

"Reva told me."

"It was on the obituary page," she offered. "We don't go on over such things. A fifth-year medical student from Ethiopia."

"On the campus for God's sake?"

I knew Terry was enjoying my loss of control, coolly he repeated what Reva had told him; "She was found lying on the grass between the reference library and the main building. Throat cut."

"And raped," Reva added.

I blurted, "No one even mentioned it. Is murder a common event?"

"Rare, but less so since the Communists lost out."

"A medical student from Ethiopia, black? Any suspects?"

Reva simpered and called me Sherlock Holmes.

Walking home, she pointed to graffiti on a wall with the letters Sz-D-Sz top and bottom. In the middle was the Star of David. Reva explained the Sz-D-Sz was the party of Free Democrats, said to consist mostly of Jews. "During the Nazi days, my aunt's husband, Uncle Svolt, had to wear one of those stars."

7. Murder in the Seminar

Sunday, September 13.

Another bright day. Interminable. I walked an asphalt path in a direction away from the university and found the zoo. It was near a toy railroad track and amusement park. I went on, ambling down the forest road, onto the playing fields which I could not believe. I counted seven soccer set-ups, one in a sizable stadium. Close by was another stadium, a track for race horses, an outdoor skating rink, and an indoor gymnasium. I spotted a small al fresco café in a grove of trees and had lunch - - pickled beef, impossible to have a bad meal in Hungary.

Starting back, I became pleasantly lost. At last I glimpsed the tram through the trees. Heading for it, I discovered the Copacabana, a huge public house fronting an artificial lake. Families were in paddle boats. All was placid, even the children pedaled quietly.

Just before the tram tracks, I came upon a triangle of grass bordered in fall flowers. Two hefty brass sculptures occupied the middle, powerfully muscled nude women in ambiguous poses; one seated, the other standing, offering brass flowers to each other. Circling around, I was fascinated by the changing relationships, the two figures were attracting and repelling, opening and closing to each other, sexually inviting and prohibiting, dainty and forceful.

Monday, September 14.

I share an office with Reva at the forsaken headquarters of the Communist Party, our off-campus institute building on Simonyi. It is a deceptively large structure with extensions behind. A lawn with a willow tree stretches from the street to its ominous front windows trimmed in delicate terra cotta, suggesting graceful terrors the former tenants were said to perpetrate.

The university has totally refurbished it in cheap contemporary, each office having two desk and chair sets, and two cushioned chairs with coffee table. No lamps. Reva had supplied one. She has also pleaded my case for a typewriter. An electric German machine with unfathomable features now sits atop my desk alongside two cartons of textbooks, which should have arrived a month ago. Her desk, opposite, is empty except for several old anthologies. Tom Riedel offices next door. My seminar room is down the hall.

One carton of books yields ten copies of "Racism in America." "Don't despair!" Andros Kiros advises. He has just taken over the institute. One student has signed up belatedly for the racism course and a few others who must take the 5th year option are still on teaching assignments somewhere on the Alfold.

"But the course is already cancelled."

"Too early for pessimism," Andros insists.

Another carton contains six copies of texts ordered for my American Reformation seminar, Volume One: 1640-1865. Of course, all pertinent information takes place in Volume Two: 1865 – Present!

Eight students show up for the Reformation seminar, three bright young ladies among them. One of the males - - all look clean and industrious - - wears a suit and tie. I am no sooner introducing the American Progressive Party than his hand shoots up. He conceived of these progressives as America's socialists in the very early part of the century. He is Istvan, articulate, suave, polished, something of a politician.

"Actually the movement was generated in Wisconsin," I said, "but possibly influenced by European socialism."

"Inspired by race?"

"Not in Wisconsin." I was suddenly reminded of the murder on campus, and asked, "Was the murder of the Ethiopian student racial?"

They appeared puzzled. Istvan was the only one that seemed to know about it. "Very unusual for Debrecen," he responded with diplomatic glaze. Aha! Protecting his country's image from the foreigner's eye.

"Unusual?" I asked him. "Murder? Or this particular murder? Of a black?"

A young lady in jeans and badly dyed hair offered, "I think murder is more common now after our release from past rigidities." Equally articulate, but not as smooth.

"She means the Communists," another blurted.

"What I mean," responded the first, "is the freedom that Leatherstocking takes - - we studied Cooper last term - - his self-assertion of a moral law that may result in individual justice but also in tragic act."

Faces had gone from puzzlement to utter consternation. "Can you explain?" I asked

Istvan, who had also read Cooper's novel in the same class last term, came to her rescue, "Leatherstocking's first principle was responsibility to himself and his god. So, guided only by natural law, he took matters into his own hands. Natural law was his law. When it conflicted with society's laws, crime resulted, murder!"

"Leatherstocking only killed a deer," the first student corrected, "out of season."

"Your American individualism," muttered another student sarcastically. He wore a slight mustache and had a meek demeanor.

"Nothing new about American individualism," said a female student in an embroidered peasant's blouse. "Hungary has a bloody history. Murder was always the way to settle things. The state murdered people under every regime."

"Official murder," I said, "is not a matter of individuality."

She shrugged. "Killing is killing. State approved or not. That is my moral law."

"You are against war?"

"You are not? It's all murder!"

They were getting out of hand. "So you see," I said, "there are two sides even to Leatherstocking's natural law." And turned the discussion back to the Progressive Party of Wisconsin. Before the class was over, I learned that not all Hungarian students appreciate American individualism as touted in our literature.

As the students were leaving, Istvan told me he might have to miss some of our sessions in order to attend meetings of the City Council. "I am elected."

The cafeteria served students and faculty alike; a choice of two levas and four main dishes, none appetizing. All the meats seemed grey and ground, the vegetables cooked colorless. Choosing a levas, I asked Reva, "Anything about the murder?" She shrugged indifferently. Yesterday's event was non-political, so all but forgotten today. "Do you know just where they found the body?"

She stopped a passing student and chatted, then said, "Yes. I'll show you" Reva giggled, "But you're too late, Sherlock. Someone's already been arrested."

It was a very public spot on the lawn beside the main building not far from the arcing waters. I expected to see a police cordon. "Doesn't seem the police were here." I looked for clues, differences in the way the grass laid, a fragment of clothing, a cigarette stub in the bushes.

"Not necessary. They have the culprit."

"That was in the newspaper?"

"Today's. Not on the first page. You have to look for it."

"The front page is for politics, I know."

"And the second and a few more for politics and business and the war in Bosnia and you know, like American newspapers."

"And who is the suspect?"

"Her Ethiopian boyfriend, also a fifth-year med student."

"Why do they suspect him?"

"He was seen with her on the night of the murder."

Walking alone to the centrum, I toyed with the murder. Was it witnessed? Reva said the student was raped. Why would the boyfriend need to do that? Who else could be involved? Was it racial? A white somehow? A skinhead catching her out alone? Was she attractive? Shapely? Ethiopian, fifth-year med student - - that was the total description. The scrawl on the Simonyi red bench flashed in my brain: POWER WHITE ONLY. NO NIGGER.

8. Peter Magua

Thursday, September 17.

I was headed for the photo shop Erika recommended to pick up my departmental snapshot. She would mount it among the other notables from England and America in the hallway gallery. Steve Ruark and Tom Riedel were already on display along with Reva's latest love, David Schwartzman. His photo had been taken at the beach, a muscular short man with a hairy body and a balding head. The nose appeared bulbous.

The photo I had chosen for the institute gallery was Dionysian, a lascivious smile, and I was in that mood as I passed a group of colorful girls on my way back. I noted the brightness of their tight skirts, yellows, reds and greens, and well above the knees.

Steve and Reka were so impressed with the Budapest performance of one Peter Maqua that they invited him to Debrecen. The announcement read:

Visit by Peter Magua, 17-19 September

Peter Magua, A Native Canadian artists, was adopted by the Ojibwa Indian Nation of Thunder Bay, Canada. An artist with major exhibitions in North America, he enjoys a growing international reputation. He will lecture and show slides:

The Survival of Indian Ritual, Customs, and Values in the Postmodern World

Friday, September 18 at 4:30 pm in Room 422

(Magua is also interested in finding students to guide him around "native parts of Hungary." He is particularly interested in seeing places where Hungarian folk art survives and in meeting Hungarian artists.)

I met them for lunch before the performance, Magua dressed in an ornamental blouse and heavy necklaces and arm bracelets. A headband bound his graying hair which dangled below his shoulders. He was acting the role of celebrity, dominating the conversation with his spiritual spins. Above all Peter was interested in meeting locals who were more prone to tribal behavior and beliefs than university sophisticates. Tom Riedel called him a fake.

But Peter himself co-opted this judgment by admitting he was white. He claimed the Ojibwas adopted him. His performance involved much smoking. The fumes caused considerable coughing. Magua's claptrap about the Indian love of earth and a living earth loving back, and of living in harmony with all your relations in the lodge house did not go down with the packed roomful of Hungarian students. I realized more than smoke was responsible for the continued coughing.

The details of Peter Magua's message may have been unfamiliar but students recognized from their own culture the universal game and character of the medicine man who delivered it. Speaking of eternal time and space which he occupied as an Indian, Peter indicated nothing whatever of their internal strife and inter-tribal warfare with its tortuous ways. "Oh boring," whispered Reka, sitting next to me. She was effusive in apology. "Peter was marvelous in Budapest. Inspirational. But you can see he's fatigued. Students had him out till early morning. I'm so disappointed!"

I was given to understand his performances were in part supported by the US Information Service. Afterward, Steve Ruark was apologetic, "Impressive in Budapest."

9. Tosca and a Chilean Quartette

Saturday, September 19.

Took the long way home from the centrum. So many broad streets, appropriate to the plains of Eastern Hungary. The tree-lined boulevard led past humble homes, ancient unkempt shacks of plaster and wood, broken occasionally by high-rise apartment houses, also unkempt, standard for the lower levels in the trades and professions. A block or two away, I could see the chimneys and sooty buildings of industry. I came to a juncture with another broad avenue which formed a great circle filled with buses, a turnabout and terminal. Grapes were growing in a few small yards; there a plum tree defied its circumstances. In contrast, the street where I lived was luxurious, neatly fenced alpine houses of stucco and polished wood, dogs behaving behind iron picket fences.

Saturday night, September 19.

I had suggested the opera to Reva. She called about six from the Opera house, wanting to make sure I'd come before buying the tickets. But dressed in jeans, she worried about propriety, "I won't wear a tie."

It was the first night of "Tosca," which accounted for a few tuxedoes among the scattering of blue jeans. A mix of opera aficionados was gratifying.

A South American baritone sang the male lead. He wore high heeled boots to approach the height of his female counterpart. She towered over everyone on stage, in poorly faked red hair and tarnished period dress. The parody her appearance suggested evaporated with the first note of the aria she sang. The magnificent timber and control of her voice were matched by her acting, natural, paced, emotionally subtle. Unlike the male, she did not pause for appreciation after each solo flight, but the applause began before she was through, in the rhythm of a cheering section.

Each of the three acts had its own set, each more exciting than the last, which was the brooding blue jail yard where the artist is executed. Marvelous evening.

Tuesday, September 22.

Joined a crowd of 100 or so in the centrum. We formed a semi-circle on the broad sidewalk where oranges, grapes, bananas, etc. were being hawked from makeshift stands in front of the arcaded entrance to a department store. Four musicians were performing in the middle. I took them for gypsies, but closer inspection showed their hats and blouses were different. Taped cassettes of their music were on sale from a box at their feet. The cassette covers said they were a Chilean quartet.

They swayed and stomped, beating out happy rhythms; guitars, woodwind flutes, three men and a woman who frequently broke into song. The woman's face was harshly painted. She wore tight pink pants, blazing embroidered vest, and a bright broad hat. The men dressed in looser pants and black hats with colorful bands. Another hat was on the ground and the crowd was tossing in forints and fillers. The adjacent stand, pyramided with oranges, enjoyed a banner day.

A veiled bride in white satin and her tuxedoed groom emerged from the photo shop. Surrounded by celebrants, they slowly proceeded to a waiting taxi. The alert musicians switched to a wedding march. A legless old man in a wheelchair, grey and decrepit, rolled up to the taxi and pushed a bouquet of flowers at the couple. Fillers poured on him as the taxi whisked away.

10. My Neighbor from Coral Gables

Wednesday, September 23.

Another sunny day. After my half-mile hike to the bakery, I exulted a moment in the aroma and sweets, then hiked back through the tree-lined neighborhood to eat the crispy rolls on my rear balcony. New morning light colored the trees and berry bushes in the surrounding yards. The light breeze smelled of cedar and musk.

Preparing lessons. Emerson is still beguiling, and of course full of bull. Transcendendant irresponsibility! Missing Roberta. I still the longing with a Budapest guide book, planning for her visit. Long walk through the forest. Tonight I'll appease myself with a sugar-free hot chocolate (I still have two dozen packs Roberta sent) and Camille Paglia's "Sexual Personae," her "clthonian woman," blood and mud. Yuk! She really has fingered (right word?) my poetess, emphasizing Miss Emily's violence. "Dismembering body parts"? Did I miss this Emily Dickinson? Paglia - - a mind only de Sade could love!

The old man across the way has introduced himself in mildly accented English. Peter Eglan. He is well-dressed, well-kept and on social security; he's returned from Coral Gables after 30 years. The Debrecen golf course, I learn, is only nine holes with little challenge except for rough greens. He has difficulty finding players.

Since I can't read the Hungarian newspapers, he tries to keep me informed. The Ethiopian medical student held for his compatriot's murder has been shipped home. "That's how Hungarian police do. Keeps our records clean." He showed me the notice, an inch and a half above the obituaries and ads on the next to the last page.

His wife was in the hospital. "She was born in Subotica. I won't live there, so she settled for Debrecen. I was born here." But his heart was in Coral Gables. "The university hospital's as good as any in Florida." The prognosis was not good. "Avril wants to die in her birthplace." That was somehow key to her salvation.

"But Subotica is not Hungary," I said uncertainly.

"Subotica is a Hungarian city in Vojvodina, an independent province of Serbia." A touch of emotion had crept into his voice, as if he were girding against insult. "Until 1918, Subotica was Hungarian territory." Then he seemed to realize he had overreacted, and shook his head, "What does that matter? I am American, a citizen. I only wait for my wife to get better and I go home to Coral Gables."

My neighbor said Debrecen was a pleasant enough place to wait, but Subotica was not. It was many years since he'd been there. As he recalled, it consisted of streets lined with one story houses packed together, drifting into the empty prairie. Except for their color and trim they were all alike, long and narrow, the backs serving as barn, chicken house, or pig pen and extending into the family plow land.

"You don't care for Serbia?"

His head lifted and his eyes sharpened, perceiving, it seemed a hint of prejudice in my question. "You mean now? Fighting with Bosnia?"

"That's not what I meant, but - - what do you think of that butchery?"

"Not what you want to hear." He leaned forward. It was apparent he welcomed the opportunity to speak out. "You think Bosnia is really a country?"

I chuckled, "Of course, I've never heard it questioned."

"And the Bosnians are really Muslims?" He did not wait for my response. "They are Serbs, same as the men they fight, except they converted under the Turks. The one's you call Bosnian Serbs did not. For five centuries, Ottomans ruled them, if not the Turks then the Hapsburgs; after that, Yugoslav royalty, Croats - - Ustache Nazis - - until Tito. So Bosnia is a country?"

I knew the history he recited; he was following the tragic error of still living it. He was excited. I was a fellow American, a rare chance to let out the steam. And right next door. "Can you understand why a Serb risks his life and his family in the hills around Sarajevo? You think he is mad! An animal! Those are his hills, where he was born."

History mandates behavior, I thought. "Both sides could use a lesson in history." His brow lifted and he leaned forward. "Vengeance is an endless cycle."

"Americans do not remember atrocities?"

"You are American," I reminded him.

"But not like you. I don't forget the terrible things that happened ten years ago, not even ten thousand years ago." I nodded understandingly though oblivious to his references.

"Serbs and Muslims are children fighting over a candy bar," I continued. "They need a mommy who will teach them to share."

"Ah, what a dream! Everybody's beautiful dream, but only that. The world is not a democracy, my friend."

Silently I agreed. After my neighbor had gone and I was in bed, I reflected, the world is thousands of begrudging tribes like Bosnia's crammed into - - how many, maybe two hundred countries?

I shuttered at the ugly thought that he was quietly and politely waiting for his Serbian wife to die so he could return home.

11. Gypsy Nymph with Golden Child

Thursday, September 24

Julia called from Turkey. (My step-daughter, the engineer.) She'll be delayed a week. The plan is to detour on her way home via Frankfort and relieve what she insists is my homesickness. Debrecen is at least a thousand miles out of the way. But such is her devotion. The delay means she'll arrive the evening after the first Poetry Club meeting, chez moi!

Determined to reawaken my powers of observation while on my balcony this morning, I studied the details on the roofs and treetops, but saw only the accumulation of yellowing and reddening leaves beginning their blaze to death against the cracked red tiles. Poe saw physical beauty in the dying, also the grotesque. For Emily Dickinson, death was always ghastly, up to that last puny hiss. Internal. Mental. Not what I mean.

Educated patterns in my head defeat my observation. I do not observe the moment before my eyes. I must freeze time to attend the moment, neither past nor future, not see through my filters. Nonsense. Not possible! What a foolish quest. For raw existence. Even Thoreau had to envision nature.

Saturday, September 26.

Found it! The rathskeller off the high street where Reva had taken Terry and me to lunch. Once more I dipped into a gross bowl of thick gulyas and bit into chewy dark bread. Satisfied, I meandered down Voros Hadsereg, the high street with the aftertaste on my tongue. A sight arrested me.

The hustling Saturday crowd on the broad sidewalk seemed indifferent. I was enrapt by an absolutely corrupt beauty, a gypsy nymph out of costume in a dusty black dress that clung to her nubile body, her small breasts firm and her waist tiny. The black eyes radiated mischievous innocence. Only a protruding brow marred the perfection of the dingy doll face.

She was unloading a huge bundle from her back onto a cement planter in the middle of the walk. Then standing erect, she released a babe whose legs had been clutching her hip. The child was about a year old and brilliantly blonde, apparently the result of a North European encounter. When she set this golden creature in the filth and debris of the sidewalk, I saw no underpants, bare flesh. The child fell back, kicking her legs in the air. The genitalia appeared swollen. The nymph busied herself rearranging her worldly possessions, mostly wrinkled clothes. She organized them into two bundles. Then hoisting them to her back with one hand, she grabbed the babe's arm with the other, jerked it to her hip and trudged on. Heading for a gypsy camp somewhere on the town fringe where someone cared? It was a frozen moment of life, caught in transit. A tram came by, she broke into a run. The tram stopped, then started again; our Neanderthal nymph caught a pole as she leaped, struggling aboard with her burdens, so forlorn.

12. Tom and the other Reva

Sunday, September 27.

Dinner at Tom Riedel's last night, actually at his new Reva's. He has decided to stay coupled in her small apartment rather than share mine. Gulyas again, but quite another dish, served with spiced beef. Reva disdained praise. "Nothing, we all cook that way, Hungarian mothers teach their daughters."

The apartment was also tasteful, furnished with cream-colored leather sofa and chairs, lined with books as I expected of academics. Reva was also studious, closing in on her "kis doctorate" while teaching English at the medical college. Hungarian universities actually offer three Ph.D.s in English. "Kis" is the first.

She is not as pretty as Tom's former Reva, but her face is equally strong, the bones more pronounced, a Magyar face, and her shapely figure is fuller, more athletic. Like the other Reva, her dark hair is uncolored, combed and shiny; the cosmetics spare. Her face exudes intelligence. She's well-spoken and confident, a friend of Reva Milany, "who will not speak to poor Tom, even walks out of a room to avoid his company. You'd think she'd get with it."

On the ottoman I noticed a Budapest newspaper written in English. "Last week's," Tom said. "If you lived in Budapest you'd always be up on Hungarian politics, blacker than we can know in Debrecen. Istvan Csurka, a former communist writer and now Deputy Premier - - "

"Matt Palmer's told me about him."

"In the last issue of the house organ he edits, Churka called the ball game. He criticized his party and prime minister, Josef Antall. Used a lot of Nazi buzzwords like 'genetic roots' to make his point, which was simply the Magyar cause. Antall's a sick man, according to Csurka, a tragic hero with cancer."

Tom took up the English language newspaper and read, "'Pick Antall's successor now! It is the Democratic Forum's last chance. The party must quit compromising, quit bargaining with degenerates who run our TV; snuff out their insolence, threaten consequences, destroy all forces that sabotage our goals.'"

Tom was an effective actor. His pitch grew more strident as he continued, "'Life in this country must proceed as we demand, not as leftover communists allow. We are the Forum party of all Hungary, the party that embodies Hungarianism! We are the volk. All others on Hungarian soil are alien; communists, liberals, Jews, gypsies.'"

Reva brought more coffee and observed that Csurka was particularly rankled by President Arpod Gonez, who had rejected the government appointees to chief TV positions. "Why did Arpod refuse them?" She grimaced playfully, "Csurka says he had orders from his communist liaisons in Paris, New York and Tel Aviv."

"They can't stand prosperity?" I asked.

"Too much expansion too fast," she responded. "A frenzy of new entrepreneurs in Budapest."

"God tempered the winds for the shorn lamb," said Tom, "and the lamb became a bull. Now its Budapest in the fast lane, so who's listening to Csurka?"

"Too many," said Reva, "even outside Budapest. Most of us still scratch for bread. The economy's worse than it was with the communists.

13. Sex and Amour

Monday, September 28.

Reva Milany called - - the Civic film series was showing an English language movie. We walked down to the sprawling Cultural Center and just got in the blackened theatre as the credits rolled. Neither of us knew the title. The screen showed, "Yugoslavia," in Cyrillic. Few lines of dialogue were in English.

The opening scene was an orgy of flashing buttocks and privates, followed by the face of a benign old fellow. "Dr. Reich," announced a narrator with a sardonic twinge. The subtitle read, "Dr. Reich's Orgasm Corporation. Orgasms are promoted here in a cooperative arrangement, a therapy that allows freer breathing." The film turned out to be a communist spoof, produced underground during the old regime.

It was orgy as ritual, another opiate. Sexual display soon took the backstage, but hardly a scene without an accompaniment of intercourse. A fresh young female occupied the center. She was a party stalwart who lost her head to a virile and virtuous blonde demi-god, both Nazi and communist. Once turned on to the violence of sex, our Apollo goes crazy for it until he has her head, that is, severed. At the end the detached head forgives him - - at least that is what I made out of the garbled subtitles, which had been Hungarian interpretations of the Serbian and retranslated into English.

Over late night tea at Matya's, I said such explicit satire would not be appreciated in America.

"Because Americans haven't quite lost their virginity?"

"That's long gone. It's too crude, I mean politically."

"I think so too." Usually when Reva spoke her eyes were straight into yours. Now she looked down, into her tea. "I thought it was an English language film," she offered apologetically, her face flushed. "David would have liked it. Weird films were intellectual challenges to David. You knew he taught film?" When her eyes did return to me, I saw sadness and confusion.

"At the university?"

She nodded. "They asked him to stop. Hateful, all of them."

"I'm told he couldn't express himself. Too confounding, argumentative, abstract."

"David was brighter than any of them. Did Tom Riedel talk about him? Don't listen. Riedel's venomous."

"He showed me a reprint of David's lecture for the institute. I couldn't follow it either. David got twisted up in critical theory, deconstruction, tried to make sense out of nonsense."

Reva was not hearing me. "Riedel has spread the worst tales about David and me. Jealousy's eaten him. But he's had that Smithsonian, a senior fellow. They respect him; they listen to him, Imre, Andros and the rest, even Ruark. They didn't renew David."

"No chance they'll have him back?"

"None. They never got to know him. He's been looking in Germany, Finland, even Turkey."

"If he finds something you will go to him?"

"He'll find nothing. Riedel can send a nasty letter."

"You know that's nonsense. Is David working in America?"

"He's been sitting in Iowa, applying. We plan to live in Europe, anywhere he gets a job."

222

David's department photo shows a balding man with a smirk, certain shrewdness. I sensed he was not just sitting there in Iowa. "You trust him?" She smiled evasively.

We walked the rest of the way under the dim yellow glow of the street lights. It was dark when we turned off Simonyi and followed the glimmer of houses to her gate. She began to unlock it. "I must go."

She said nothing. Her eyes reflected the glimmer of the houses. Finally, she responded, "I love you." We stood quietly, trying to see each other. Hesitantly she reached for my hand. Her body seemed to lean into me, emitting vibrations. I'm married, I told myself, and too old for this. Reva had admitted to thirty-five years. "Sizzling," was Tom's opinion. I squeezed her hand and let go.

Tuesday, September 29.

Reva was already working on our German typewriter at my desk. I sat on the fake leather chair alongside the coffee table and began shuffling my notes. Hardly stopping, certainly without looking she mumbled, "Pity." What? I responded with astonishment. She rose, smiling ambiguously, gathered her books and notes for class, and went to the door. "Have a good class, Daniel."

Wednesday, September 30.

I am the wanderer, old medieval loner, seeking and rejecting duplicitous human society. But I'm no long haired hermit in a cave, I must be near, must know the news, the gossip. I have straggled through, nauseated with my fellows babble and ever-thrusting vanities, an unsuspected solitaire. I've deceived them, everyone. Debrecen is no exception. Alone, I've wandered in the midst of cities, gaping at the architecture, intrigued but irritated with glimpses of the human race through windows. Only with a loved one do I flow.

I suspect Reva of the same orientation. She performs academically as if obligated, dutifully accepting committee assignments and managing activities. But she prefers herself removed from society, which she condemns as fraudulent. She scours for a like soul. I

223

understand her need to share her inner richness, anyone half genteel, equally alone, a Tom, a David will do just fine.

Thursday, October 1.

Reva's asked to borrow my copy of Camille Paglia's "Sexual Personae." I warned her that I agreed with the "New York Times" "Paglia is stimulating but exasperating, a craven sexual animal with a Barnum and Bailey spirit. Her mythic knowledge is vast."

Saturday, October 3.

She was aghast and overwhelmed, "Ugly, ugly, vile, too much," after reading only the Emily Dickinson chapter. "Have to put it down till I catch my breath." Reva was angered by the author's reading of Dickinson's poems as "sterile androgynes." Paglia was a "case of reductio ad absurdum."

My judgment was much the same. I assured Reva, "Paglia's mind is wholly mythical and her book is overly researched."

"Her research I like, what I can trust, but she's off the wall. Something's missing from her analysis."

"Amour?"

"The possibility of it, the spiritual side. She reduces love to sexual polarity and woman's mucky earthiness."

"Woman's 'clthonian nature.'"

"Did you look up 'clthonian'? I had to."

As Reva's critique rolled out, I entertained a notion of her as a Hungarian Dickinson, less accentuated and non-poetic, but an evanescent and ambiguous isolato, forever yearning for and evading another. Dickinson had a penchant for asking males correspondents to be her "preceptor." She signed letters, "Your scholar," and confessed, "I haven't the confidence in fraud which many exercise."

Sunday, October 4.

I've devoured two jars of sugarless jam with these chewy rolls. Sad compensation for the forbidden Hungarian pastries. One jar left. Julia is bringing more from Turkey.

A light morning patter. I enjoy the dry comfort, watching the glistening leaves from under the hood of my balcony. Thinking again of Reva, "lips may be silent, but fingertips chatter." Freud wrote that.

She has asked me to accompany her to Goeff Gibson's big bash. Goeff is formerly of the Institute and now a major player at the three year college established by the British Council for training English teachers, the CETT. He's just returned from a summer in England with his Hungarian wife and children. The party celebrates the house they rented in the new section on the edge of town.

14. Yet Another Reva

Monday, October 5.

Passing Tom's open office door, I glimpsed a wondrous shape in blue jeans and high heels. He motioned me in, then introduced her, yet another Reva. All were about the same age. It must have been the Hungarian fashion in names three decades back. This one was as pretty as she was shapely, very lively, quick-witted, and aware of the world. Her face was Hollywood.

To avoid misconceptions, she told me they had acted together two years ago in a not so amateurish musical production at the opera house. Reva was a professional singer and dancer, "enthralled with Tom's Indian prancing."

When she had gone, Riedel assured me, "We're just friends. Reva's got a lover. She wants to try graduate school and I'm advising her."

Ironically, I said, "I wouldn't suspect you of being an actor."

"It was a Broadway musical, Imrè-Bali was also in it."

I couldn't fathom the institute head, now university dean, as a stage actor. "Imrè's idea to put it on. Reva was his English student."

"Did you do your Indian dance?"

He became sheepish. "Well, yes I did. That's how we became friends. I taught her a few steps."

A foxy smile displaced Tom's sheepishness. He broke the awkwardness by getting out some poems he had published in lesser literary journals. I had offered to read them. The poems were not as wretched as I had anticipated; actually, the metaphors were arresting, but always internal, which did not surprise me. The writing was not insincere. It exuded pain.

His poems revealed the source of his pain was the frustration of language itself, the essential tool that humanizes and deceives us. Language forever masks the essence of things. His poems obsessed over the raw terrors of human history and behavior that language disguised in its renderings.

The most anguished poem addressed his profession. Tom was an anthropologist, a scientist, and objective observer. The poem quarreled with this posture. Modern science fostered mindless worship of its methodical objectivity, its promise of progress, and its narrow specialization. It is all consuming. Plato and Aristotle were taught now only as relics of intuition and reason. In its specialized spheres, "science compartmentalizes thought and grows myopic"; knowledge carried by language "bulges each sphere till it halves/and again halves, and again."

Tom refused scientific comfort; he refused to diminish that way. He belonged to no school, his philosophy was not business as usual.

15. Precise Observation

Tuesday, October 16.

Less than two weeks since I resolved the enigma of my observing eye. For a moment I thought I was capable of meticulously examining objects whether in my rooms or in the forest. I meant without pre-conceptions, which is impossible of course, given our experiential and mental generators of habit. This exactness is scientific delusion. What I can do is observe an oak conscientiously and make rather sharp approximations about the pattern in the bark. But I can observe only a minute or two before 'attention deficit' sets in, before the object reveals itself as a process. Then, surreptitiously, my mind slips back to glossing. My habit of generalizing is too deeply grooved.

Walking back from the centrum yesterday, a burly fellow mumbled something as he passed. I determined to pay attention, to observe precisely. His face was ruddy but his eyes were cold and blue. Waiting for my answer, he asked, "Anglulol? Anglulol?" (English, English). The blue eyes widened for a moment with consternation, then, sensing the failure of communication, narrowed like a beam. I saw the language of hatred twist across the face, and following his example, leapt to judgment: the world is populated with a substratum of devils, my mind snapped. (A super strata of devils, he might be thinking.). Other casual encounters on Debrecen streets have had less severe endings. Unable to respond with the correct direction or the time of day, I've been dismissed with a shrug or wave of the hand, a worthless foreigner.

Wednesday, October 7.

Strolling through the forest, I observe others on the path, but do not see. I do not read faces. I am no Thoreau. Nor did he see faces; he read flora and fauna, and the higher laws. Was he one of Camille Paglia's Apollos? Dionysians? She divided mankind between them, her equivalents of homo or hetero. But womankind is quite another brew, all clthonian, of blood and mud, of mother earth, menstruating women. Again I work to observe precisely.

Girls passing on the forest path have high hems. One is prettier than the other, flusher cheeks. Unornamented. One wears a sweeter expression, beyond virginal claptrap but unscathed by whatever brushed her cheek. The beauty of mild manners contours her face. Would anybody consider this observation? It's not even description. Its representation, arrangement of my perceptions. My action. My narration. Description is too deadly, lifeless.

16. Academic Vagabonds

Saturday, October 10.

After we picked up Judit, the taxi headed for a newly developed section where the choice of shrubs distinguished one new house from another. "America has come to Debrecen," said Judit.

Goeff's house was brightly stucco'd; the interior was ornamented with dark wooded beams. Three or four bedrooms, up and down, rec room, standard European or American middle mod. The living and dining rooms were stuffed, people against walls and tables, knees on chairs. No one sat.

Goeff was in the rear yard, barbequing chicken wings, a tall jolly fellow who juggled utensils to free one hand. We shook and I felt his warmth immediately. He made a frivolous comment about my recent book on 19th Century literature, which he mistook as puritanical. His smile and happy voice were altogether disarming.

A statuesque Hungarian came up beside us. She held a tray of orange fish eggs and giggled as she offered them. Elene, his wife. Her

231

welcoming face was brilliant yet soft. An unadorned gown clung to her slightly plump body. Colored a simple chocolate, the gown shimmered uncertainly, like her sophisticated smile. This formidable woman had been Reva's very close chum at Kossuth University only eight years before. Goeff had been their English instructor and since marrying him, Elene lived in Bristol where she acquired two children and a touch of international grace before returning with her husband.

Spotting Istvan Ratz, I went to him as to a port. He was by far the most inviting of the native faculty. Ratz had been the first to make me comfortable in the institute office, taking time to explain the workings of the curriculum, the numbers and kinds of majors we serviced, what rooms held what volumes of the institute library, how the copy machine worked. At first his name was bothersome, sounded like 'rats.' His obsequious manner and appearance reinforced the impression. Ratz was a slight man of forty or so with a goatee on a thin face. The voice was soft and his English was very British, I almost preferred his Hungarian. Ratz had recently returned from a year at the University of East Anglia where he had interviewed the writer, Ray Bradbury, for the institute's "Hungarian Studies in English." He had also been a major booster of the poetry club.

Most foreign faculty - - the academic vagabonds - - mixed well with the Hungarians, including our institute's head in his perennial turtleneck, now dean. Andros Kiros, Imrè's replacement as head, was nervously attempting a svelte posture. Everything overwhelmed him; big decisions were delayed until forced by Imrè or Erica, the institute secretary, or by a special committee. Small decisions, on the other hand, were disposed with dictatorial finesse. Matt Palmer was sure Kiros relished the pain his negatives inflicted on younger instructors.

Csontos Pàl was sharply featured like a rugged movie star with a week's beard. Excessively polite and accommodating. Pàl was Tom Riedel's office mate. His English was so American I was not sure for a while that he was Hungarian. Whenever I stopped by for a few words with Tom, Pal's nose was in a book. Now he was surprisingly gregarious, and entertaining.

Among the cluster surrounding Pàl were two strong looking women, one in jeans was rather pop-eyed with rich auburn hair - - the

Canadian I had heard about, Andres Goffart; the other, turning grey, slender and slinky in sheer silk pajamas was Gwen Jones, a fireball.

Gwen floated risqué stories about her derring do escapades. A Welsh woman approaching middle years, she had held numerous positions with the British Council, coming to Debrecen a year ago from Cairo. Not quite past flirtation, she lorded her womanhood over polite and subdued Csontos Pàl.

Like other "advanced" members of her sex, Gwen was into Camille Paglia, a literary name unknown to Csontos who took pride in the currency of his scholarship. I heard Jones in mischief and joy paraphrase her new mother earth: " 'Maleness is merely shadow . . .' You do understand, Csontos, mother love smothers what it embraces. Motherhood blankets existence."

Hearing that Reva had a copy of "Sexual Personae," Andrea Goffart made an urgent request for it. She had switched her attention from Csontos Pàl to Daniel Price, a dramatic arts graduate from Bristol who dressed in the mode, wearing a knit fisherman's cap over his long yellow hair. He rarely removed it. Daniel was teaching conversational English but his real job was directing students in the production of "Antigone." Yes, he had enough actors; in fact he had a student from York who had done a number of Greek dramas at home. The play was to be performed on the huge mezzanine overlooking the grand concourse.

I met a dull American psychologist, a thorough scholar also on Fulbright, and an intriguing Hungarian who was now an American citizen. Janos Pinter had taken a Ph.D. and become a professor of political science at Ohio University. He was enjoying his Fulbright in the country of his birth.

Janos had been invited to attend the national congress of "Fidesz" in Debrecen, and was still excited. "Fidesz" is the Hungarian acronym of the Alliance of Young Democrats, Hungary's most popular opposition party, born in the wane of communist rule. Membership is limited to those under thirty-five years; European and American newspapers had taken note. The town council member in my American Reformation seminar is a "Fidesz" politician. His frequent absence deflects my judgment of his classroom performance.

At the Debrecen congress, Janos told me, Fidesz determined to broaden its appeal for the spring parliamentary elections by removing the age limit. Ruefully the party's 29 year old president, Viktor Orban, admitted, "We cannot continue to believe that the age limit itself will be our source of authority." Janos lamented the consequences, the loss of brashness and unswerving honesty.

"For the past two years," Janos said, "'Fidesz' has outstripped not only the ruling party, but the major opposition as well." Party posters proclaiming "We're Growing Older," showed a member embracing his children before a birthday cake with five candles.

Two lovelies in their middle years asked who I was. Both were from small colleges in New England. They were on two year teaching stints for the Peace Corps. Carol was assigned full time to the teachers college (CITT); she was short, heavy, and exceedingly congenial. The one called Muffy was a touch more understated. Her time was shared between Kossuth and the teachers college. Muffy was proud of the "dreadfully large" apartment she had lucked into, fully furnished with four-posters, silver, plate, lace and stuff. Her husband would be coming for Christmas to help fill it up. But in the meantime, she chuckled, her four-poster needed a comforter. Muffy rhapsodized about the mature students in her conversational English class, former teachers of Russian "hopping the English bandwagon."

Alistair Wood was so small I might not have seen him had Ansca, his Hungarian live-in lady, not made a point of meeting me. He was Jack Sprat to her Lady Fat, a flirtatious one. She insisted we dance. Helplessly, I obliged. Ansca was effusive about America. She would be going there one day. For the moment she was a school secretary, but Alistair was manipulating a position for her at the institute. As Erika's assistant? "As office manager!" To Alistair she announced, "He must come for dinner." Alistair was quiet and excessively polite, a Scotsman working for the British Council.

Leslie Burton was also paid from the British Council, abusively intellectual. Apparently he had no time for anything not expressed in the latest academic jargon. I was wrong. Later, he loosened, got groovy, talking about his sweetie from Warsaw with an eye roving towards Reva. And there was George Koster, an absolute curmudgeon, just arrived at the teacher's college from Germany - - CITT accepted almost everyone, they were so pressured by former Russian teachers clamoring for English.

George was a large overstuffed fellow whose shirt would not stay in his pants. He had come with his svelte German maiden, who wandered around as if lost. He made a show of ordering her about. She was obedient, bringing him wine and chicken wings. He pointed out the house they shared on the hill overlooking Goeff's yard. George had not been home to England in 18 years and it would be another 18 before he gave it a thought. "I hate it," he said bluntly. "I hate everything British." He had clearly enjoyed teaching in Darmstadt. Why he left was not clear.

After the party, the taxi took us to Judit's apartment for brandy. We listened to her audio of Margaret Atwood stories. Judit was convinced that current Canadian writers were the most adventuresome North America was producing. "Because you've chosen Canadian lit as your specialty," I insisted. "But why? Why would any respectable Hungarian professor do that?" Judit responded defensively, making vague references to the Hungarian intellectual spirit, the freedom to choose as she pleased, a freedom they fought for since the 1848 revolution. "The Hungarians lost that one," I said smartly. Was I unaware that "freedom" was the essence of Hungarian spirit? Judit was no doubt unconscious of her North American immersion.

"We've never won a war, but we've never lost our independent spirit," whereupon she put in my hands a short translated history of the 1848 revolt. "Read."

235

17. Presence of the Past

Sunday, October 10

Gray and rainy. No rolls and bakery's closed. I made do with half a loaf of stale bread for breakfast, then took a long bath and spent the day between Hungary's 1848 revolution and TV - - soccer and tennis from London, rap and hip-hop from Berlin.

Frequently its called the peasant revolt, but peasants have been revolting ever since Hungary settled into a feudal state. The first great peasant insurgence (1514) occurred when they took up arms under the Sign of the Cross, not against the heathens but their own nobles. The Leader of these Christian soldiers was a lesser noble, the Transylvanian Szekely, Gyorgy Dozsa. Believing the laws of God opposed unequal distribution of property, Dozsa's zealous peasants bathed the country in blood. Fields and manor houses were ablaze. The magnates cowered behind their castle battlements.

Eventually the nobles overpowered their peasants and arrested Dozsa. As his lieutenants watched, they seated this "king of the

237

peasants" on a red-hot iron throne, and placed a burning iron crown upon his head. Then his men were forced to eat their leader's roasted flesh.

The revolt of 1848 was less a local conflagration than a prime explosion of the revolutionary shock wave that jolted all Europe. Driven east by the Austrians beyond Buda and Pest, the Hungarian insurgents set up a provisional government in Debrecen. They announced dethronement of a 16-year old Emperor Francis Joseph and proclaimed their fiery Adonis-like leader, Lajos Kossuth, their regent.

For a few weeks it seemed the Hungarian army for independence might succeed against the imperial forces. But then Czar Nickolas I, whose interventions against revolutionary movements earned him the title, "Europe's gendarme," rushed in to avoid catastrophe and preserve the principle of monarchical dominance. Meeting in Warsaw, the grateful boy, Francis Joseph, kissed the Czar's hand. Kossuth resigned and fled to the West, leaving in charge his commanding general, Artur Gorgey, as abstinent and vain as himself (they had battled constantly).

Gorgey's quick surrender to the Russian forces in Arad County (Transylvania) was suspicious. Was Artur Gorgey a traitor? He trusted the amnesty promised by the Russian generals. Ironically, on the very day of surrender, the Austrian Council of Ministers instructed their army to begin negotiations on favorable terms. But when the news of Gorgey's surrender reached them, they withdrew the decision and ordered reprisals, to the disgust of the Russian generals.

An Austrian field marshal named Hayneau, called the 'Hyena of Brescia' for his cruelties in Poland, arrested thousands of Hungarians and executed thirteen of their generals. Then the beast celebrated with his officers, their bloody hands clinking beer mugs through the night.

I'd been glimpsing the TV occasionally as I read. Looking out, I noticed the rain had dwindled. I turned off the TV, and put on my old all-weather coat and went in search of food. My mind returned to Judit. What did she mean? Attempting to justify her specialty in Canadian literature, Judit had careened wildly, confusing it with her country's cruel history. But what did they have in common? History, it appeared, was ever ready in the Hungarian psyche to validate behavior. How could the Austrian suppressions, still vivid after a hundred-fifty years, explain her Canadian specialization that I found so peculiar for a Hungarian?

What would Tom say? Specializations that half and half again. Wasn't literature of the English language enough specialization for Hungarian students? Surely he would find the little garden spot of Canadian literature no less myopic than the minute specializations of science.

I was passing Rudolph's, the brightly lit pastry and ice cream shop at the end of the street. The name rattled my mind and popped an association with the historical Rudolf who helped the Arpàd king defeat Otto of Bohemia and establish the House of Hapsburg in 1278. The ice cream shop typified a later Hungary, however, with its alpine roof, curlicue wood and colorful signs. Judit's logic, I suddenly realized, was not so confused, not any more than mine just now. It was Hungarian. Her logic clung to Hungary's history. She was symbiotic with it, a comfort.

18. Avril is Dead

Sunday night, October 11.

The history I'd been reading had slipped to the floor and I was dozing off when I heard the knock. It was Peter Eglan, my neighbor, standing in the dark hall in shirt and tie, his ashen face sharply angled and almost ghoulish in the small light from my doorway. He was leaving in the morning, too early to awaken me, and wanted to say goodbye. Yes, it was sudden. His wife was dead. "I buried her yesterday. How I hate those depressing churches!" The sharp face seemed in a clench, the head nodding like a keening Irish granny.

There had been no signs. No relatives coming and going. No flowers, nothing. "I'm sorry."

"Buried her in Subotica. I just drove back." He had an old Fiat which he seldom used. "It's for the best. She no longer suffers." He resumed the nodding, obviously not ready to go to his empty apartment.

"Come in."

"You don't mind?"

"I'll put on tea."

"She was Slav, you know." How was that related?

He sat on the Poesque couch, picked up the history I'd dropped (on T. Roosevelt) and put it down as if struggling to break out of death's aura. When I returned from the kitchen, he was not quite squirming but uncomfortable.

"She wished to be buried where she was born." His hands were fidgeting on the arm rest. "Family's from a piece of Hungary given to the Yugoslavs after the war. Now its Serbia."

"Yes." He'd already told me.

"Those Slavs were not Magyars but always Hungarian."

I fetched the hot water kettle, teabags, and cups. He did not wait till I returned before launching into details of the funeral. "My Avril was Calvinist. We had a reform priest who read a Hungarian poem, by Endre Ady. Know him? Great poet, once he lived in Debrecen." My neighbor had the poem in hand and began reading the Hungarian verse, heavy with euphonious vowels. When he started to translate, I put up a hand. "Ok, Ok." I was too impatient. "Sorry." Again he was keening.

Eglan's brows were low over his lids, his cheeks were caved and grooved. The creases pulled upon his lips, baring strong, carnivorous teeth. "Well, she's gone. . . so now I go home. . .to Florida."

It was a chance to stand and lead him out, but I maintained civility, "You're giving up the apartment?"

"It's for sale. Maybe I'll rent, come to check up once a year, enough Hungary for me."

"You are not proud of being Hungarian?"

He drew back and looked at me, hard. "Of course I am." Then he was nodding again. "Satisfied me, like my girls and grandchildren. But living here makes me nervous. I do nothing. Play golf. Awful course. Nobody to play."

"This is your homeland. You must have other interests."

"Florida is my homeland. I was just born here. Avril and I were married here, when I came on vacation. When I retired, she wanted to come back. It was cheap, she said, but I have a pension and social security, so why? 'For my heart's sake,' she says."

Ten million Hungarians in this country and eleven million scattered through Europe and America, eager to return, I thought, like

Zionists to Israel. But my neighbor, Peter Eglan, wished to go the other way.

"I'm easy, so I go along," he continued, "just so I'm comfortable and secure.

"What did you do in America?"

"Maintenance, for Martin Marietta. Good life. Who needs to be a plutocrat? You get rich, then dull, then because you're rich you can't stand being dull; so you make trouble. Big men make big trouble when they get clogged with honey and can't fly anymore."

I must have blinked. If this man had come from the peasantry as I had assumed, it was a poetic peasantry. "But you also enjoy the easy life," I responded, "You just said as much. I don't suspect you make much trouble."

"Because I don't have ambition to claw and climb the ladder." He held a finger in the air. "Hungarian proverb: Set a beggar on a horse's back and he rides to the devil. Over human bone and flesh. So beggar or rich man! Only beggar has no easy life to bore him."

The man's wife had just died. Had he no sense of propriety? "Maybe I shouldn't say this, but at a time like - - "

He was quick, "Avril is dead. That struggle is over. I don't pretend great sorrow." Mr. Eglan put down his tea cup. I began to hope he would leave. But my neighbor had come to talk.

"More tea?" In many cultures, the offer of a second cup is an invitation to depart. Unfortunately he accepted.

I put another tea bag in his cup and poured from the still warm kettle. Soon he was chattering about the foolish and bloody distinctions between the Orthodox, the Catholic, and the Muslim. "All Slavs. This family feud in Bosnia, who started it? You and me are American, so we say the Serbs. Or it doesn't matter, you say? You remember Ustache? General Ratko Mladic remembers. You know who he is, leader of the Bosnian Serbs. He says he's protecting Serb territory and the people who have lived there for centuries."

"The Muslims have also lived there for centuries."

An ironic grin split my neighbor's hard face. "I have a friend who fought with Mladic and saw on his barrack wall a fading poster of soldiers in swastika armbands. The general said they were Ustache, who devastated his valley and tortured his father when he was two. Fifty

243

years ago, and Mladic is still on fire with hatred. Today's enemy is still the Ustache."

Out of bewilderment, I asked, "Is Mladic a relation?"

"We are all one family, we never forget fascists. They also killed my wife's uncles. Do you know how many Serbs lost their lives to these Croatian Nazis? More than the Jews. Nearly every Serb family lost someone. Forgive and forget?"

I was quiet, my mind working on my own Croatian memories, mostly of my friend, Josip Lerinc. Croatia was still a Yugoslavian republic then. I recalled him shutting down discussion whenever it turned towards the devastating inflation or the country's unstable politics. (I had written that I would visit him.)

"Did you know," he went on, as if unable to control himself, "that in 1991, Franjo Tudjman, the Croatian president, bulldozed the holocaust museum at Janenovic and wanted to replace it with a memorial to the Croatian victims of Tito? And something else I can tell you. Tudjman is not the worst thing in Eastern Europe. Know what is?"

"I have no idea." I yawned, needing to get back to bed.

"Green paint." I failed to respond. "Green is for Islam. The paint is spilling over the Blue Flag of Europe."

"Like the Ottomans five hundred years ago?"

My neighbor did not crack a smile. "Their hordes dominate Bosnia and Kosovo."

"And Montenegro, Macedonia?" Why should it matter to him? I stood up. Finally, he moved toward the door. "Really sorry about your wife." I meant it, and extended a hand. He shrugged as he left.

19. Performances

Friday, October 16.

"Bully," shouts Teddy Roosevelt from the auditorium of the Teacher's Reformed College in Eger. "If you're bullish on the American past," says the brochure, "come spend an evening with the Roughrider. (He carries no stick, his words are big.)" The man behind the mustache on the brochure is the Fulbrighter, Chuck Chalberg, historian, actor, and friend of Tom Riedel and Matt Palmer.

Tom returned from a visit with boundless enthusiasm. Chalberg was now performing H.L. Menken instead of T. Roosevelt. "He promised he'd do a night for us."

We sent Matt to beard our institute head, Andros Kiros. He proposed an evening with H.L.Menken for expenses only. - - rail fare, meals, hotel. Andros evaded and finally made the standard excuse, events budget used up, maybe next year. "He can bunk at my place," Matt bargained. "How about just travel, a few forints?" Andros wouldn't budge.

"Andros has favorites," Matt protested. "He gave Steve Ruark funds for that fake Indian, Magua." We sat on the patio of the café where the forest meets Simonyi. After lengthy discussion we aimed a heavier gun at a more potent target, the former head and now dean. Having been friends and co-actors, Tom expected Imrè-Bali to be forthcoming, generous, if possible.

Imrè-Bali reeled off a few reasons for rejection - - Menken was hardly known outside the United States, he was not a major figure, really just a journalist, a curmudgeon. Then he revealed the true reason, "Frankly Tom, he was an intellectual elitist and a fascist who supported Germany through the thirties."

"So did Hungary."

"Yes, but we had to, and resented it. Our support was geographical, Menken's was ideological."

"The university ought to be an open forum."

"It is, but it also has limits."

"A few forints."

"I don't mean what we'd pay, but what we'd lose. It would be foolish to offer a platform for fascist thought. We could be accused of propagandizing; we'd be out more than funds."

Matt was upset when Tom reported his meeting, not so much from the rejection as from Tom's admitting that Menken did lean to the fascists. "So did your T.S. Eliot and Ezra Pound. A host of American writers flirted with fascism, ours too. Imrè-Bali was just name-calling. He's suppressing free speech." Matt was climbing his idealistic ladder, but Tom and I had to agree. Now we had a moral purpose which drove us to bring Chalberg's impressions to Debrecen.

We sat, a sour trio, on the patio under the warm overcast. Suddenly Matt brightened. "Why don't we support him ourselves?"

Chuck appreciated Matt's offer of a bed; he insisted we let him contribute his own rail fare. Goeff Gibson and Gwen Jones arranged for space at CETT, a large second floor chamber with tables. They also cajoled the college into providing refreshment, big bottles of Coke, no ice. Tom advised against asking Reva Milany to draw up posters. Gwen volunteered and also managed their distribution. Within days, the posters appeared in conspicuous spots at Kossuth and CETT:

MARDER-PALMER-RIDEL PRODUCTIONS
Present
H. L. MENKEN
The Sage of Baltimore and Critic of America
Performed by Dr. 'Chuck' Chalberg
Thursday, October 15 8:00 PM CETT

The three-year college was in the corner building of the vast military grounds taken over by the Soviets after the Germans had fled and again abandoned when the old regime was ousted. These grounds were now dust and rust, except for greenery around this old grey building with pleasant trim.

Multicolored streamers hung from the ceiling. The tables were decorated with large Coke bottles and paper cups. Around them sat nearly eighty or so faculty and students from both institutions.

Chuck was an unassuming academic until he donned stripped pants and gold-rimmed spectacles. Then he was transformed into the witty and dyspeptic antagonist of middle class America.

He was especially virulent in attacking the popular lady novelists and distinguished men of letter who fed the "booboisie." Most American tradition was stultifying and false. It lacked "civilized aristocracy." The puritan ideal was his straw man and he kept picking at it. His targets were the Christian moral code and government by the people, whether democratic or socialist. He was a puritan arisen to challenge puritans, a scholar to dispute professors. Life was a duel between doubt and dogma. Courage was required to doubt, cowards hid in dogma. He went the way of Nietzsche's superman, in the other way lay the doldrums of Marx. His was the "howl of a lone wolf in the wilderness of hypocrisy."

Chalberg's dramatic performance monologue arrested their attention but did little for their comprehension. The Hungarian faces were fascinated, also screwed with bewilderment. Imrè-Bali had his point.

Saturday, October 17.

Another performance - - Daniel Price's students in his production of *ANTIGONE*. No one dressed for the classic occasion. Reva wore jeans. We arrived late and had to swim through a sea of students for a place on the marble floor of the grand mezzanine. They were also squeezed into the long rows of benches and chairs arranged haphazardly against the marble balustrade overlooking the concourse. As we searched for a place, students recognized us and offered their bench seats.

Square columns at the rear of the mezzanine supported a recessed balcony, giving Daniel the advantage of two stage levels. King Creon was the principle occupant and when he vacated, the chorus, who shared the main stage with Antigone, took his place. This shifting provided most of the physical action. A wisp of a girl played Antigone and the student Daniel had imported from England did the king. Often her voice was lost to the poor acoustics but his was so strong, it projected through the multi-storied hall.

Bright spots isolated each actor in turn against the blackened stage where they poised stoically on wooden boxes. Statue replaced character; oration replaced dialogue. A triumph of spectacle! If that was the effect Daniel wished to render, he succeeded.

But his tragedy would succeed even if the staging was less artistic. This English graduate student had achieved a triumph of organization, leadership and timing. Here it was before our eyes, in less than two months time, Hungarian students turned classic thespians in their Greek robes, lights designed to subtly heighten their fates, a grand theatre magically produced from a concourse mezzanine.

The king fell, the chorus moaned, and the lights blacked out. When they came up, the thespians were students again, and Daniel Price stood among them, beaming in his black knit fisherman's cap. The audience thronged the stage area, and we waited our turn to offer congratulations.

Reva kissed Daniel.

"Isn't it amazing?" the dramatist asked, stealing my line.

20. Eger.

Monday, October 19.

Matt Palmer met Erika and me in the bursar's office for his monthly rental allowance. As a junior Soros appointment, he let me know that he received less, "Because you are American and I'm only English." Erika noised her amusement and Matt accused her of guffawing in Hungarian.

He had taught conversational English at several Hungarian institutions while pursuing a doctorate in Art History at Budapest. At the Reformed Teachers College in Eger, Matt became engaged to Kauty, his third fiancé in six years of vagabond teaching. He was also completing his dissertation on the design of three Gothic churches in Transylvania, a static pursuit which belied his vitality.

At least once every year he visited the sites of his study, which was to determine the original designs of the churches from alterations through the centuries. At that rate, I estimated he would complete the work in less than a hundred years. He also bicycled home to Sussex every year where his father was a government librarian and his mother a secondary school teacher. The last time, Kauty, the fiancé, bicycled with him across Hungary, Austria, Germany and France.

Often he was taken as Magyar, which delighted him, having mastered the language, acquired the culture, and read the history. Usually he spent weekends in Eger, in the refreshing air of the Matra and Bukk mountains. He no longer counted expenses in quid but forints. Everywhere Hungarians were moved by his knowledge and sense of caring. Matt exuded curiosity and wonder. His preference for formative Hungarian ways charmed them, in spite of the stubble on his face, his unkempt hair, careless clothes, and blunt opinions.

We were quickly friends and Matt invited me to share a weekend in the mountains.

Friday, October 23.

We climbed through streets lined with Eger's baroque and rococo buildings. The Czakos, Kauty's family, lived in a modern apartment complex on a hill overlooking Dobo Ter (after General Istvan Dobo who beat back the Turks in 1552).

Spotlights on St. Anthony's in the square splayed onto the busy balcony, illuminating laundry that flapped among the discards and junk.

I sat on the sofa next to Kauty's uncle who looked young enough to be her brother. He spoke no English. Interpreting, Matt said Uncle Eric was honored to be sitting beside an American professor in his own house. Kauty served tea, while a little boy with yellow hair who had hugged Matt's legs when we entered, ran from one to another performing tricks like a pet dog. Matt caught him and sat him on his lap. They seemed overjoyed.

After a shy introduction, Mother Czako disappeared into the kitchen, then emerged for approval of a pastry Kauty was now passing about. As anticipated, she was rotund in a flowery smock. Kauty was shapely in clinging tan slacks. A white blouse pulled about her small bosom. Dark hair surrounded her round peaches and cream cheeks. Her face carried only a hint of cosmetic.

Matt continued playing with the child. I speculated about the boy's parents until his mother, Kauty's sister, appeared. She was a thinner version with drawn cheeks and yellow hair.

Seven of us squeezed about the table in the tiny dining room. Mrs. Czakos served thick levas (chicken noodle), pork cutlets, rice, more pastry. Then Kauty's sister took her child to her own apartment. (Purchased with annuities the Czakos had the foresight to provide the daughters.)

That left five. The father would return from his construction job in the Matras Mountains at about three, giving him an hour with Mrs. Czakos before she left for her bakery on Dobo Ter. Only two bedrooms. Did Kauty share her mattress? Arrangements appeared insignificant to everyone.

It began sprinkling just as we started for a simple neon, reading "Palace Hotel," about a block up the street. Matt didn't think reservations were necessary, but under the crystal chandelier in the Louis XVI corridor which served as a lobby, the liveried clerk had to call several other places before he found accommodation. It was on the other side of town.

Rain poured as a taxi delivered us to the "Venus." I was shown to a room with two cots on opposite sides against the walls, a large wardrobe, a shaky desk and a chair. Worn linoleum covered the floor. But there was a bathroom and a window opening to the street. It overlooked an automobile repair shop.

Wanting to celebrate, we braved the rain for several hundred yards to a tavern. Kauty would not hear my diabetic protest and insisted I taste just one glass of Eger's famous bull's blood wine. She also called it "Erlauer," after the German name for the old city. "In all Hungary, only Tokay has richer wine, and no where is wine so heroic." Kauty recited the old Eger legend of General Dobo sustaining his soldiers with the vintage. It gave them super strength and stained their beards so bloody red, the Turks were frightened and fled.

For herself, Kauty ordered beer, then held the mug against her chest, refusing to clink glasses with Matt and me. "Homage to the thirteen martyrs of Arad," Matt explained. "After the slaughter, Field Marshal Haynau celebrated through the night, clinking beer mugs with his officers. Hungarians still drink beer, but never clink mugs."

Saturday, October 24.

Salami sliced so thin it was mostly essence, more odor than taste. Served with cheese, bread, coffee and American hip-hop from the TV perched on the corner shelf.

The clouds were high, not threatening. Meeting at the station, Matt and I boarded the red two-car for a 17 mile journey to Szilvasvarad in the wooded Bukk Mountains. It was much the same train as the communist shuttle Croatians took in Osijek to shop for Hungarian goods in Pec. The little two-car no longer wore the red star but it hadn't been painted either.

The people of Eger went to stroll the woods at Szilvasvarad, to ride the horses and carts and eat trout. The streams were full of them. Climbing the path from the station to the woods, we passed a newly constructed alpine house, plush and conspicuous in the simple countryside. "Made of all native materials." Matt was facetiously alluding to a current exhibit at the University demonstrating the use of all Hungarian architecture and materials, including straw. Two Mercedes sedans were parked in the circular drive.

Our path led past a round neo-classic church perched above the brush, apparently abandoned. Why was such a structure built in such a place? Matt, my cathedral expert, had no answer. I had to inspect. The white walls were flaking, the palladin columns rotting. Walking on, we passed prosperous, well-spaced houses. In front of each plot was a newly-painted blue post with handle. "They look like water pumps."

"They are," Matt said, "The wells are communal; county paints them every spring."

"But they let that church rot?"

"Same thing's been happening all over rural England."

Well into the trees, we glimpsed horse riders on another path. Forest green horse carts with drivers in Tyrol hats hauled touring parties through the woods. Then we saw them, the Lipizzaner studs, famous Austrian dressage horses; tall white elitists, prancing and cantering, proud trainers in dungarees reining their heads high. I had seen them on the Italian border and in a Croatian village near Osijek, both places claiming the originals.

Among the turning colors, we came upon a stand of poplars; a blue lake within. The hills rose spectacularly behind. I fancied presences, wraiths, we were not quite alone. Soothed brows of old Magyar warriors reflected among the brilliant heights in the blue lake. I saw them resting their short horses, bowstrings slackened, cleaning dried blood from their jeweled broadswords.

A stone maiden occupied a hollow in the brush along our way. Legs folded beneath, she sat with an arm stretched as if caressing the woods. Her expression was stolid grace, Grecian beauty appealing to crude nature. Couples passed by, pushing baby carriages, and lovers arm in arm.

Our rising path turned into an avenue of shacks, makeshift restaurants smelling of trout just taken from the stream. Kauty's mother had sent along sandwiches, apples, and wine. A whiff of the grilling trout, and we agreed to abandon our packed lunch. Anxious as traitors, we waited at the plank table. Matt exchanged Hungarian jovialities with the waiter in a grease-splattered apron until the golden crisp fish arrived. It did not appear as it smelled; tiny grease globules clung to the golden skin. But when I took a bite, o' heavenly tang, not to be described! The mountain stream freshness and succulence of that trout overcame me.

We paused before a small waterfall, and again my mind wondered to the old Magyar warriors in richly brocaded tunics, perhaps mesmerized as I was by the whitened cascades of water. A group of children were playing on the plateau at the top of the mountain. Their supervisor sat at a table in an open-sided log shelter. Another adult was gathering more children near a plank platform marked by a post and schedule board. Approaching, I noticed the narrow gauge railroad track.

"Should we take the toy train down the hill?" I asked Matt. He read the schedule, 'It won't come for another quarter-hour."

Matt inhaled deeply as we began meandering down. "You feel the essence of Hungary up here."

"Or any mountaintop."

"I include the people, the pace."

"The simplicity." My slightly specious tone did not faze him.

Again, he took in the keen air with exaggerated pleasure, then exhaled to exhaustion. "How delicious." Suddenly he frowned. "The

253

trout was delicious. Everything's 'delicious.' I need another word for the air."

"Savory? How about delectable? Ambrosial?"

"Naw, words can't do it."

Sunday, October 25.

Thin slices of salami and cheese, bread and coffee. When the orchestra on TV finished Bartok, I returned to my room and watched the rain hitting the gutter in front of the automobile repair shop. Then I put on my old black all-weather, and took off for St. Anthony's on Dobo Ter to meet Matt at nine. I hugged the buildings.

The twin belfries of the pink cathedral rose above the square. Reaching it, I waited inside the vestibule. (That afternoon Matt informed me that St. Anthony's was not a cathedral but a Minorite church erected in 1771, and considered among the most beautiful baroque buildings in Hungary. Peeking in, I was disappointed with the usual, marble columns and tableau.)

Horseless, General Dobo dominated the square. He was posed gallantly atop a high pedestal, his sword thrashing the air. Behind him I glimpsed the oblong tower of the castle fortress, topped by a steep roof that suggested prisons or concentration camps. The bronze horses were snorting and stomping on the other side of the square, frozen in a ferocious charge, their Magyar riders grimacing ruthlessly in glorious tribute.

As I waited in the vestibule, the few early parishioners emerged, scrubbed, pressed, and sanctified, none young. They hesitated before the rain, then unfurling umbrellas, went off by twos and crossed the square to the pastry shop where Mrs. Czako worked. I intended to pay my visit when the sanctuary was cleared; hoping to locate a saint's relic like the kidney preserved in St. Anthony's of Padua, to which this church was dedicated. Matt appeared before I could. "Kauty has to study."

"Didn't expect her." He opened an umbrella for the two of us. The rain let up as we scurried past General Dobo; it stopped by the time we reached the cobblestone lane leading to the castle fortress. The wetted gravel shone bright grey as if it had been airbrushed. Erected in the 13th Century for protection against the Mongol invaders, the octagonal fortress was a marvel of that time. Turks occupied it in 1596 when Eger became their provincial capital, the Ottoman's northernmost outpost. Much of the fortress was destroyed with the rest of the city in the 19th Century during the Austrian suppression. It was renovated at the turn of the century.

The cobblestone path ended in a short passageway where a large bronze relief on the fortress wall portrayed the Eger women of 1552 pouring cauldrons of hot oil on the Turks who fell writhing from their scaling ladders.

"Did the bloody red beards frighten the Turks away or was it the fury of these women?"

Matt said he would have to ask Kauty.

A souvenir shop worked into a cave opposite displayed the novel, "Eclipse of the Crescent Mood," which told the story of Eger locals fighting as Dobo's warriors. Actually it is an adventure story for adolescents grown into legend and required reading in district schools. Two thousand Hungarian defenders routed 150,000 Turks brandishing superior weapons. The Eger victory was the first over the Ottoman Empire since the disastrous Battle of Mohacs (1526) led to Turkish domination of the Danube basin.

In 1897 the writer Geza Gardonyi retreated from his journalistic turmoil in Budapest to an isolated house overlooking the fortress ruins. He had attended the Reformed Teacher's College and was returning to the placid life of this cathedral town. Two years later, "Eclipse" began appearing in a Budapest newspaper.

The citizen warriors of 1552 are enshrined in the Bishop's palace, a Renaissance building (1470) with Gothic arches, also rebuilt. The bishopric was one of five founded by St. Stephen in the early tenth century; nine centuries later, it graduated to an archbishopric. The statues are of this century, sculpted in Soviet heroic fashion, gilded figures some ten feet tall, mammoth muscles in stiff postures, some with hammers, some with broadswords, all wearing craftsmen's aprons, women and men distinguished only by their hair style.

In the center of the chamber is an aged bier, reduced to normal size, containing the remains of General Istvan Dobo. The overwrought warriors diminish Dobo's corpse, represented by a stunted unpolished bronze relief on the lid, holding a battle helmet.

The bishopric itself left a greater imprint on Eger than General Dobo. Faith, hope, and charity are the motifs wrought into the filigreed black iron gates at the County Hall. The gates are marked number 9 on Kossuth Lajos Ut, an avenue of baroque and rococo buildings. They were constructed when Eger was revamped, a hundred fifty years before the name, Kossuth, appeared in Hungarian annuls.

Matt, who had never seen inside the courtyard, puzzled over the identity of the tall building opposite the County Hall. Pinioned on its cream-colored wall was an oversized statue of a crucified Christ flanked below by his two fellow sufferers on Calvary. The icons gleamed in fresh black paint against the soft cream wall. Bars on the windows were also painted black. "A prison?" Matt asked, but he was somber only a moment, "Sinners in the bosom of their agonized lord."

We tarried along the 18th Century gems on Kossuth Lajos. Number 14 was a Franciscan church built in 1755 on the site of a mosque. Coming to a shopping mall that obscured the orthodox synagogue at number 17, we turned and retraced our steps. Matt pretended to gasp at the rococo extravaganza of number 4, the Minor Canon's residence.

"I'm getting toured out," I said

"You haven't seen Teachers College."

Matt waved a hand. "Totally different. You'll feel more like it after we eat something. How about Szepasszonyvolgy? It means, 'valley of beautiful women,' a street lined with wine cellars."

It was a twenty-minute walk to Bela Bartok Ter, then down Szepasszonyvolgy Ut. We chose the wine cellar at No 38. No one sat at the outside tables. Violins played in the cellar. A heavy woman in an embroidered sheepskin vest drew the wine from casks through large glass tubes. Matt drank leanyka, 'young girl,' a dry white. "Tastes like honey," he said. A plate of stuffed peppers and dumplings restored my enthusiasm.

We headed for Eszterhazy Square. Matt said the pile of stones to be found there was the original Romanesque cathedral. It had been devastated in the Tartar invasion of the 12th Century and rebuilt in Gothic style during the 15th. Vaguely I made out a foundation but the history had gone out of these old stones. Along side them is the monolithic new cathedral built from the ground up in the classical style.

"Ugly," said Matt, "those square columns," Telling more than I wished to know, he called it a neo-classic design by Joseph Hild who later improved on it when he built Hungary's largest and most imposing cathedral of the Cardinal Primate in Estergom. No, I didn't want to go in, "Matt, I'm beginning to resent these ubiquitous churches hogging history."

Across the way, twelve stories in Louis XVI style, the Reformed Teacher's Training College hovered over Eszterhazy Square.

257

21. Maria Teresa's University

The empress of Hungary was only the archduchess of Austria because, Hapsburg though she was, a woman could not wear the crown of the Holy Roman Empire. In 1741, aware of agitation among the Hungarian serfs, a disconcerted Maria Teresa sought protection from the Hungarian Estates of the Realm. Reasserting the law that proclaimed a permanent serfdom, they pledged their empress "our lives and our blood," and added an ingrained Hungarian wit, "but not our oats."

Hungary won her gratitude and consequent favors; one was a plan for the Catholic University in Eger, to be the greatest in all the Hapsburg Empire. It was finally constructed as a lyceum, and falling under Calvinist influence became the Reformed Teachers Training College until the advent of communists, when it was renamed Ho Chi Minh Teachers Training College. Matt said the archbishopric still battles the government to regain possession. It is now named for Karoly Eszterhazy, a founder, though to most, it's just 'Teachers College.'

The interior is without color, except for white. A grand marble stairway curls down to the lobby. The stairs rise to perhaps fifty feet,

259

surrounded by Gothic arches over a raised walkway. Matt stopped me as I started up the marble stairs. "For officials only."

"Who are the officials?"

"School administration and visiting dignitaries."

"Not faculty?"

Matt led me to another set of stairs in the rear, "For students and faculty." The stone steps were deeply grooved.

Muttering "Hapsburgs be damned," I turned back and led Matt up the marble steps. "We're visiting dignitaries."

We entered the library, a lofty hexagon with books almost as high as the domed ceiling. Ladders reached over a balcony about half way up the shelves. Most volumes were like oversized accounting ledgers, leather covers frayed and cracked.

We stood roped off in the middle. Behind the rope was a glass case with illustrated manuscripts and codices. A librarian stood beside a desk, well worn in her occupation.

Stiffly she recognized Matt, then reminded him that a permit from the rector was required for access to the books. Scholars applied mostly from Germanic and Slavic countries. "They work in there." She pointed to a poorly disguised secret door in the shelves. "We have 20,000 volumes in this chamber and near 100,000 in there. Students are allowed at certain times and under conditions."

What conditions? I didn't ask. I felt the authority in the air and speculated on the nature of scholarship that thrived in such disciplined atmosphere; centuries of devotion to these volumes. External restrictions must have generated internal freedoms that produced the great works. I felt the tug of fancy, an urge to meld with these old manuscripts, to touch and turn the crisped pages, to indulge in the physical sensations of scholarship, if not in its essence.

Matt was looking at the peculiar fresco painted on the domed ceiling. "By Johan Lukas Kracker," the librarian said, "the Bohemian who also painted the altarpiece in St. Anthony's, of Virgin Mary with the saint. This is Kracker's Council of Trent."

The fresco portrayed the cardinals in red robes and hats. Disdainfully, they gaze down at a pile of confiscated books as a bolt of lightening set them ablaze. One holds a rod pointing to the burning books, acid satisfaction on his vinegary face.

I took my camera from its case. "No, no," she held up a hand, "Forbidden," then offered a post card from the pile on her desk. I laid down a forint and took the card. Matt chuckled, also laying down a forint for one. The picture was far superior to any I could have snapped.

Stone replaced marble as we continued, passing floors of closed classroom doors. The staircase was cluttered with rough hewn building blocks, ladders, ropes and pulleys. I was dragging when we reached the astronomical museum on the sixth level. Mothers sat on old wood benches or inspected star-gazing instrument, Galileo telescopes, compasses, model solar systems, while their young gathered about the clownish robes decorated with stars, crescent moons, and the tall coned hats of medieval magicians and soothsayers. Only Dr. Faust was missing.

Matt knew this museum attendant also and conversed as I caught breath. He came back to the bench and said we had to hurry, "The camera obscura closes at five. It's on the twelfth floor." We had less than ten minutes. He raced while I chugged along as the stairs narrowed and the clutter increased. The building blocks seemed bigger, corners jutting into the stairway. On the 11th floor I passed a small office with a short man in Tyrol hat looking back at me from the open doorway. I nodded and he tipped his hat. Just as I crawled to the final landing, Matt put out his hands," Too late." The thick oak door was chained and padlocked. We heard a rustling below and Matt leaped down the stair. He was speaking Hungarian with the little man by the time I arrived, panting.

The Hungarian stood to Matt's arm pit. He wore a leather tie and leather jacket. A feather in his Tyrol lent a jaunty look. He was smooth shaven except for a barbered brown and grey mustache; the skin was also smooth. His body appeared hard, tight. A small-featured face was chiseled, a Magyar in miniature. He could be no more than 60.

Matt pointed to his watch, just a minute past five. The little man was intrigued with my companion's Hungarian but remained adamant. Finally he permitted us to observe the city from his parapet, opening the glass doors and following us out. St. Anthony's was easy to locate and on the hill overlooking it, Kauty's apartment house. Realizing we were not ordinary tourists, our host asked us who we were."

"Professors from Kossuth University in Debrecen."

His blue eyes became vivid. He knew the university well, he said, worked many years for them, in maintenance, until he retired and came to the teachers college.

"When was that?"

I was stunned when Matt translated his answer, "After the war, in 1949." He was caretaker in charge here until three years ago when they confined him to the top two floors.

"How old could he be?"

Matt asked, and shaking his head, told me, "Going on eighty-six."

"Does he walk up and down these twelve floors every day?"

This question was put and answered, "Twice a day when he forgets to bring lunch."

Basking in our admiration, the little Hungarian grasped his ring of keys and invited us upstairs.

The camera obscura was an aged contraption, a large milky disk in a darkened room. Above it, a hole in the roof let in a narrow shaft of light when the little man pulled on a rope that opened it. An arrangement of mirrors reflected the light, casting images of the city onto the disk, a quadrant at a time. His whole body perked up, like a cock in a henhouse, proud of the medieval mechanism, the most magnificent ever devised.

The lone minaret was easy to pick out, just west of the castle fortress. Matt had climbed it two years ago. "Very tight steps, 96 of them winding to the top. It's no longer allowed. Unsafe."

Going down twelve flights - - students and faculty - - the little man kept talking, a conquest of Matt's charm.

Monday, October 26.

Kauty's mother insisted I come for lunch and proper goodbyes. She served another big meal, levas, of course, then stuffed cabbage, pork steaks and potatoes. Kauty was staying another day but would see us to the train. The uncle had returned, and imagining his niece also leaving, gave her a clownish kiss, then chuckled at his mistake.

Mrs. Czako hugged Matt and kissed him full on the lips. I felt her unlimited generosity. Then she planted one on me. She handed each of

262

us an aluminum foil packed for the train, more pork cutlets, plus apples
and a bottle of bull's blood

22. The Poetry Club

Tuesday, October 27.

I put sheets in the other bedroom for Julia tomorrow night, then prepared for the Poetry Club tonight, sweeping the kitchen and vacuuming the rugs. At the centrum, I had purchased Szeged salami ('the salami capital of the world,' Szeged boasts) cheese, halsalata (herring salad) biscuits of a sort, grapes, apples, bananas, langos (a pancake fried in oil) and wine. Roberta had sent along a jar of peanut butter (not for me, it contained sugar) as a treat for the Hungarians. The Yugoslavs had fussed over it. I opened the jar and set it on the coffee table with thin slices of kenyer (bread), a sort of centerpiece.

Istvan Ratz was first to arrive, after Reva of course. A meek but outgoing, compliant man of inner resources and steel resolve, he did not flinch as I anticipated upon confronting my Poesque parlor and beholding the forest mural dominating it. Behind his pointed brush beard, Ratz was imperturbable. He brought white wine.

265

David and Reka stopped by on the way to another affair merely to say they couldn't come. I was happy to greet two students in jeans from the medical school, and a suave good-looking couple from the CETT. They surveyed the mural without comment. Then Anna appeared with two male students. "That forest on the wall is supposed to be Nagyerdei," I blurted out before they were quite in the room. I hadn't seen Anna since my arrival in Budapest and was delighted but a touch nervous: Would the food hold out? I dragged in the rickety dining room chairs.

No more appeared. Reva's posters had announced the literary fare and she had prepared copies of Dickinson's poems, but most brought their own.

I said a few words about the poet's devotion to family and poetry, and her isolation, out of which she created her 'estate.' Then I read the poems Reva had copied, including the one about the 'trembling emblems', and mentioned her dominant theme of evanescence, nature's comings and goings. "About a third of her poems deal with death," I said, "but death is not all she is about."

To get discussion rolling, I asked Ratz for a comment.

He quoted Dickinson's 'earth was made for lovers.' "I find nothing clthonian about her, no blood and shit, as Camille Paglia insists."

"Paglia is off the wall," said Reva, but the suave woman from CETT felt otherwise, her partner nodding in agreement. She referred to a necrophilic poem of Dickinson as though it were a bloom in her garden. "Dickinson's scarred tombstone is a passive phallus," soft, spaced words from a finely-honed English face. Deliberately, she asked Ratz, who had written on the English romantics, what Lord Byron might make of it.

He was embarrassed, "It?"

"Dickinson's passive phallus."

Ratz quickly recovered, 'You know my field is English literature, not American. I'm not too familiar with Dickinson."

Anna contributed, "She's a sexual monolith, a slab of aggression frozen between potency and paralysis."

My brain was whirling. I recognized these comments as quotes from Paglia, but they were undigested, without context, confused.

266

The woman from CETT and Anna were in congenial agreement, the English one waxing, "To paraphrase Paglia, Dickinson fluctuates between active and passive sex." Anna added her own profundity, "Echoing de Sade. He inverts exotic confrontation where an individual both penetrates and is penetrated." Anna still wore the virginal mask, pure and unblemished, honeyed hair combed straight, the wholesome countenance that greeted me in Budapest.

Enthusiasm darted briefly across the suave brows of the woman from CETT. "Dickinson is a totem of phallic force," and she quoted, "My life is a loaded gun."

"Is a loaded gun passive?" I asked. Logic was out of place, I was ignored.

Anna picked it up, "But she's only a genuine poet when she's sadistic, throwing body parts around, when she can satisfy her sweet tooth for horror. The phallus must be detached before her passive womb can accept it."

The women were self-inspiring and excluded the men. Reva too surprised me, "A womb hosting a phallus is not passive! Not even Dickinson's. Think about her 'Wild Nights, Wild Nights,' and she's only dreaming.

I had lost control of the Poetry Club. The jar of peanut butter was untouched.

23. Julia

Wednesday, October 28.

    My step-daughter, the engineer, is strong willed. Roberta said independence was her earliest sign of personality. Julia determined I would be lonely. So going home, she arranged to fly a thousand miles out of her way - - Istanbul to Frankfort and back to Budapest, then by rail to Debrecen - - to comfort me, although her husband was waiting in America.

    They had just married that summer in Key West, and Julia had rushed back to complete her assignment in Turkey. Il Hami, also an engineer, remained to set up his import/export business. His American dream was practical, of the sort of wealth his profession seldom provides.

    Julia's train would arrive at 5:30; I was anxious. She was short, strong-shouldered (from swimming on the high school team) and a bit heavier, as I recalled. At last sight, her round, unpainted face was also fuller, but her blondish hair was still untouched and stringy.

269

I left early for the station in order to dawdle along the way, and stopped for tea at the tables outside the Golden Bull. Mindlessly I doodled with its name. It had nothing to do with stock markets, and was little related to the Pope's pronouncements or Papal papers, but it was a document, and of enduring force. In 1217, the profligate and abusive King Andrew II had, among his extravagances, equipped and dispatched a crusade to the East at the expense of his frustrated nobles. Five years later, these freemen drew up a contract reasserting rights their forefathers had extracted from St. Stephen, and forced Andrew to sign it. The Golden Bull is to Hungary what the Magna Carta is to Britain.

Living in this history while taking tea al fresco at the Golden Bull, I was for the moment a self-satisfied Hungarian. I paid up and moved on.

Around the corner from the honky tonk behind the hotel, where the ghetto had been, I found a yellow brick synagogue built since Hitler's day. The hue was a poor approximation of empire gold. It was an inconspicuous ugly square building, no match for the Catholic basilica on Szechenyi Ut. whose grounds were green and decorated with saintly statues. The golden building had several stepped entrances adorned with iron filigree.

Cement surrounded the synagogue, encircled by a spike iron fence. From a corner of the roof a small Star of David, seemingly made of sticks, poked into the sky.

Walking back to the high street (the tramway from Nagyerdei forest to the railroad station), I discovered another synagogue, abandoned. It was constructed as three bold gables, originally white with red eaves. A large Star of David topped the point of each gabled section, and another perched on the iron fence. What history here? There was no obvious molestation, and darkened windows were intact. No vandals? Peculiar - -so were the blank stares whenever I mentioned Hitler in the classroom. Rise ye skinheads, lift up your chalk and beat the boards!

A square white tower rises at the city's center, where Szechenyi, (a hero of the 1848 revolution) becomes Kossuth (another hero of 1848), and crosses the high street. Clocks on each side are stopped at different times; the tower is newly scaffolded. A bulletin box announces this is a Lutheran church; it gives a pastor's Germanic name.

Seeing an open door, I am curious and peek in, at workmen in a dust filled sanctuary. Inside, my breath is stifled. The nave is stuffed with ladders, carpentry horses, wooden panels, lumber, tubs of plaster. Dust covers the pews stacked against one wall. Machines are grinding at another. Plasterers work the ceiling. The dust whirls. I walk on the board planks over the uncovered floor smelling of freed dirt. Foolishly I find myself regretting that tiles must soon again suffocate the refreshed earth. I am myself suffocating. I must leave for sweeter air.

The crowd is thickest here. Vendor stalls impede the sidewalk traffic, pedestrians stopping to feel the leather of a jacket or purse, or to sample anything from a Hungarian edition of "Playboy" to a translated chapter of "Pride and Prejudice."

Further on, I encounter seedy buildings, old hotels, used clothing and grocery stores with greasy windows. In the midst I confront the town hall where Kossuth lived, another neo-classic structure in 'Hungarian style.' Through the grime, I can barely make out the coloring of the tiles. Then suddenly, an opening. A green space, another park appears, just before the station, where the trams complete their run in a great turnaround. The column rising from the fountain in the middle of the park hoists a granite airplane, World War II vintage, multi-engine bomber, German or Soviet.

I lean against the railing above the stairway coming from the train platforms. A crowd emerges at 5:20, dragging bags and children and waving to greeters. Julia's train is on time. Another crowd climbs the steps. No Julia. The 6:16 arrives, still no Julia. I hang on, though no more trains are scheduled from Budapest. Reluctantly I give in. Probably she's been trying to call me. No uneasy thoughts. Passing the fruit stands in front of the station, I look back and see the first of another wave begin to flood the depot. I rush back and in the midst of arrivals, spot my step-daughter, struggling with an oversized black duffle bag.

In the taxi Julia explained she missed her train but caught the next one. "You missed that one too. The one you did catch wasn't even scheduled. Very resourceful, Julia."

I couldn't follow her explanation which involved transfers. The train that delivered her did not originate in Budapest.

271

Thursday, October 29.

Julia was bringing jewelry and gems from Istanbul, for Il Hami to sell. "Don't get the idea he's going into the flea market. Il Hami's into procurement, military stuff for the Turkish Air Force." The pieces she was transporting were filigreed silver bracelets and necklaces with jade and onyx, just starters. "You should buy one for mom's birthday."

"I've already picked out a vase, but I'll take one of those bracelets. Can you carry the vase back for me?"

That morning we searched for the shop. The vase was a Szasz, a Debrecen potter whose porcelains were known throughout Hungary. Black line drawings against milky blue porcelain showed young women in the fields, full breasts bursting from their tunics. The vase was on display among other Szasz works in a barred window on the plaza, to be purchased at another address.

"That vase won't embarrass mom?"

We found the shop - - a small window on a narrow lane tied up with truck traffic. Within, however, was a showplace of porcelain and crystal. Julia was attracted to a figurine that cost three times what I could afford.

In the market, she bought cucumbers, tomatoes, other garden vegetables, and olive oil. She cut the vegetables into small bits, poured on the oil and served up "Turkish salad."

Julia was tired. She would visit the university tomorrow. What she really wanted to see was the Roman ruins and aqueduct at Obuda in Northern Budapest. She slept until Reva came, then we walked the mile or two down Simonyi to Matya's. Reva was indifferent to Julia's exotic jewelry but impressed to learn she was an engineer and excited to discover she worked in Turkey. "I'd just as soon work here," Julia said, without enthusiasm. I believe she had been surprised by the colorful contrasts and sharp beauty of Reva's face, and particularly her thin figure, surprised and perhaps curious. Julia was certainly a curiosity to Reva.

"What do you do in Turkey?"

"Work on G.E. Engines.'

"General Electric," I explained.

"Is it lonely?"

"It was, even with the good old boys pinching my behind, until I got married."

"Her husband is Turkish," I said. "He is in America."

"You married for love? Or out of loneliness?" Julia brought out a photo of Il Hami. "My God! Omar Sharif!"

"Maybe if I worked in Hungary, I'd marry a Hungarian."

This, I assumed, was in deference to Reva.

"Will you be having a baby?"

Julia gasped. "My biological clock is ticking."

"Oh, I wish I could be married."

"How old are you?"

"Thirty-five."

24. Budapest

Saturday, October 31

She emerged from the phone booth outside Nyugati with a broad smile. "The Citadella is holding a room for us."

The taxi wound up Gellert Hill, the highest in Buda, and dropped us before a tall arch in the fortress wall. A souvenir stall stood on one side, and a casino some yards down on the other. Austrians built the Citadella on the crown of the hill after the revolution of 1848 to discourage further notions of independence, but never was a cannon fired from its portals.

We hauled our luggage through the arch, then climbed the stone steps leading to a cemented plateau and the plain hotel entrance. The plateau overlooked the Danube and Pest beyond; at the edge, we saw the mammoth silhouette of a monument and the shadow it cast on the cemented ground. We were viewing the backside of Liberation Memorial, the heroic figure of a female, both arms raised triumphantly over her head, holding an elongated wreath or was it a broadsword? The

275

enormous statue, face to the Danube, commemorates the Soviet soldiers who fell in the seven week siege at the end of World War II. It is better known as the Reoccupation Memorial.

In spite of the bulky hobnail furniture and the relics of medieval wars lining the lobby and corridors, our room was comfortable, graced with two modern bedsteads, large wardrobes, and a sink with towels. The toilet and shower were down the hall. Julia was immediately attracted to the window, a glazed gun port in a wall three feet thick. The window looked out on the deep valley and the rise of Castle Hill.

Needing to walk, I refused the taxi. Not selfish as it turned out; Julia also wanted the exercise. The path curved down through the brush in the valley for a long time before turning up Castle Hill. As we approached, I gasped, not for breath as much as the dramatic aspect of the massive wall, the ramparts that surround the Hill.

Reaching the enormous terrace of the Royal Palace, Julia pointed to a golden bird on a column. "Eagle's a long way from home, isn't he?" Its wings spread as if protecting the nation; the column stood at the end of a very ornate wall and gate.

I corrected her, 'That's not an American eagle, it's a turel," and feeling sheepish for throwing off such a tidbit, I shut down.

"OK, so what's a turel?"

I was uncertain. "A kind of buzzard or turkey. It's mythical, a la Leda and the Swan; the turel impregnated some ancestral mother who gave birth to the first Magyar."

The information was not in Julia's guidebook. She read as we strolled the terrace overlooking the Danube, dominated by an equestrian statue. (Eugene of Savoy, said her guide book, commander of an army fighting the Turks at the end of the 17th Century.)

The Soviet siege transformed the whole district into a vast acreage of ruins. Falling back, the Germans blew up all the bridges and made their final stand from the Royal Palace, from this same terrace we so nonchalantly strolled upon. The old castle was the home of Holy Roman Emperor Sigismund and sainted King Matthais Corvina. Matthais rebuilt it into a Renaissance showpiece in the 15th Century. When the Germans surrendered, the walls were reduced to a few blackened statues and bullet-riddled pillars poking up from the burned ruins.

Restoration began immediately. It was painstaking, but rewarding. Archaeologists sifted through some twenty feet of rubble, often scratching with their fingernails. Castle walls of the Arpàd and Anjou dynasties were uncovered along with Renaissance ramparts, and partially restored. One relic on display was an "Apostle,' found among Gothic statuary from the Anjou period (14th Century), a painted figure with a flowing beard and robe.

"Perfect except for a missing hand," said Julia, "Kindly face."

"Do you suppose it was just tossed out? Discarded because it fell out of fashion?" I chuckled, "Or was it buried carefully so it wouldn't become a victim of the Turks? You know they destroyed images of the human form."

"Nonsense. You don't know Turks."

My trivia was not appreciated.

The palace was restored to the Baroque splendor acquired under the dual monarchy when Emperor Francis Joseph remodeled and refurbished it, a constant, ongoing enterprise. Now it is a vast culture center and museum complex. We spent a few moments with '1000 Years of our Capital,' a permanent exhibit in the Budapest History Museum.

The plateau of Castle Hill is long and narrow, lined by a few medieval churches, miniature palaces, mansions, and the Hilton Hotel, which incorporates remnants of the oldest sanctuary on the Hill, St. Nickolas, built in the 13th Century by Dominican friars. A tower and wall survived World War II; Hilton's modern architecture blended them harmoniously.

A few hundred yards and we encountered a lacy, convoluted column in the middle of a cobblestone turnabout, (though private cars have been forbidden except for those at the Hilton.) Looming behind is the Matthais or Coronation Church where kings are crowned. The gingerbread and candy spectacle was rebuilt after World War II. It had suffered attacks since mid-13th Century. In 1686, after serving 150 years as a Turkish mosque, it was severely damaged in the recapture of Buda.

In the 19th Century, Matthais was totally reconstructed with one spire high, one low, and a rose window. At that time, the excavated tombs of Bella III and his queen were re-interred. His father, Bela II, was blinded in infancy to prevent his ascension to the throne, but Blind

Bela ruled 60 years. We viewed their burial crowns, rings, a scepter and cross.

Behind Matthais, St. Stephen rides his horse atop a high pedestal, dominating the yard of Fisherman's Bastian. The domes and stairways of the Bastian curl about him to no apparent purpose; nothing about this elf-like fortification banked high above the Danube suggests or smells of real fish. It was erected in homage to river toilers who rose in defense of the city.

Julia loved the views of Pest from the Bastian steps, especially of the English imitation parliament building, its lacy dome and spires shining on the oily Danube.

On Tancsics Mihaly Ut., we stood before the Baroque building that masked the dungeon imprisoning Kossuth Lajos for three years; Beethoven stayed next door in 1800 when he conducted in Buda at the Castle Theatre (recently rebuilt).

"Look, Julia, grass!" A lawn suddenly appeared about a golden mansion on Orscaghaz Ut. The statue of a man in 19th Century dress stood on the corner with the name Szèchenyi on a plaque. Another plaque beside the entrance read in Hungarian and English, "Hungarian Academy of Science."

At once I knew the name; Szèchenyi was the aristocrat who shared leadership with Kossuth in the 1848 revolution. That was not all. He fathered steamboat navigation on the inland waterways, engineered a giant flood control project, regulated rivers, redesigned city streets, and promoted a permanent bridge to link Buda and Pest. In the philanthropic spirit of his family, who founded the National Museum and National Library, he gave a huge sum to establish the Hungarian Academy of Science.

"Great engineer," I said, pointing, "but wasted in passion." I related his sad ending. Upon his brother's death Szèchenyi married his widowed sister-in-law, whom he'd cherished silently through the years. But he was soon miserable, grew ill, despondent, his mind vacillating between the hells of madness and clear-sightedness, perhaps greater hell. Broken in body and spirit, recluse, he committed suicide in a Viennese mental clinic.

A larger statue of Szèchenyi stands before the Hungarian Academy of Sciences in Pest near the foot of the Chain Bridge (officially Szèchenyi Lanchild). We stood before the Academy's guest house, where I would spend several days on my way home. Reva made the arrangements.

On Uri Ut, we encountered a huge hole in the ground circumscribed by deep foundation walls and filled with loose brick, rubble, rotting boards, bits of decayed plaster, remains of the Castle Hill Synagogue. The excavation had continued on and off since the bombing in 1945.

Examining it, we had a peculiar encounter. A man of mid-years wearing a tie and fedora came out of the pit, walking on a wooden plank. He brushed dust off his jacket and pants. After a casual moment of exchange, he asked in clean English, "Have you been to Plot 301?"

Julia mumbled, "Lost his marbles?" and asked, "What's there?"

"The cemetery. Easy to find, over the Chain Bridge, down to Rakocsi, up to Rottenbiller Ut. Why go? For the memorial honoring Istvan Agnyal. Who is Agnyal? The Jewish martyr who led the revolt in 1956. The Soviets executed him."

"As much as we'd like to - - "

"You must! No foreigner should miss it."

"Never heard of him," said Julia.

"Yes, yes, I know that!" he almost shouted. "You must go. Already they deny Angyal even existed."

"Who?"

"Who? Fascists, skinheads, nationalists. The world must know what happened here. Go! Read the sign on the gate to Plot 301. It says, 'Only Hungarians with souls step through this gate.' They put it up. Take a photo. Everyone in America should see it."

We extricated ourselves only by promising we'd try to visit Plot 301.

"What was he doing in that hole in the ground?"

"Looking for visitors," I answered smartly, though I had been moved by the outrage he emanated, and I reflected on a nationalist movement strong enough to drive a rational-seeming fellow to such distraction.

TV and newspapers were full of the Hungarian reburials of their martyrs in 1989. Julia also remembered. The 1989 ceremony was a grand repudiation of the communists. Until then the cemetery had been a weedy field where over 250 victims of the Soviet executions were planted, including Imrè Nagy, the hanged prime minister. All attempts to maintain the graves had been stymied.

"Let's talk about something more cheerful."

Strolling on, we came upon a bronze of the Polish General Joseph Bem, who led a Transylvania force against the Hapsburgs in 1848. "Bem closed his life as a Turkish Pasha, a Mohammedan convert in Aleppo. It was here" I went on, "Before Bem's statue that a demonstration for Polish reform ended in the tragic uprising of 1956."

"That's better?" The past was cheerless.

We walked along the river, past cross streets with flights of steps climbing the hill like old Montmarte. At last we reached Elizabeth Bridge at the foot of Gellert. I was tired and hungry. Julia suggested a taxi up to the Citadella.

Clear and balmy air on the hilltop. After dinner of paprika'd river fish in the cave-like restaurant, complete with violins, Julia went to our room and I strolled out the bluff to look down on the necklace of lights on Elizabeth Bridge. Grace, delicacy - - I wanted language to describe the slender arch. For many months after the Germans left, only pontoon bridges connected the city. 'Erzsebethid' was the last to be restored.

Its namesake was an extraordinarily beautiful and tragic woman. An abiding melancholy enhanced her enigmatic appeal and her sensuality. Her husband, Francis Joseph, was ultra-conservative, and though an emperor, petty and pedantic. Elizabeth was quite the opposite, sensitive, freedom-loving and a touch psychotic.

Longing for emancipation and embittered by her husband's ethnic-hating mother, Elizabeth gave her sympathies to the Hungarians. She learned the language, studied the history, and succumbed, it is said, to the charming Count Gyula Andrassy, the most attractive Hungarian statesmen of the time. (Sentenced to death in 1851, he returned from exile as the first prime minister under the dual monarchy.)

In 1858, Elizabeth bore Francis Joseph a son, Rudolph, who grew into a nervous, intellectual mother's child. Rudolph was thoroughly repelled by his father's cold dogmatism and sense of duty; Elizabeth added to her son's revulsion by telling him of the emperor's sexual capers. She admitted recommending a surrogate, a silly petty bourgeois, contrary to the refined and decadent empress. Rudolph favored notorious Viennese prostitutes until a 17-year old Baroness, Maria Vetsera, enraptured him.

In January, 1889, at a hunting lodge called Mayerling, they died together. Was it a pact? The emperor had cast them out. Did he order them murdered? Rudolph was tortured with syphilis; Maria was hemorrhaging from a botched abortion. Legends of Mayerling and the 'good prince' sprang up everywhere.

Within a decade, the beautiful Elizabeth also lay dead. A wild anarchist plunged a sharpened wood file into her emptied heart. 'A deliverance,' people called the tragic act.

The cousin, Archduke Francis Ferdinand, who took Rudolph's place, ran into bad luck in Sarajevo on June 14, 1914.

Sunday, November 1.

Rather than listen to the splendid orchestra and choir at the Matthais church on Castle Hill, we agreed to peek in at the 8:30 service in the cave chapel on a cliffside across from the Gellert Hotel. Our hotel man said the chapel had been walled up until a year ago. He had regarded it as a bugging center for the communist secret police.

After the chapel, we'd catch a tram for the Roman ruins at Obuda. Going down the hill in the taxi, Julia suddenly erupted. She pointed to the meter and shouted to the driver that it was racing. "Two hundred already!" The driver looked and shrugged. "Stop!" He did as bid. "It was only 300 coming up."

She was clutching two hundred-forint notes ($1.60) and threw them. The notes fluttered to his seat. The driver, pretending to no English, picked them up and tried to return them.

Julia was out of the taxi and looking for another. He charged out after her and I followed, prepared to defend my step-daughter, though bewildered by her behavior. Infuriated, the driver threw the notes back at her. One settled on the pavement, the other on the taxi trunk. It fell off as the taxi driver gunned down the hill. The next taxi had a Turkish driver and proved Julia right. They exchanged Turkish phrases. She was all sugar. I had to register disapproval. "Turkey has taught you to assert yourself."

"I don't like to be tooled."

281

"Hungary is not Turkey. These people are like us."

Julia cast a hard, meaningful stare and suddenly my residual bigotry was choking me with guilt. "I didn't mean that."

"Reva warned me about taxis in Budapest."

"Me too! I laughed, breaking the tension. She softened, gradually.

The chapel and monastery were perched on the cliff side. In 1989 a new government returned them to the 700-year Paulite order of White Monks (color of their robes). At the entrance, rusted cables protrude from a chunk of concrete bearing a Hungarian inscription. The driver, who followed us up the walkway, put it into Turkish and Julia translated for me: "Momento! Remnant of concrete that communists used to wall up the cliff temple."

We poked our noses into a small outer chamber. Rough walls amplified elderly voices singing hymns further in. The organ fit into a rock outcropping.

The Turkish driver took us roundabout to Mosckva Ter where he would point out the tram for Obuda. First, he wanted to show us the 'turbe' of Gul Baba. We had already passed the unremarkable Gothic building on Uri Ut. Containing the tomb of Abdurrahman Ali, last pasha to rule Buda, but Gul Baba was a dervish and poet, the 'Father of Roses.' His tomb was decorated with stone foliation surrounding four oval windows. It continued to be the object of pilgrimages long after the Turks were ejected from Hungary.

Mosckva Ter is a fecund warren of human pandering and transportation. Tram tracks lay thick, switching and cross crossing. The square is a kaleidoscope of yellow trams, multicolored buses and taxis. Stalls hawk everything from hamburgers to pornographic videos. Vendors offer perestroika watches, Lenin busts, and pizza, side by side. Next to transport, the most important business in the square is the "human market," the temporary black market in employment. An army of the young and not so young holding tool bags swirl around illicit job jockeys who scatter their clients at the approach of police checking passports.

The driver pointed to the tram for Batthyany Ter where we could change for the Obuda railcar. It ran along the river toward Margaret Island. "Named for the younger of the two Margarets," I informed Julia.

During the Tartar peril, went the story, Bela III dedicated his maiden daughter to Christ and put her into a monastery. Then out of dynastic interest, he changed his mind, offering her to an importune Bohemian king, Otokar II., who was bewitched by the young nun's beauty. But she was not willing to exchange her barren cell for the royal throne and marriage bed. "Margaret was sainted," I finished, "Adding to the holies in the House of Arpàd."

"For that?"

Margaret Island is a sleek green oval dividing the Danube. Bridges connect to the city at either end, Margaret on the south and Arpod on the north. Towards the end of 1944, the Nazis blew up the Margaret Bridge at a vulnerable moment, when rush-hour traffic was streaming across. With the bridge restored, the island's spas, resort hotels, and sports arenas resumed a prosperity begin in 1873, the year Old Buda (Obuda) joined with Buda and Pest to become Budapest.

25. Obuda and the Holy Crown

Running parallel with the Danube, we were engulfed by a vast apartment complex then released into the open air and the ruins. The six lanes of heavy traffic were divided by grass and a series of stone stumps which had been supports of the aqueduct. They were followed by six wholly reconstructed arches bearing a trough. To the side of the roadway we barely made out walls of the amphitheatre, which had formed the center of the civilian town of Aquincum. The military camp to the south had an amphitheatre of its own.

On the other side of busy Szentendrei Ut sprawled the ruins of the ancient city. Acres of foundations, gravel pits of anthropological interest. "Just stones now," I said, "like any other." Julia was engrossed and did not hear.

A small Romanesque museum marked with neoclassic columns sits slightly above the ruins. Behind, two colonnades stretch the length of the preserve. They're lined with stone tablets illustrating the Romans at chores; planting crops, tending cattle, cooking. We were nearing the end when a tablet startled me. It portrayed a farmer and his wife staring straight out at the viewer with the most serious and wholesome of faces. "Grant Wood," I called, "'American Gothic,' sans pitchfork."

Julia laughed, "And no spectacles."

A little shop at an exit sold souvenirs. Julia fussed over the coins and finally purchased a few that seemed genuine. The old vendor asked if we intended to visit Hadrian's palace on Shipyard Island. The sumptuous showplace was built before the proconsul became emperor. Then he shook his head. It was no longer worth the trip out. Part was destroyed and the rest was hidden under land occupied by the defunct Ganz-Danibius shipyards.

We got off the tram at Batthyany Ter and took the metro under the river to Vorosmarty Ter, devoted to pedestrian traffic in the fashionable heart of Pest. Stumbling into Gerbeaud's, the famous chocolate and pastry shop, I mustered the will to resist the exquisite cakes and settled for a sugarless muffin, while Julia splurged.

Strolling, we were attracted to a jeweled arcade formed by Gothic arches of glass tiles. It was stories tall. Art deco chandeliers extended on chains, casting dim yellow light on the marble columns and creating shadowy nooks and crannies. The medieval aura was blighted by the computers and big board we observed through a glass window - - the Budapest Stock Exchange. The first to reopen in Eastern Europe and the most active, it bears only a modest resemblance to the huge exchange of the 19th Century. The youthful brokers could just as well be in New York or Tokyo, frenetically prowling the floor and trading on their cellular phones.

Down the Corso along the Danube, Julia pretended to shutter as we passed an incongruous monolith, the Duna-Intercontinental Hotel. We turned off onto the maze of narrow streets behind it, the walled city of medieval times, where the houses and old churches are packed together. Dutifully, I followed her into the Inner City Parish Church, the oldest in Pest, dating to the 12th Century. Nonchalantly, we toured the original lattice work that still decorates the nave. Renaissance alterpieces and red marble tabernacles ornament the side chapels. A 'mihab,' Muslim prayer niche, testifies to the Turkish intrusion. Liszt often played the organ; he lived only a few doors down where he held 'musical Sundays.'

Wandering, we found ourselves before the National Museum. My interest sparked - - here was the Holy Crown. Reva had shown me the University's replica and hoped I'd treat myself to the original.

Four guards attended the glass cube in the darkened chamber as crystalline light beamed on the crown. It sits on a black velvet bed. Goldsmiths fashioned the crude crown with jewels and icons of the Byzantine world. A broad band of dull gold dangles panels of female-appearing saints alternating with huge precious stones. Medallions of gems on gold chains hang down the sides. Two more ornate bands intersect on top and hold the famous crooked cross, which has never been explained, according to Reva. As the 11th Century began, either Pope Sylvester or Otto III, emperor of the Holy Roman Empire, sent the Holy Crown for King Stephen's coronation.

Reva claimed the importance of this crown is unmatched in history. Magically it bestows sovereignty to whoever possesses it. Seizing the crown was equivalent to grasping the actual power of the state; its absence cast doubt on a ruler's legitimacy. The House of Arpàd intermarried so frequently during the 11th, 12th, and 13th Centuries that its blood no longer flowed in the last kings. The Holy Crown alone symbolized Hungarian sovereignty.

Someone at the Citadella told Julia about the Markem off Mosckva Ter and she wanted to have supper there. "It's really a pizza place, no violins."

A stylized red star is the only sign to mark the small basement restaurant. A huge factory sprawls on the other side of the cobblestone street. "A white elephant," said the owner, an art historian. Julia was told to ask for him. He had been in business nearly two years. "Cozy colors, no?" It was difficult to hear in the competition of canned rap and hip-hop reverberating off the industrial grey walls and blazing red ventilation pipes. The barstools and ashtrays were all in hot red. "For the proletariat," he said. The booths were not filled. Students bunched together at the bar. We ate pizza topped with herring and onions beside a wall decorated with communist banners, a three-foot red star, and a photo of Lenin. It was stolen, the owner said, "from the Ministry of Industry."

26. Heroes' Square

Monday, November 2.

The air was chill and windy. Still, I wanted to walk the Grand Boulevard, a half-circle about the Danube, until it intersects half way with Nepkoztarsaz Utja, the most glorious street.

Nepokztarsaz was Budapest's Broadway before decay. It contains most of the theatres, reputed cafes, elegant old hotels, the State Opera House, Ferenc Erkel Theatre, and the Drechsler Palace, home of the National Ballet School. Mansions sit in blemished splendor among the ornate facades along Nepkoztarsag, which leads straight to Heroes' Square and City Park. Initially, it was called Andrassy Ut, after the first Hungarian prime minister of the dual empire and rumored lover of the murdered Elizabeth; inevitably, for a time, it was Stalin Avenue.

Too cold and windy for Julia. She suggested the Number One underground which runs the length of the grand avenue. That would also be adventurous, since it is the original Budapest subway and the first in Europe. We caught the Number One line at Deak Square.

289

The wind gusted as we emerged from the underground. A vast field of blue-grey tile geometrically designed with white lines confronted us. On opposite sides of this square are the Museum of Fine Arts, rich in old masters including the best Spanish collection outside Spain, and the Art Gallery, host to current exhibitions.

The Millenary Monument rose towards the far end of the square. Two arcs form a semi-circle and seem to embrace a pillar hoisting the Archangel Gabriel to the heavens in celebration. At the pillar's base rides Arpàd surrounded by his seven chieftains whose blood was let into a common vessel to originate the nation. Columns in the arcs create niches, seven in each, holding the heroes - - St. Stephan anchors one end, Francis Joseph the other. Originally the only woman was Maria Teresa. After World War II, she was removed with other Hapsburg monarchs (the first removals followed World War I) to make room for neglected Hungarians, including Lajos Kossuth.

Construction of the monument started in 1896 when the Hungarians put on a massive celebration to commemorate the thousandth anniversary of the Magyar conquest. As reported, the Millennium was dazzling, with Hungarians wearing panther and leopard skin capes, pipings, shakoes, gem-studded plumes, boots, spurs, and dress swords. Chests gloated with decorations. The air shook with regimental music, inexhaustible fireworks. Now, foreign dignitaries somberly lay wreaths.

Women from Transylvania were offering wares in the mammoth square; their embroidered tablecloths, shawls, skirts and vests vibrating in the wind. Julia was bargaining for a green-trimmed table set, napkins and spread, when suddenly it was thrust into a bag and her young vendor disappeared. They all vanished on the instant as police cars squealed and stopped, violating the blue tiles of the square. Officers emerged, eager for culprits but the alacrity of the Transylvanians, young and old, frustrated them. Moving towards the park, I thought I recognized Julia's tall and round vendor holding a child's hand, disguised as an innocent bystander.

The park was on the other side of a two-laned bridge over a lagoon. "A statue of George Washington is somewhere over there," Julia reminded me. Her guidebook said it was erected in 1906, the gift of thankful Hungarians who had immigrated to the United States. A sign to the side of the bridge read, AGRICULTURAL MUSEUM, and an arrow pointed down a broad lane lined with tables of trinkets. A Soviet watch attracted me, made of reused metal with a large red face bearing in a semicircle the words, 'Perestroika' and "Glasnost.' I held it to my ear. It ran. So I gave the vendor 1600 forint ($20).

The Agricultural Museum is a huge, ornate castle incongruously devoted to animal husbandry, forestry, horticulture. The castle jams together the history of Hungarian architecture. Actually, it is Transylvanian; a replica of Vajdahunyad Castle duplicated 500 years later for the Millennium celebration. The original was the center of Janos Hunyadi's enormous estates, which originated as a modest structure given by the king to Valk, Hunyadi's Wallachian father.

"His story is not in your guidebook, Julia. Hunyadi is the most celebrated Hungarian of them all."

"Transylvanian?"

"They were all Hungarians then. Anyway, it is said he was a natural son of King Sigismund of Luxemburg, who later became the Holy Roman Emperor." I waded into Hunyadi's story - - his rise from low rank to most eminent general of the 15th Century and the champion of Christendom. His most significant triumph was the rout of Mohammed II before Belgrade in 1456, which blunted Ottoman expansion for nearly a century. Hunyadi's deliverance was celebrated every noon by the tolling of church bells throughout the Catholic world. A few weeks later, they rang for Hunyadi as well; he lay dead of the plague raging through his camp. I concluded, "The bells are still ringing."

I spared my step-daughter the horror story of Hunyadi's successor, his eldest son, Lazlo, beheaded by the Hapsburg emperor.

The Transylvanian women were hawking their shawls and tablecloths again as we returned to the square. Julia pretended no interest passing by the fluttering embroideries. Actually she wanted to play fair, and was looking for the young mother she had bargained with. The woman found her. Behind the shelter of a tour bus parked on the street, Julia paid 6000 forints for two creamy linen table sets embroidered blue and yellow.

Monday eve, November 2.

Julia would not leave Budapest without a taste of nightlife. (In America she is a faithful of the Grateful Dead.) Alongside the restaurant at the Citadella, a word scripted in green neon spelled "CASINO." The atmosphere inside was green felt, not glamorous as I imagined the gambling palace at the Gellert but equally quiet. Gamblers the world over are serious at play.

Some dressed fashionably, women in Italian gowns and a few men in evening dress. Smoke was thick, fetid and suffocating. Not only do Hungarians remain heavy smokers in spite of health notices, but they prefer their own high nicotine tobacco. The rancid smoke curled up to the tall dark ceilings. We idled around rooms of roulette, craps, poker, and blackjack, observing the joyless winners and dour losers. One sleek old dame won two hands of blackjack in a row without moving a muscle in her face. "Not what I had in mind," said Julia.

A taxi driver told us the trendy bars and clubs are on the Pest side. Julia agreed, having checked the map for a few places listed in the English language newspaper. "Trocadero," she directed the driver, 15 Szent Ivan Korut.'

The street shone with the lights of Nugati. At night Eiffel's railroad station becomes a crystal palace. The Trocadero is across the way, a dimly-lit basement two stories deep, steel girders overhead. A mural of bright yellows and greens serves as a backdrop for the band, thankfully not raucous. A few middle-aged couples were dancing on the tiny square floor space provided at the expense of the pool tables. We ordered the specialty, pina coladas, and left without finishing them; not lively enough for Julia.

As the husky doorkeeper called a taxi, she asked if he knew about the 'Piaf.' "Paris in Budapest," he told her. In the taxi, I wanted to know why the 'Piaf.' "Actors go there after the shows."

We heard the jazz from the street. The walls of 'Piaf' were covered with blown up photos of an earlier Budapest. Rattan tables and chairs were spaced comfortably. I anticipated songs of Edith Piaf but not even a photograph of the chanteuse from the Paris streets appeared. The feel was more of a French possession than of France, Casablanca rather than Paris. The crowd was younger and paid more attention to the music;

men dressed in slouchy leather and denim crunched at the bottom like American hip-hoppers; women in tank tops and skimpy skirts. Prepared to sacrifice my pleasure for Julia's on her last night in Hungary, I found myself thoroughly enjoying it.

27. The Alfold

Tuesday, November 3.

My first class car was in fair condition, nothing deluxe, but nothing torn, fixtures in place, not crowded. One other person occupied the cabin, a man who kept looking up from his book and making slight gestures as if to speak then holding back. Old, he was dressed immaculately in a colorless western suit, shirt and tie. A black lamb's fur covered his head. The grey hair along the sides of his face had yellowed like his skin. Bulbous lips dominated his face, the eyes a weary blue. I was tempted to relieve his anxiety by opening conversation, but did he speak English? By the time I decided to try, he was looking through the window at the Alfold.

Little to see, not even stones. The spare, sun baked houses are of earth and brick. At one time the great plain was swampland that monks drained to make agriculture flourish. But their work languished and the land reverted to its primitive state until the nineteenth century. Now we rumble past stretches of tilled field and pasture with an occasional sight of water, a thin sheet of a pond, where once storks frolicked among the frogs. Nearer Debrecen, villages occur more frequently; the grassy puszta has a wilder, more alien air. I spotted a few cattle and looked for csikòs who entertain tourists with their splendid horses.

The csikòs are said to be nomad cowboys following their ancestors' calling. They lead contemplative lives, certainly know more than most about the mysterious gulf between man, beasts, and stars. Nights they squat around their fires in large embroidered sheepskin coats, their tanned, furrowed faces silently chewing pipe stems. Sometimes an old story will be told, reminiscence, in half uttered sentences, laconic pauses. Some attend the village tavern. A fight will emerge. It's said their blood is fiery. The fight is usually over a woman, often a 'menylske,' a married one.

The village streets are narrow and straight, bordered with acacia trees, sweet smelling in the spring. The houses are whitewashed, colorful stripes painted at the base, golden tile roofs, flower boxes under the windows.

At last the immaculate old man gathered the courage to speak. He asked, "You are not Hungarian. What country?"

"America."

He nodded approvingly. "I will go to America before the end."

I sympathized and looked away at the darkening fields. His hand was hitting my knee. "You American? Where you going?"

"I'm a visiting professor in Debrecen."

"Professor? Ah. Me too, at Debrecen. I used to be." A sly withered smile spread his tight face. "What you teach?"

"Literature. You taught at Kossuth?"

Nodding, he said, "German language." He pointed to himself, "How old?" I refused to play the guessing game. "Eighty-five. You?" I told him sixty-nine but he wouldn't believe it. He stared at me without a word for awhile, and then he confessed in a soft voice, as if giving me a revered prize, "I write history. Admiral Horthy."

I had read a memoir of the Hungarian regent and also an account of his wretched relations with Hitler. How many lives of Miklós Horthy were needed? "Why?" I asked.

"Horthy and the Jews," he responded.

"That hasn't been told?"

His head shook. The weary eyes had come alive with appreciation for my concern. We could barely see each other in the dark car. I pointed to the unlit lamp in the ceiling. He shrugged and emitted an old man's giggle, then quickly a store of Horthy material began spilling out of him. The old professor had found an audience.

His history of Admiral Horthy began in 1867, decades before the regent was born. With relish he described the beating of the Austrian Empire by the Prussians and Italians, and chortled at the subsequent plight of the Hapsburgs. "Bismarck kicked them out of the German Reich. So they turned to good friends," he took a deep breath, "who they suppressed for centuries. They make deal. One empire, Austria-Hungary."

I nodded, acknowledging the dual monarchy.

"After three centuries, Magyars are again their own masters."

"Not quite."

He admitted the Austrians still dominated foreign policy and the military. "No matter," he said with a touch of vehemence. "Language! Sacred Magyar language. We make it compulsory."

The language was their identity. But the aged professor conceded that Magyarization went too far, and that his English was rusty.

Now he deliberated over his words and uttered them almost in monotone. Hungarians played the role of "the gentleman class," lording over their minorities, harping on their cultural superiority.

"Mistake. We deserved upbraiding."

They got it when the largest Hungarian army in history marched under the imperial flag in World War I and lost. As the Kaiser's evil accomplice, Hungary shared blame and was punished.

The cabin was completely dark. I found a switch beside the sliding door and turned it. "Might we go in dark?" I switched off the light. Occasionally, as he continued, streetlamps of a passing village flashed across the cabin, enflaming the old eyes.

"Western leaders punished Hungary by declaring our minorities oppressed and liberating them." They found an exiled Czech, Tomas Masyrk, who articulated a plan. He proposed a Slavic bulwark, a "New Europe" of nation states, established on land forfeited by the German and Hungarian powers. "Hungary a power? It is a joke, no?"

297

The Hungarian spokesman was Mihaly Karoyli, head of the National Council and a promoter of Bolshevik fervor. He had instigated the assassination of his predecessor, Count Tisza, who he accused of promoting the war. Four revolutionary soldiers entered Count Tisza's villa, seized him unarmed, and executed him before his wife's horrified eyes.

Impatient with the peace process, the Czechs moved troops into the Slovak region and upper Hungary. After a few skirmishes, Count Karoyli withdrew. "The democrat was confident in the fairness of Western democracies." The old man sneered. "Romania was so impatient. They march through Transylvania, take half of pre-war Hungary."

When the Allies legitimized the Romanian seizure as a "neutral zone," Karoyli complained, and was told to withdraw further, to the Tisza River. "He resigned in favor of Bela Kun, a Hungarian Jew just returned from Moscow. Kun had fled to Russia after a court martial for stealing from fellow soldiers in the Austrian army. He was schooled in Moscow to incite masses." The Hungarian proletariat leaped in popularity, and so did the opposition; "the 'white terror' ran wild, led by anti-communist, anti-Semite Arrow Cross party."

In May 1919, a coalition of Social Democrats and communists proclaimed a Hungarian Soviet Republic under the leadership of Bela Kun who believed world revolution would dissolve Hungary's minorities.

The professor sighed in the darkness. "Nine months and Bela Kun is finished. In France they sign Treaty of Trianon. Devastation complete!" Statistics were at his fingertips: "Treaty take two-thirds Hungarian land. Over three million forced into lower cultures."

Kun's Bolsheviks railed against the Treaty while their atrocities horrified the country. Gangs pillaged the villages, holding kangaroo courts. Wartime heroes wearing Kaiser's gold medals were sought out and hanged. Citizens were shot with flimsy reason, thrown into the Danube at night; skinned alive in the cellar of Count Batthyany's palace, punctured with nails, "All tricks of torture learned from Russians. 'Terror is the weapon of our regime!' cried Kun's executioner."

Anti-Semitism soared. Even tolerant Hungarians would not deny that Jews had been too prominent. They played dominant roles in finance and commerce. They were blamed for the terror that offended even Kun's fellows. Kun resigned when the Romanians advanced beyond their Trianon borders and marched on Budapest. "Romanian lorries were idling just outside the city, to carry loot away."

Enter Admiral Horthy. The Hungarian nobles invited him in. "Count Teleki asks his aristocrat to stage counter-revolution, restore order." The professor chuckled sadly, 'French occupiers invite Admiral of Hapsburg Navy to form Army." His head shook at this paradox. "Hungarian National Army"

"Horthy ride white horse at head of troops into Budapest, up to Gellert Hotel and they give him regency. City was terrible to see, ravished by Kun's Bolsheviks, unrecognizable. Hooligan bands roamed streets, louts in filthy uniforms waving red banners. The country was still half-occupied, without parliament. 'Hell has reigned here,' declared the new regent 'now national army reigns.'"

Outside, the shadows were yielding to the lights of Debrecen. Soon we were pulling up to the station platform. "This trip was too short," I said.

He was taking his bag from the overhead. "You interested, still?"

"Yes, really."

"You have phone? I call. You have name?"

We exchanged names and I gave my phone number. Professor Miklos Katona had no phone.

299

28. Josip

Tuesday night, November 3.

The phone was ringing as I entered the apartment. Josip. When was I coming to Osijek? That is the old Roman outpost of Murcia and the major city of Slovenia, Croatia's eastern sector which the Serbs had just pounded. On the map you could go straight south to Pecs, then over the border at Beli Manastir and again south some 50 kilometers to Osijek. On my Fulbright three years before, I had often taken Roberta and Danya to Pecs in the red two-car railroad, painted with a communist star, Roberta was enthralled with the ancient Magyar city.

At that time, somber Hungarian guards patrolled the border with machine guns on their backs. They unsettled us the first time when the rest of the passengers were allowed off the cars. We sat stiffly, a trifle alarmed. For nearly a half-hour we looked out at the station and the guards. Finally one of them came in, accompanied by a woman toting a portable desk suspended by a chain around her neck. She offered to exchange our dollars for forints. Yugoslav dinars were beneath contempt.

The guard's face was intelligent and not yet shaven. He asked for fifteen dollars each, explaining that it was the price of a visa, a service his government kindly provided at this remote border. "Entrance fee?" No smile. He gave us a receipt for the forty-five dollars and stamped our passports. Returning them, he observed, "Professor? What you teach?" I responded brusquely and he became a beamish boy. "I learn American literature. School." We were allowed off the train.

Roberta had brought Josip to our one-room apartment in Osijek. He was a psychologist with the postal department and they had met at a psychology conference staged by "itinerant promoters." (That was my wife's professional opinion.) Josip was hungry for any professional contact. He kindled the friendship which deepened when he learned that my mother was Hungarian born. Josip's Hungarian family name was Lerinc which was also the name of an outstanding student in my senior seminar. "Yes, my daughter." Typically, he feigned disinterest in the subject of his pride.

The Lerinc apartment was in the same complex as ours but much larger, three bedrooms. Durinca, Josip's hefty wife, was all for physical fitness. She would lead us around the new stadium track just beyond the complex at a fast trot, then serve us dinner, a pork roast or chicken. She had unquenchable thirst for off color jokes. One evening we were guests with their close friends, the Drs. Janos, a medical couple. When the jokes ran out, they resorted to blurting sexual words, body party and naughties, roaring hilariously while Roberta and I sat with frozen smiles.

Josip had asked for professional publications from America and I had sent back issues of PSYCHOLOGY TODAY even though the articles were popularized. On the phone, he thanked me and asked for more. "That magazine's defunct," I told him. I would look for something else when I got home.

"Home? You mean without coming to Osijek?"

"We have a long break this month. I'll try." This was a fib. The All Saints break started three days ago. I had agreed on going to Transylvania with Matt. Josip asked how I would come. "No train goes directly to Pecs," I equivocated.

Josip laughed at me. "You know Osijek is surrounded by Serb army?" I had seen television shots of familiar places reduced to rubble and a former student had written while the fight was still raging how they ran in spurts between buildings and walls to go shopping. But I thought the Serbs had relented. I didn't realize Osijek was still surrounded. "They make deal." Josip told me, "Serbs sit on three borders. Only the road west is open. Take train across border to Zagreb then bus."

"Directly to Osijek?"

"Route changes all the time. Two buses, maybe three. You will get here.

Instantly, Transylvania was more alluring. But I had no heart for dampening his enthusiasm. "Your family is OK? Everybody made it through ok?"

"Thank God we all survived that awful war. Now everything will be better. Standard of living is low, but better than a year ago when our "brothers" treated us with hundreds of shells every day. The post office is still here, with me in it. And you will recognize Osijek, because the USA did so. They didn't recognize the Serbs, you know. Osijek is changing more and more to its previous shape." He went on about our chess and brandy breaks at the Lerinc cottage, his "weeken' house" in the village of Samatovci.

Josip wanted me to know something and he was carried away with it. He had taken a second job as a teacher. "I know I'm too old to do anything new. Anyway, I'll do my best to become a good teacher. I hope you don't mind to help me when you come. If we put together your rich experience and my big wish, we attain something. Well, I'm not such an amateur in everything. Am I not good in brandy production? I'm not bad even in foreign languages. I understand your mother tongue."

"You mean my mother's tongue? She never spoke Hungarian. Came to America as an infant."

"What a conceited person I am! Hope I'm not. What about my barbeque? Remember it? I'm not bad in chess.! Josip was a master and kindly accommodated my ineptness. "So come! There is enough Szlivovitz at Samatovic, the brandy that speaks many languages. You liked our talks? For me it's important to have a clever conversationalist like you." He said that I wrote him with the wrong address, not

303

Vizenacvi Suk 89; that was a partisan name. "Such names are not in fashion any more," but Szenjak 89. He did not say what the names meant.

29. Reva's Troubles

Wednesday, November 4.

Reva called. I was on my balcony in the chill evening air, bathing in guilt for deceiving Josip. She had just finished her aerobics class and was at a pay phone on Simonyi two blocks away. "I must see you, immediately. Glad you're back." The deep voice was laden with crisis. I heard her withholding tears.

Her straight black hair shone about the wan Magyar face. She seemed a Chinese movie maiden. "Have a good workout?" She sat on the sofa. Plump trees in the forest mural at her back accented her thinness.

"Oh Daniel, I thought you'd never get back."

"What is it?" Did Tom Riedel insult her? Did Andros cancel her contract? Was her dissertation subject rejected (how on earth does a Hungarian girl chose a dissertation about Toni Morrison, an American black)?

"It's David." She had been confiding in me after each weekly chat with her fiancé in Iowa. I sensed the relationship had altered, the calls and letters were less frequent. David was tiring of his game. Reva was too easy a mark.

"He's turned down an offer from Ankara." A university in Turkish Cypress had already been rejected. Reva had also applied to the universities in those places.

"You still think he's serious about coming back?" She was unmoved by my skepticism, maintaining that David was the more ardent. "He still loves you of course?"

"He wants me to come to America and marry him"

"He does?"

"I've received notice from the US Embassy and application forms to obtain a fiancée visa, but I didn't send them back because I wasn't sure David was serious. Now I don't know what to do."

I was a moment before I could reverse attitudes. Didn't she want to be married? Isn't that what she indicated to Julia? And wasn't David her love? She was alone. Marriage is usually seen as a remedy for that, if nothing else. Not knowing what to say, I offered diffidently, "The forms are only to get a visa."

"But I feel they're a commitment, a notification that we're engaged. I just don't want to play with it. David does not want me for a visit only, he wants me to stay."

"David is not Muslim and America is not Iran. You can always go home."

"If I had money. He has the money, and gives no assurance when I might come back to see my family." (Her father was a retired physician, living with Reva's sickly mother; they had just moved to Vamosperce, the village of her birth outside Debrecen. Her married sister lived in Budapest with her husband and three-year old daughter.) "David wants to marry me as soon as I get there. That's what we quarreled over. I told him I would prefer living with him again to see if it would work. 'It's for the rest of our lives,' I said. But he won't have it that way."

"You are asking for advice?" My tone surely told her what it would be. I was tempted to remind her of a trite tale she told about people's natures in which a man saves a baby anaconda from death, feeds and cares for it until one day the snake bites him. Dying, the man asks, 'Why: I've been so good to you!' The anaconda replies, 'You should have known I was just a snake.' And the man of course was just a nurturer, like Reva.

It was her nature to undertake the care and protection of David Schwartzman, a Jewish stereotype and intellectual castoff in the swirl of academic combat, as it was her nature to gravitate towards Toni Morrison, authoress of the American underprivileged, the denied. And to an extent, perhaps, toward me and other visiting professors like Tom Riedel, just a touch outside, at least until they were fully grounded in the center of academic affairs at Kossuth and could bite.

She ignored my question. "How can I drop everything and fly away? I've just taken off for the last flight with Toni Morrison." ("The People Could Fly: Images of Flight in Toni Morrison's Novels" was the title of a paper Reva delivered with spellbinding success at an international conference that summer, arousing excitement with the inclusion of magical words Africans chant before they fly.) "I force myself to do nothing else but compose paragraphs and jog in the evenings."

"Other than teaching classes, you mean, and seeing to my welfare?"

"The dissertation requires all of my self control. Usually, I'm hopping from one thing to another." She had been in charge of Kossuth's Modern Philological Society, for which I had promised a paper, involved with the Poetry Club, and occasionally recruited students for the University in Budapest. (Only the upper four percent qualified.) "But I've set a deadline. This dissertation must be finished before the end of June so I can spend the summer studying for exams."

David had been cloying; I welcomed another subject, "What exams are you taking?"

"Twentieth Century Black Writing. I'm up on that and also Feminism. The hellish one's going to be Theories of Metaphor. Andros chose that one."

I was astonished. "Those are your general field exams?"

"For the kis doctorate."

"Shouldn't they test you more broadly?"

"In recognized areas of literature?" Her eyes flashed and her face tightened. "Daniel, you disappoint me."

"You propose to call yourself a doctor of philosophy in American literature with those puny offshoots? They're more sociology than literature. Look at the canon!"

Murmuring something about the canon being autocratic and arbitrary, she demurred, then immediately resumed her sorrowful plight. "If I went to join David, even with the little doctorate, I couldn't get a job. Being from Central Europe would hinder my chances. They just won't credit my experience and knowledge."

"When you are ready - - "

"The US Embassy will support me for a seminar at a US university, if I want."

"But you don't?"

"I do want to get out of Debrecen for a while, but not to America, not to David. What I'd like is to get away from the situation."

"You're sure a situation exists?"

"Oh yes, Riedel's gossip is childish, unprofessional, but does have repercussions. His idle tongue raises suspicions that I'm setting my teeth for him."

I was instantly defensive. "I've not spoken to anyone about the 'situation' as you call it."

"Anyway, that's part of the reason I would like to get away, at least until the gossipy professor leaves. Sometimes I feel the need for a person like David to protect me - - I don't mean that. I can protect myself. I am strong, you know, and perseverant."

"And arbitrary?"

"And arbitrary," she conceded. "David has been in and out of the picture. I am very hesitant about what is happening or what should happen. He has enormous need for me. It's frightening. I have memories of loving him."

"Maybe your loving was the ticking of your bio clock?" Her eyes grew tender. "Since you want advice, I'll say this, Reva. You seem to flit between accepting what is possible and demanding utopia."

"My longings are not practical, I know that, they've been frustrated too long."

"Is that typically Hungarian?"

"Hungarians can be utopian."

"Most accept what's at hand."

"You mean 'tolerate,' don't you? Toleration is not good enough."

"Better than a life of missed opportunities, wasted capacities."

"Oh, what can come of it? Shouldn't I give it a try?"

"After you finish the dissertation, of course."

"I'll still be undecided."

We went to "Matya's Pince" for tea a few blocks down Simonyi, where the soft lighting drained her tension. The entry was a simple portal on the street leading down a spiral stairwell. I especially liked the light piano music, a reprieve from the passionate violins that pollute most cozy places.

30. The Ruarks

Thursday, November 5.

The Ruarks own a one bedroom apartment on the fifth (top) floor of an ugly cement-block building near Reva's place, and a second apartment on the floor below which they use for storage. Apparently, Steve Ruark is making his home in his wife's native land, though he still holds a professorship at his university in Illinois and intends to return next year rather than forfeit it. We had met in 1968 at an MLA conference for new department heads ("chairs" was not the universal designation back then). He impressed me as very young for a position of academic leadership, but he was sharp, diligent, over polite, and lacking the usual arrogance.

Twenty years later I was startled to see him board a special bus in Ljubljana for professors attending an international meeting in Lake Bled, Slovenia. I had come to give a paper extracted from EXILES AT HOME, a book I'd published three years earlier. Steve had discovered notices in USIA European publications. I responded self-consciously, "I thought my book was like most, no sooner released than flushed down a black hole." He confessed that he hadn't read it; he was too busy with his own book, a collection of Irish humor, including James Joyce. His wife was co-editor. Steve pointed to her sitting a few rows away.

The name of Steve's second wife is Reka Grosz. At Lake Bled in 1988 she appeared girlish and shy, a total misreading I discovered. Then she was an instructor in Eger where Steve had been granted his first Fulbright; now she is a full-fledged professor at Kossuth, and has been invited to lecture at London University, while Steve returns for his required stints in America. Her face is still as full and colorful; the brightness in her brown eyes undiminished. Reka speaks out boldly. Politics, she explains apologetically, is in her family blood; her brother, Pàl, now fills the parliamentary seat her father recently vacated.

The senior Grosz had been much maligned by the Hungarian communists. "He was adept at avoiding prison," Reka said. "Party members remark on it." She loathes the party in consequence. In retirement, her father concentrates on his painting, to which she is devoted.

They hang all over the apartment, except the bathroom which is cluttered as Hungarian bathrooms usually are; mops, brooms, wash buckets, ladders, stools, tools, barely room to slip down your pants.

Mr. Grosz' suffocating colors darken the study and bedroom walls. These chambers are also cramped with books and papers, research for the couple's steady publication. A cross bearing Jesus hangs over the bed, a duplicate of the one on Steve's office wall in the Simonyi building. By contrast, that office is uncluttered. It's furnished with cream colored leather sofa and easy chair plus ottoman, the cause of consternation and envy among his colleagues.

Most of the paintings depict spirals, the colors brightening, purples to reds and orange, as they spin out toward some heavenly goal. A few are semi-figurative, pleading limbs stretching up from the murk to vague violet. The textures are coarse, the lines crude. Nevertheless, I found complimentary words.

"You can't really tell much from these," said Reka. "His best work will be hanging in the Great Church on the square next month. You will come."

"The Reform Church?"

She nodded. "We've stored some below, in our other apartment, but it's too late to see in there. The electricity's off." She went to stir a pot in the tiny kitchen.

"He's given up on Budapest," Steve said. "They won't recognize anything from the provinces. I've tried a number of people myself. I should have some influence as Chair of the Fulbright Committee. They do know him, after all he was in parliament many years, painting all the time."

"Maybe Budapest has its own idea of sophistication," I offered. Did Steve really appreciate his father-in-law's work or was he merely Reka's man? "Shouldn't the church show satisfy him?"

"Artists are artists the world over, and at all ages - - blind, unrelenting egos" Ah! If Steve had the wisdom to satisfy his wife, he still held an opinion or two.

She called us to the kitchen, where we stretched and twisted to fit ourselves around a little table. Reka had prepared lamb stuffed peppers and chicken paprikas. "A dish my mother served," I asserted. She smiled in acknowledgement. "According to Reva," I said, "I mean Tom Riedel's Reva; all Hungarian mothers teach their daughters how to make paprikas."

"True. Is he still living with her? I understood he was moving in with you?"

Though the Institute's rumor mill was broad and fast, I was surprised that Tom's living arrangement created a ripple. "He's decided to stay there."

Reka made no effort to mask her frown.

Not for an instant had I given a thought to her moral fixations or her religion.

She had also invited Matt, hearing of our plan to visit Transylvania. Considering it a piece of the homeland, Reka had visited many times and had many tips. But how could another body fit into that tiny crammed kitchen? Matt asked me to offer his apology. Other than a grunt she was not visibly offended. I complimented her graceful composure and compared it with the Hungarian President's at his recent booing on the steps of the Parliament building. It was merely a gesture of courtliness, but she took it up. "Hungarians are easily roused," she replied.

"It's the Magyar's great fault," said Steve. "They love political embroilments. Usually they lose sight of high principle and drift into party politics."

"Like our Democrats and Republicans, and the Irish."

Reka did not laugh. She pursued my reference to the Hungarian President. "You and your American colleagues should not be appalled to hear our President booed."

"I think Daniel is more upset with the party vice-president, with Churka's strident attacks," said Steve.

"His call for a pure Hungary? It's annoying, smacks of the fascists. But I'm all cheers when Churka demands the restoration of Hungarian living space."

"All of us are," Steve added, "before the Romanians completely wipe out Hungarian culture in Transylvania."

"Even socialists would shed blood for that," Reka said.

"Even? Socialists are not Hungarians?"

It was a mildly facetious question. Actually I was upset with their instant willingness to let blood for the Transylvanians. My tone had not escaped her; she answered, "Most are communist retreads," and began clearing the dishes.

I was tempted to put the question, 'By which you mean the impure - - Jews and Gypsies?' Instead, I asked, "Socialists are still strong?"

"Very." Steve brought out a map of Romania with red circles around Koloszvar and other Transylvanian towns populated with Székelys. We returned to the living room. "You know who Székelys are?"

"The abused minority in Romania."

"Hungarians who came to the Carpathians with Arpàd and settled while he pushed on. Hungarians say they're the root descendents, fierce warriors. They're honest Magyars, actually naïve, noble and heroic. Matt hasn't mentioned them?"

I detected a trace of antagonism, but had no idea Steve was aware of our young colleague's disparagements. To Matt, Steve and Reka seemed blatant nationalists who were busily pushing each other up the academic ladder with time out only for sexual athletics.

From the kitchen, she called, "Szèkelys are unspoiled by the excesses of Western civilization. They fought beside King Stephan in 1003 when he slew Guyla the Vlach."

"I'm lost."

"The Vlaches are the Wallachians," Steve explained, "who are Romanians, who claim to be Romans originally." He offered brandy.

"Dacians originally," Reka corrected, wiping her hands on a towel as she came into the living room. She accepted the brandy.

"And because Stephen slew Guyla," I tried, "Transylvania is Hungarian?"

My simplification brought a slight smile to Reka's serious face. "Today, Transylvania is Romanian," she admitted, "a shell of a glorious Hungarian kingdom. When you get to Koloszvar - - the Romanians were calling it Cluj until they discovered the Roman name for it was Napoca, so now its Cluj Napoka - - when you get there, you'll laugh at the hilarious statue of Romulus and Remus suckling the wolf, a perfect reproduction from Rome., I mean, really, yet there it is, asking to be taken seriously.

Soberly, Steve said, "People have been taken away for poking fun at it. Too much of the country's energy is spent maintaining lies like the one of Roman descent. Museums have to exhibit at least one Roman ruin. Of course they hoak it up. History books are burned or banished if they don't reflect the big lie, the unity of all Romanians and their antiquity. You know the Treaty of Trianon put the country together in 1920, out of bits and pieces of principalities."

I accepted a spot of something Steve thought truly Hungarian, took a sip and put it down. It tasted like olive oil. "We were there just before Ceausescu was executed," he went on. "Koloszvar smelled, I mean literally, it stunk! Offal in the alleys, vomit in the bus stations, decay everywhere in a country that Ceausescu bragged was the glory of scientific socialism. We went again two years ago, after his lieutenant, Ion Iliescu, installed himself with his National Salvation Front. Koloszvar still smelled. The bread lines were just as long and the gas, water, and electricity just as erratic. But conditions were slightly improved. Not all the country's produce was being shipped out, people were allowed to eat some. Iliescu had also improved on Ceausescu's sophisticated electronic surveillance."

315

"In your hotel room?"

"Always check for devices. They're easy to find. Keystone cops are very clumsy."

"And crude," Reka said. "Once, on the border, we were checked by the notorious fat lady. She spoke no English and very little Hungarian. Without a word of greeting, she blurted in Romanian, 'Show me everything.' Her fat hand plunged into my pack and my heart sank. I knew what she was searching for, and she was going to find it. She opened my portfolio case to see if I was hiding any letters. Hungarians usually sneak them in since Romanian mail is intercepted and sometimes thrown away. In her fat hand plunged, beneath my carefully layers skirts and blouses which covered the paperbacks. Suddenly she stopped and gave me a scathing look. Grunting the equivalent of "I gotcha." her hand came out holding a book. In it went and came up with another." Reka shook her head.

"In Piggy's police eyes," Steve said, "these books were terrible things, about Hungarian folk beliefs, customs, songs, as important to Szèkelys as Bibles to condemned zealots. All outlawed in that country where by law everyone is Romanian. But all this was just a prelude to the big search that delayed the train for over an hour."

"She sniffed treasure," Reka continued, "ripped into everything, mine and my brother's, who was along. Helter-skelter she flung out stuff on the cement floor, clothing, foodstuffs, books. 'Where you going?' the fat one asked. 'Who you go see?' 'Several places,' I told her. 'Ha! You think so? You go off this train, that is where you go.'"

Obviously, Reka enjoyed her imitation of the fat guard. So did I.

"They ignored Steve but threatened my brother, Pàl, and me. They took our passports. I was frightened of being in official hands in that country. Suddenly, I thought to say, 'My American husband.' Magic words. So we had a conference with the other inspectors and were allowed to stay on the train. A few days later Pàl was permitted to pick up the confiscated books on his way back to Hungary. The foodstuffs were not returned. He says the keystone kops shadowed him until five o'clock which was quitting time. But don't fool with them. They may be stupid; they're not harmless."

"But they hardly looked a my stuff," said Steve, "I concealed a few copies of Reka's new book on Yeats for Miklós and Irina. They're friends who publish the best Hungarian journal in Romania, actually the only one left. They've shut down Székely radio and TV along with the theatre and newspapers. And most Hungarian schools, only one university still teaches the literature."

"I suppose they want residents to read and speak only Romanian. Some Americans want only English spoken in our schools."

"Not the same," said Reka. "This is total elimination. Székelys can't even give their babies Hungarian names. The government provides a list of 80 names to choose from. If you stay in a Székely home, do you know it will be illegal?"

"The basis of Hungarian life," Steve said, "is the village, and they're being bulldozed off the map. They're getting concrete housing blocks with communal kitchens and toilets instead of houses and churches.

Steve and Reka were too heavy.

"Bring plenty of food with you and books."

"Matt's taking care of that."

She went right on, "Romanians resent foreigners bearing gifts. Stings their pride, but they'll barely search an American. They need coffee, chocolates, cocoa, cheese, tomato paste, spices - - paprika is rare for some reason - - soap, candles, razors, novels. They like the American naturalists, especially Steinbeck and Dreiser."

Saying good night, Steve assured me, "You'll enjoy it. Transylvania is incredibly beautiful, and the Székely people are brave and determined. They're losing the little they have. When you get back you'll appreciate your precious vote and your freedoms." He was so serious.

"I might even be tempted to join the ACLU."

He did not crack a smile.

The October air was balmy as I walked back to the apartment. Heavy clouds blew across the sky and a half moon occasionally peeped through. I felt myself freed of the Ruarks gloom, afloat in the warm wind. I was a little boy of many moons ago, with wings. They carried my spirit over Steve's patriotic sobriety and Reka's Hungarian melancholy. I was unattached. Seldom was I so free, so uplifted at being at American in Europe.

Canadian literature was close enough, and she was Reva's bosom friend. Besides I'd been a guest at her place.

The meal was a triumph. I had secured two huge turkey legs at the market next to the laundry on Egyetem Utca. As I turned from the meat counter, the butcher came out of the back and plopped a legless and wingless turkey carcass on the block. "That too," I called, pointing, "I want that." Thanksgiving turkey was cooked in two pots with potatoes and carrots, and presented with enormous pride.

I brought out the Transylvanian photographs: In Brasov, buildings on the plaza backed to a peakless Tampa Mountain that hovered like the wings of a gigantic bat; a long line of people stretching from a bread truck unloading the daily loaves; crumbling citadel walls now encompassing a tennis court; three purple peeks seen through naked fall brush from a mountain top restaurant, where another Dracula castle is supposed to be.

Reka could barely make out my tiny image atop the mountain next to a flagpole. It flew a scrawny Romanian pennant, blue, yellow and red bands sewn together in an oversized shawl. Reka's face flushed. Then she took the photograph in hand, breathed deeply for control, then flung it to the rug. "Matt snapped it?" Obviously, who else was there? "Especially for me?"

"Matt's a devil." said Judit. I felt again the impishness of that moment.

Reka lost it once more - - when she came to the photos of Csikscereda where we stayed with the Székely family of Edit, Imrò and their two boys. She admired my shot of frozen action before the sports area, an aluminum statue of two hockey players racing for the puck; and of salamis on hooks in an empty food store. What reddened her face now was a shot of an ostentatious orthodox church, white with black trim. She snarled, "Greek Oriental," and the Orthodox Church joined the Romanian flag on my fake oriental rug.

Judit asked, "What did you think of the trains?" She allowed no time to answer, but launched into an earlier period when her father had taken her second class, "the peasants singing and playing their pipes and rams horns, stamping on the carriage floor with the holes in it."

"And the foul smell of garlic and onion," Reka added.

"No more singing now," Steve said. "They're all wearing walkmans."

"You can still tell Hungarian passengers from Romanian," said Reka. "Romanians board the train with turkeys and geese in baskets, hens under their arms, and their pigs and lambs in sacks. Once I traveled with a pig who woke to squeal at every stop. His master stroked him and crooned him to sleep again."

A tired anecdote, I let it pass, "We didn't see any of that."

"But most Hungarians won't offend your sensibilities that way," Reka continued, "They respect others."

"You mean the better classes," Judit corrected. "Hungarian peasants are just as boorish as Romanian. They respect only those above them."

Steve agreed. "And those below are treated like dogs,"

Upset, Reka charged her husband, "So there's no difference?"

"Of course, in other ways, many other ways." Steve looked about, embarrassed. I changed the subject.

"We stayed with Matt's Szèkely friends, except the first night,"

"What happened the first night?" Reka asked. "Matt couldn't round up anyone?"

"We intended to stay with his Saxon friend, Harry Cloos, but Harry said he already had guests."

"A Szèkely would never do that."

"They're too generous," I agreed. "The next night we stayed with another Szèkely family. They were upset, all the Szèkelys were. The police were brutalizing them."

Steve said they'd heard about the recent police murders including the father of a 15-year-old whose head was smashed against a wall when he tried to stop a policeman from raping his daughter."

"As bad as the Serbs," Reva commented

"Not at all," said Steve.

"Serbs are particularly heinous," she insisted, "and not just in Bosnia or Croatia. Two days ago I read in a Budapest newspaper that a 19-year-old girl in Belgrade was gang-raped by fellow workers at a party celebrating her promotion."

"At least the rapists weren't the police," Steve answered.

"Bosnia is a family feud between the Orthodox Serbs and the Muslims," said Reka. "Both are still communist." She began her family travails at communist hands, and abruptly cut herself off, "Communists are hateful beasts," she finished.

I asked, "They were never popular in Hungary?"

"Bela Kun's regime lasted only 133 days after the first World War," she answered, "and even before Gorbechev, we forced the Soviets to allow us free enterprise, our NEM."

"New Economic Mechanism," Steve explained before I could ask. "Hungary's capitalists were off and running by the time the communists were kicked out."

32. Riedel's Trouble

Tuesday, December 1.

Passing through the sleazy showplaces behind the Golden Bull, I was startled by a life-size poster of a near-nude posed on her haunches, slim and full-breasted. A perfect starlet body with the pert face of Tom's actress - - Reva Three! I looked again. Still Reva Three. The lush skin on the photo was probably enhanced. It did not arouse me, but I was affected, maybe because it was of one I knew.

Back at the Simonyi building Riedel was in his office. I was bursting to tell him, but his face was already woeful. "My wife's coming for the holidays."

"She didn't show up last year?"

"Not here!" He almost shouted it. "I met Lily in Germany."

"She's able to get around?"

"With a little help. She doesn't dwell on her paralysis. I can't let her poach here."

"Didn't you tell me you had an understanding?"

"Yes, with her, but not with Reva."

"Reva's expecting to marry you?" I didn't intend a tone of approbation.

"I suppose. Milany did. Lily wanted to see Debrecen last year too. Wasn't easy to keep her away. She's got a will of steel."

He had promised Reva Milany that he would divorce Lily.

"Impossible," he told me. Lily needed him, and he felt very close to her. Love enough for Tom, but he has also a sexual being. And rolling around as he did, he required the medical benefits her university professorship provided the spouse.

Leaving, I mentioned almost as an afterthought that a near-nude of his actress friend was on display in the centrum. "Can't be!" Dropping his troubles, Tom rushed out. From my window, I saw him catch a tram just before its doors closed.

I did a batch of papers till he returned.

"Not her. I knew it wasn't."

"Ok."

"Reva's an actress, not a shill."

"Why does it matter?"

His face colored a touch. He was quiet a moment, then casually said, "Just ran into Judit. She told me Dr. Milany died."

"Reva's father?" I never met the man, but it was upsetting.

"She's gone to her sister's in Budapest." Riedel ruminated at his desk, looking out the window.

I broke the silence, "Know him?"

"Two years ago I helped him plant his spring garden. A very practical man, not at all into popular beliefs." Tom let out a weak bubble of laughter. "Churches and prayers were testimony to mankind's insanity and cowardice. He bent my ear on that. Guess no one else would listen."

"Know when they'll bury him?"

Wednesday, December 2

I stopped by Reva's apartment yesterday. Her neighbor managed to let me know in poor English that she was still in mourning at her sister's in Budapest. She'd be back for the funeral on Friday.

326

As I was plundering the TV tonight for something in English other than black 'rap,' Professor Miklós Katrona rang and within the hour appeared at my door. He pushed a thin folder into my arms, "Isaac Ferenc helped translate." In a moment I realized he was talking about our famed linguist. "My friend many years."

"Don't know him too well," I said, recalling a tennis match in which Muffy and Carole, the Peace Corps ladies, joined in for mixed doubles. Isaac and Carole trounced Muffy and me three sets in a row. Later I learned he had been a professional player.

"Tea?" I asked. He wondered if I might have brandy about. As I fetched a half-empty bottle from my inherited stock and poured, he began reciting from his manuscript. His high-pitched voice contributed to my irritation with the TV and a senseless guilt because I could not reach Reva to share her sadness. I was in no mood for Professor Katrona's history or biography, whatever it was.

Copiously, Professor Katrona discoursed on Hungary's mangling after the war, "the fragment's slow resuscitation." Fields were freshly tilled and harvested. Rhythms of peasant life penetrated the whole nation, drawing strength from its soil. One by one factories were rebuilt. "By 1927, Horthy institutes compulsory insurance for widows and orphans; by 1936 he provided old age insurance for estate manager, pension for agriculture worker. By 1940, Green Cross, public health service, covers the whole country."

While he paused, I jumped in, "Too much work tonight. I'll read it later, if it's not all statistics." He cast an apprehensive eye, then quietly finished his brandy, said goodnight, and left.

33. The Deri.

Thursday, December 3

Balmy December day. Gates to the botanical garden were open, so I went in and walked the rows of dried plants, inviting a melancholy suitable to death. Nothing but phony sentiments came to mind. What was I doing there? I hurried out.

Unwilling to deny myself the breezy air, I meandered through the forest, skirting the medical village. I circled the tall cement cylinder that shoots above the trees like an ultra-modern church tower. It was the observatory. How utterly adequate was this university, complete, comfortable, pleasant, like Debrecen itself. The city even included museums, which I hadn't seen, not till that afternoon.

The Deri sits in the park-like area behind the Great Church near the old Calvinist College (that became Kossuth University.) A wide gravel path lined with benches between elfin and fawn-like statues leads to a broad stone stairway. It cuts through a sculpted fountain and flowerbed. Larger than life female and male statues grace each side.

Unlike outsized communist grotesques, they offer aesthetic introduction to the art within. The female sits, leaning on an arm, and contemplates a miniature man in her hand.

The collection, started by the college in the middle of the 18th Century, became a museum in 1902. After the World War, Frigyes Deri, a Hungarian who ran a silk factory in Vienna, gave his private collection to the city of Debrecen. The empire-style museum was constructed two years after his death in 1924.

Anticipating the usual - - pottery dug from the ages, bits of precious metal pounded into trinkets, portraits and farm implements - - I was fascinated by the vivid contrast. Relics of war going back to 850, when the city was walled in, juxtaposed with satirical drawings of the human comedy by a Marie Kopozu, who died in 1940. Egyptian tablets and tombs had made their way from the Nile to Debrecen. One mummy was opened. The face had hardened and aged into the brown linen binding.

A mural made of panels ran the top of the wall, flat figures, of course, of women with straight black tresses rowing barks with curled bows and sterns. Next, men at field work and at war, then flutists and harpists, all pancakes but the last. This one jolted me. A fleshed out, voluptuous and erotic female nude except for the legs. She leans into a man, her head upon his lap, eyes clearly anticipating. Her legs are wrapped in cloth, an indeterminate blanket or robe which was of no interest to the artist.

To the side another set of full figures, a woman, her fleshy back to the viewer, an erotically curved backside. Her arm is frozen in mid-dance, swinging in the air. A stern, disapproving face peeps from behind her body. A Calvinist harpy? But this is Egypt!

Then scenes from the Japanese countryside, a collection of enamels. Just what were they doing in a museum in a secondary city near the edge of the Hungarian plain? Some were large, vivid, exquisite and delicate, as expected from Japanese of any period. These were followed by a gallery devoted to medieval warfare - - armor, harness, shields, weapons - - but again a surprise, not the usual lances and swords, rather the warring gear of Samari warriors, complete with their flappy helmets.

It seemed there was no escape from Japan in the Deri Museum. I was standing in a chamber of Japanese artifacts, getting weary, seeing less than I observed amid the cooking pots, dishes, furnishings, fabrics, hoes, harvesting implements, wine presses . . . variations of the human's universal creations.

After a near miss with a two-foot metal stork perched uncannily in the middle of the aisle, I trudged to the second floor. Hungary at last! The Old Gallery - - paintings of national romanticism, cultural resistance to Austrian suppression that followed the 1848-9 War of Independence. The gallery was also a tribute to lost glory - - the Arpàd dynasty, Hunyadi's conquest of the Turks, the humanistic reign of King Matthais.

Another vigorous outburst of national romanticism was popular genre painting; the artist's discovery of the common people, not the true and crude peasant, but the idealized, poetic version of outlaw, gypsy and goat herder. These saccharine depictions ranged from Janos Janko's exotic "Scenes from the Life of the Gypsies,' to the excessively sentimental, "grieving Shepherd," an early painting by Mihaly Munkacsy who later enhanced the reputation of Hungarian art during several decades in Paris where urbanity gradually overcame his plebian themes. Wandering through these sentiments, my attention was taken by a country girl with a bursting bodice, glowing with rosy freshness. It was the freshness itself which attracted me, that seemed so alive, so breathtaking, among the common people.

The country girl was actually exhibited in the New Hungarian Gallery, which I had entered unawares. Here were the great plain painters of the early Twentieth Century, the puszta, the Alfold, open air contrast to studio art, as well as representations from the mountain-encircled Nagybanya Colony, which aimed at forms and colors invigorated by the ever-changing light effects of the sun. Native romantics were behind me, impressionists and realists astride.

"Peasant Girl" shows a demure young maid expectantly waiting inside a peasant dwelling. She is dressed in her Sunday best. Her homely ambience suggests she waits in vain. She is one of sixty in a series, "Life of People in Poverty," by Adolph Fenyes, marked "critical realism."

Nearly all the Great Plains painters were well traveled. As a group they aimed to present Europe a Twentieth Century portrait of Hungary's Alfold. Acquainted with the works and traditions of Europe's great artists, these sophisticates came back to the plains because "the fog is thickest here." As one of them, Viko Tornyai, said, "It is here that the fog has to be broken and blown away." Tornyai's puszta landscapes show the fight against the wind, sand, and storm with such expressiveness that I could feel the plainsmen futilely wrestling their fates. The atmosphere is empty.

I learned of a separate museum that Debrecen had devoted to one Great Plains painter, Laszlo Hollo, but was too burned out to pursue it. He dedicated his work, I was told, to the drama of the poor between the world wars.

34. Dr. Milany's Funeral

Friday, December 4.

Dr. Milany was buried today in the Debrecen cemetery. Reva insisted that Vamospercs was too remote, even for her mother. Burial in the village would be like stowing her father in another country.

Reva and her sister stood in traditional black with their mother among aunts, cousins, and a scattering of neighbors and her father's colleagues from both Debrecen and Vamospercs. The sun hung small in a cloudy sky; the day was chill and dull.

Tom was silent. We stood on the other side of the pit, opened into the pebbly and weedy ground. No other faculty showed up. (Judit was at a conference in Budapest.) With soulful eyes, Tom gazed at Reva across the divide. She bobbed her head in our direction once, then turned away, having recognized us but not inviting our approach.

Behind, we heard the grinding of carriage wheels on the paved road. In one continuous motion, four men wearing blue frocks hoisted the box from the carriage, hauled it to the pit, and lowered it in. Nothing

333

was said. Reva followed her mother and sister in throwing handfuls of dirt on the lid, and then the men in frocks started shoveling.

Tom's feet shifted impatiently. His eyes sought Reva's, which were obscured by a shawl. Still no one stepped forward to offer a word. His throat moved and finally he emitted in a high-pitched squeal, less than a shout, "Is nothing to be said?" The digger stopped and looked up. The mourners cast wounded stares, as if Tom had violated the sacred moment. Reva may have been the only one to understand his language. Perhaps he was addressing her.

"A life," he began, unsteady, stepping to the pit's edge, "All civilizations honor a human life as it passes." His voice was a touch admonishing, his face strained. "Dr. Milany's life was unique . . .as any. And I knew him only a little." Obviously seeking proper words, Tom examined his audience for clues that he was connecting, but all heads were bowed as in prayer.

"This day," he went on, looking to heaven as a preacher might, "is not especially dark or sad, though a man departs. It is indifferent. Dr. Milany would want that said, if anything. But we are not indifferent. We know the sun that set last night and rose this morning. We know it will not repeat for him. And we know that one day it will fail each of us; the sun will not cycle again, rising and setting, the rhythm of the universe will again be indifferent. And others will stand here, mourning our loss." He looked about. A slight breeze moved a few lingering leaves. But not a human limb moved. If he was not communicating, perhaps he was communing. He sighed. "This is the lot of life."

I knew Tom wrote poetry; it was his spontaneity that amazed me. When his words were no longer forthcoming, the mourners lifted their heads and a murmuring was heard, a response. I also, "Amen."

The frocked men resumed shoveling dirt on the coffin. People began leaving when it was covered.

Tom followed sheepishly as I approached Reva, took her hand in both mine and tried to say how sorry I was with some trifling words that came out on the instant and instantly evaporated. We had never kissed, so I was more than ordinarily awkward.

Before Tom could express sympathy, she was introducing me to her mother and sister, who was an even prettier version of Reva. Mrs. Milany, a slim, small woman whose narrow face was pursed in grief, recognized Tom and hugged him. Reva muttered, "Mother appreciates your 'sermon,'" took a step to the side, and engaged in conversation.

On the way to the tavern, I said, "How cold."

"Reva?"

"The funeral! No ritual. No priest. Not a word of eulogy. No goodbye, except yours.

"Surely the way he would want it. Couldn't just let him go. Even barbarians did more."

"Your sincerity, Tom. Let me say it just once, it was true."

"Dr. Milany might have been a Buddhist if he had any use for religion. When we gardened together in Vamospercs, we talked. As a future son-in-law I should know what he thought of the spiritual impulse in the human race. He was sympathetic, but it was a blight, a disease of the genes. Not a scientific statement, but the conclusion of a 'barnyard philosopher,' as he called himself. 'History is genes and genes are history. Layers and layers of grandeur, fertilized with human blood.'"

"Genes explain it all?"

Tom caught my skeptical tone and shook his head. "Not all. Dr. Milany was a quiet man who understood man's limits. We talked about the enormous nothingness of space, the great absence."

"A dour soul?"

"No, contented, as any man I ever knew, with his family, his practice, his garden, and courage enough to resist the nonsense."

"But it's comforting, even beautiful at times."

"What?"

"The nonsense."

35. Parties

Thursday, December 10

Sprigs of evergreen and a few scrawny trees were appearing in the centrum, but no tall broad-branched pines or spruces. Not yet, perhaps as the season advances. The faculty is in a frenzy to finish the term, papers, tests, and parties.

Ansca remembered her off-handed invitation to dinner extended at Goeff Gibson's housewarming in September. She had mentioned it several times, but if it weighed as an obligation with her, Alistair appeared oblivious. He made no reference. For most of the term Ansca had been our office administrator, dividing functions with Erika, the secretary, but clearly in charge. Alistair spent more of his time in the institute offices.

I found their apartment among the high rises on the far side of Egyetem, a Stalin block area unappealing to my curiosity.

Alistair was a veteran of teacher training colleges in the pay of the British Council. He taught in Turkey, Germany, Austria, Australia, and had more courses at CETT than Kossuth. Literary study held no interest for him. His shelves were lined with linguistic, logic and grammar texts. He is thin, short, sallow, and obsequious.

Ansca is about half a head taller and stout. Her pudgy face is lightly complected, glowing with good humor and a touch of rouge.

Alistair took the wine from my hands and began opening it. "None for me. I shouldn't drink."

"Me neither."

"For me!" Ansca called from the kitchen. She entered the living room as I was about to sit on a flowery sofa and hugged me as though we'd been close. Alistair put on a jazz tape. "You are bad," she said coyly, her slight accent adding to the comedy of an overweight courtesan slightly offended.

"I am?"

"Why you leave before you finish?" You don't like us?"

"I've left a very generous wife and child behind," I explained one more time. "A handicapped child from a previous marriage. Can't take any more advantage. They were supposed to come for Christmas."

"Not Christmas yet," said Ansca, enthusiasm bouncing out of her.

"If Roberta changed her mind and would come, I'd stay."

"Want me to call her?"

I smiled, "Thanks."

Just before we sat down to dinner, Alistair warned me, "We are vegetarians."

The kitchen was large and more barren than the living room. An oil cloth covered a simple wood table. There were six plain chairs plus a stove and a half-sized refrigerator. Few trinkets, nothing on the walls.

Bread was sliced from one of those immense Hungarian loaves that fascinated me at the bakery. Slices were placed on the table with a large bowl of steaming red cabbage. Passing the cabbage, Ansca also passed the news that she and Alistair would be married next year, as soon as she returned from America. This was intended as a casual utterance.

"Ansca is going to study American education," Alistair added proudly, "and school administration. On a Fulbright."

"Great, Ansca! I didn't know they made such awards."

Immediately I regretted the remark, it could be taken as condescending, but apparently it flew by harmlessly. "And congratulations on the marriage. Hope I'll be back for it."

I dug into the cabbage, anticipating the surprise of the main course to follow, but there was nothing more. Coffee was served in the living room where Alistair talked about his education which began with the clay workers' children in Stoke-on-Trent. He was no public school boy. I tried to imagine the razzings and cruelties this stump of a boy must have endured from those young toughs. "From the start right through my Masters at Birmingham my education was dominated by social justice. As soon as I knew what it was, I found concern for it in every course I was reading."

Of course. Born poor and short in a menacing, tall world, he took to the socialist way. But he had company among his fellow instructors. Delicately, I phrased a question, "Does your sense of social justice extend to political activity?"

His face burst open with a smile, "So American!"

"Cowboy!" cried Ansca. Then, mischief aside, she wanted me to know that her man may be socialist but loathed communists, as she did. "Hungary suffered much until Gorbechev."

I took the occasion to show off my red-faced Perestroika-Glasnost watch. They had seen many. "It works?" she asked. I nodded. "Not for long." She was prophetic. It failed before I could get it back for show in America.

"Our communists were more like Czarists than socialists," offered Alistair. "But they were constitutional, more or less."

"Every country has a constitution," Ansca put in, then cleverly defined Hungary's under the communists, "Absolutism moderated by assassination."

His head wagged in a gentle, loving reproof. "Russian, Ansca, not Hungarian. That's a bit out of line."

I sensed emotion in Ansca's breast, probably brewed there for years for her own Hungarian experiences. Obviously she wanted to argue but took his gestures as a request to relent, and did so. I had argued with Matt and Goeff that Hungarian women made no better mates than any other. But here I could see their point.

Walking home, I felt hungry. If that cabbage represented their usual meal, plump Ansca had to be cheating.

Friday, December 11

The final session of the American Reformation seminar was held in my honor at the University Club, one of the declining mansions on Simonyi set aside for faculty and student recreation. A student jazz combo would begin playing about eight, when a fee was charged. Several nights I had passed the racket they called jazz and was glad we were meeting in the afternoon. The Poetry Club was holding a dinner for me that night at a restaurant in the centrum.

It was an occasion, and my seven students dressed for it; skirts replaced jeans and the men wore ties. "What are your impressions of Hungary?" asked a young lady who seldom volunteered responses during the term. Apparently she was set to reverse herself and our subject - - boldness instead of reticence and my personal opinions of Hungary instead of my professional observations of American reforms. "It's a huge question," I said, "Where do I begin? Hungarian reforms?" This drew subdued laughter.

She was serious. "I mean what memories are you taking back."

"Levas, gulyas, paprika, and your incredible keener." The laugher was more spirited.

Our city counselor spoke up, "As we've used the term in class, the Hungarians have been reforming since we were Magyar tribes, but the only movement we call reform is the Calvinist's. Plenty of change, though. Peasant revolts. But the old gentry is still in control."

"We're tired of them," said a young lady with badly dyed red hair who seldom attended class. Her final paper, however, was alert and precise; I suspected plagiarism.

"That won't make them go away," said a tall young man with a thin beard. He gave a quick survey of landholders great and small who maintained their fiefdoms in spite of the democratic pretenses under Horthy. He suspected Horthy was in with Hitler. The landholders persisted even under the communists and they still dominate. He cited names, events, and legalities. Again I was impressed with their

340

knowledge of Hungarian history, however they skewed it. He finished with an intended shocker, "More tiresome are American assumptions."

I took the bait. "What assumptions?"

"Assumptions and expectations. America assumes the world is eager for their brand of democracy - - "

"Out of order!" the city counselor called. "We're asking for the Professor's impressions of our country."

"If I offended you," said the tall one, "I didn't mean to. I was carried away. I'm sorry."

"His hot Magyar blood," apologized the red-haired one. (I avoid their names because I have such a hard time pronouncing them.)

Switching to a cooler subject I asked, "Did any of you attend the H.L. Menken performance at CETT?" I had noticed only two from my literature class.

They glanced at each other. "Didn't hear about it," said the counselor. "We seldom get word of such things. Wasn't Menken an aristocrat?"

Bringing up Menken was a mistake. "Only intellectually." Was he setting me up as a hypocrite?

"German, wasn't he?"

The dyed redhead must have sympathized with my situation. Facetiously, she said, "Couldn't have been much of a lover,' relieving the tension and causing laughter again.

I glanced at my Perestroika-Glasnost timepiece and displayed it. Polite shrugs. It was near six. "I have to go. Poetry Club is giving me a free dinner."

Before I could get away, someone wanted to know had I ever heard of Endre Ady. "You can't read him because the poetry does not translate well. He is like your Whitman."

Somewhere I'd read that Ady's favorite word was "somber." Hardly the effervescent Whitman, but it was too late to begin another discussion.

Friday night, December 11

One long table accommodated all nine of us. Steve and Reka joined after we had finished our pork cutlets and pastry. They could only stay a minute. Before leaving, Reka asked me to meet them tomorrow to see her father's paintings in the Great Church, third floor.

Judit Molnar said a word of appreciation and then Istvan Ratz presented a package wrapped in wrinkled tissue paper. As I unwrapped, he proclaimed proudly, "Volume twenty-one of our "Hungarian Studies in English."" It was the commemorative issue of the American Studies Symposium held in Debrecen in April of 1987. I grinned at the year 1990 printed on the cover. Judit noticed, "You're aware that the institute never rushes."

There followed a moment's critique of Andros Kiros as head, through Imrè Bali was running things between 1987 and 1990. It was agreed that events moved no swifter then, but they were more momentous, for example, the Symposium, "Artist in America."

Imrè-Bali had arranged it with the United States Information Agency (which provided an exhibit of American photography) and the prestigious Eotvos University of Budapest as sponsors. It was keynoted by the U.S. Ambassador to Hungary who also hosted a reception. Irving Howe of City University of New York presented two papers, followed by Woody Allen's "The Purple Rose of Cairo."

The publication included lectures from Reva's Modern Philology Society as well as local contributions; Steve Ruark (James Joyce) Judit (Canadian poets, of course) and Istvan (the Malcolm Bradbury interview). Istvan gladdened my heart by pointing out a page devoted to a description of the Lajos Kossuth Poetry Club. Also pleasing - - the name, Camille Paglia, did not appear, nor was it heard that night.

Saturday, December 12

A fee was demanded at the door, not for the exhibition on the third floor. The caretaker knew nothing about that. The fee was just to enter the church. Inside all was white, except the deeply varnished pews. I trudged up the broad stairway encumbered with throwaways till it ended in an all-purpose chamber on the third floor. "Oh good!" exclaimed Reka, rushing to greet me. "I wondered if you'd come." Her father's paintings were hung without identifying tags along white walls, apparently a one-man show in a make-shift gallery.

For half an hour, Steve and Reka lectured me on the political significance of the paintings, which amounted in most cases to arrested individuality caused by the loss of Hungary's gentry, the ruling class. Some were childish, like cartoons smothered in somber colors. In most, lines or human figures were reaching for some fragment or speck of light. The figures were indications, none fully developed, like the prisoners' paintings I encountered when I taught a writing course at Oklahoma's state penitentiary.

Reka decided I had to bring home authentic Hungarian music. So we spent an hour in a shop of recordings, tapes and CDs. I came away with a CD album of Bartok, whose modernity, Steve thought, echoed realities of the ancient Magyars.

Pretentious, I thought, and let slip my contrary opinion. "For me, music has no literal content. Its pure art."

He was not offended, in fact, not aware that I had derided him. Undaunted, he insisted I buy a tape to remind me of Debrecen and the Alfold, where "the flavor of the nomads can still be tasted." We tried one, but it did not live up to the cover copy, "winds that sweep up from the sands, darken the city, and stifle the air." I settled for the bizarre lament of a ram's horn and the snappy rhythm of a plains dance in "Hej, Rakoczi."

Saturday night, December 12

The only other Hungarians at Matt and Kauty's dinner party were Englishmen's native women, Ansca and Elene who was Goeff Gibson's statuesque spouse. I was the lone American, a compliment I suppose, but I felt an outsider.

Their apartment lay out along Nagyerdei Korut, where I thought the forest ended. It was furnished with a new sofa and chair in matching blue, a bright run, hi-fi, and a comfortable bedroom suite. The rest was scrounged, lamps, end tables, folding chairs. A long door was set on carpentry horses as a dining table. The party was Matt's farewell before Christmas in England. Kauty had to stay behind because of exams, but she did have a job in Sussex for the summer. "Cleaning public toilets," she announced with emphatic pride. She would bicycle with Matt. But just now he was taking the train.

An embroidered band about Elene's shiny brown hair gave the impression of a tiara. Helping serve, she radiated charm between the kitchen and dining table while her husband engaged in gossip about absent colleagues at CETT and the institute. Left out of this banter, I entertained myself with appraisals of the three Hungarian women. Two of them I had placed: Kauty was a healthy peasant from a household with fruit upon the table, and Ansca was an ambitious bourgeois climber, effectively pushing her little man before her. But Elene? Her mannerisms spoke of the gentler class, nurtured on the aesthetic and the noble and inured to the tribulations of unassisted motherhood.

After roast pork and potatoes, Dr. Leslie Burton rose to toast an impending marriage. It would occur in Eger next summer, he announced, which surprised most of us. Les added that he'd accepted the honor of serving as Matt's best man. His tone was a touch combative - - the wine in him.

He was a bantam rooster, solidly constructed with kinky red hair and thin beard. Having taught the previous year in Warsaw, Les went on to inform us of his own impending event, that is, if his "Polish princess" would yield. It was not clear whether he was actually engaged or just contemplating. Seated next to Gwen Jones, he toyed with her bodice, though little was within. He flattered as much as he annoyed her. Sitting on the other side, Goeff Gibson was uncomfortable but feigned amusement.

Les drank more wine and rose for another toast, to "Poland," then challenged the table to name a Primate of Hungary who was a Pole.

"Who?" asked Gwen, momentarily relieved.

The thinly bearded chin lifted in a pretense of intellectual scorn, "You have taught in Hungary over a year and don't know? Tom Bakocz, whose parents were Polish serfs. In the 15th Century he became bishop of Gyhor and Eger, and finally archbishop of Estyergom, Hungary's Primate."

"Pff," went Gwen, "So?"

"So history. He had also been secretary to King Mattais."

"History! I take mine with sensation."

"Very well. Do you know why Matthais' wife poisoned him?"

"The great one had a wife?"

Les charged through her sarcasm, "Because his Polish mistress, not his Viennese commoner as people supposed, bore him a bastard, John Corvina, who was groomed for the throne." His speech was slurring and Les noticed, "Anyone offended?"

"Not at all," answered Kauty smartly, passing another bottle about. "But you are offensive." I felt the good nature in her remark and joined the laughter. Kauty was just exercising grammatical variation in the language she was acquiring. Elena dashed off a Hungarian phrase.

"Unfair," Goeff called to his wife.

She corrected him, "You mean impolite," and repeated in English, "Les needs to shine more than he needs to enlighten us." Before he could respond, she added, "If more attention were paid to the driver of a bus, Les would be a bus driver."

"Maybe Matthais was a Pole?" Goeff chided.

"He was the son of Hunyadi who gave Hungary its last victory when he chased the Turks out of Belgrade.

"Pole?" Goeff persisted.

"Hunyadi's father was a Vlatch."

"So much for ethnic purity," I put in.

Lester belched and turned his attention to Elene. "Think you're Magyar?" The words were slightly garbled. "You're a Greek goddess." She wore jeans as well as the tiara-like hair band. "A goddess," he repeated more distinctly, "whose beauty demands you spend earth time in serene enjoyment and pleasure." Obviously her sophisticated loveliness challenged him and tempered his belligerence. "You share none of your husband's Teutonic traits."

"I have Teutonic traits?" asked Goeff

"Like the rest of us Britons. We are practical, energetic, we conquer obstacles. But the Greeks contemplate them. Our enjoyment of beauty is somber, reserved, in the dark; Greek beauty glistens in the sun, outside the skin."

To keep him on track, I asked, "And the Hungarians?"

He thought before he answered, "More Teutonic than Greek."

The table had broken up and I glimpsed Gwen in the living room dancing hip-hop with a bewildered Alistair. But I stayed. His brusque certainty was amusing. "Are Americans also Teutonic? We're considered more practical than most."

"You need more than that to be Teutonic. But Americans aren't Greek either. Still children, selfish, me-mes." I'm sure he meant to be seen as an intellectual tough, but his frankness emerged as rudeness. "Everything American is ephemeral, hardly any human continuity. You reverence the past, we all do, but your acts show no harmony with it." I recalled Reva's questioning Toni Morrison's "Beloved," Everything is now. It is all now." Self inspired, Les ranted on, "Instant pleasure, TV talk, nobody's fault, mistakes happen, shit happens, Nixon's no crook."

"A civilization that ignores history is doomed," I agreed and added, "So is one that doesn't."

He smiled in appreciation and went right on deriding my country, arousing a patriotic remnant I never knew existed. "No coherence, no mutual purpose, not a modicum of social rhythm."

"Nonsense!" It wasn't as loud as I imagined. Nothing stopped in the next room. "How do you suppose we win wars?"

"Oh indeed, yes, exemplary teamwork." He emitted a single laugh, a roar. "For violent sports and bloodshed!"

I turned away. Gwen had mastered the hip-hop. She was bouncing solo to the tape recording, "Rhythm, rhythm, . . . rhythm is a dancer."

With malicious enjoyment, Les asked, "Where's Reva," implying we were a pair. "Still in mourning?" I answered with a contemptuous smile and went to join Gwen in her awkward dance.

36. Hungary's Restitution

Monday, December 14

Getting my mail at the institute, I bumped into Isaac Ferenc. "How do you like Katrona's manuscript?" His owlish face had big baggy eyes, almost all cheek. Grayish hair framed his shiny pate.

Having progressed little in the manuscript, I answered sheepishly, "I can see right off you're not amateurs." Ferenc, I suspected, was responsible for the actual words on the page. "The writing is supple," I added.

"I hear you're leaving soon."

"I'm going to Budapest on the twentieth and America on the twenty-third.

"You will take it along?"

"I'll have it for Professor Katrona in a day or two, what I can read of it." I meant in the allotted time but he might have been offended.

"Only the translation is mine," he chuckled, not the history."

"More history than biography?"

347

"What is not history?"

Perfunctorily, he invited me for a brandy but understood I was eager to get into Katrona's manuscript.

<u>Horthy</u> <u>and</u> <u>the</u> <u>Jews</u> started unwisely, with statistics that would have tranquilized me had they been handled less adroitly. I've noted the most pertinent passages with few comments and quote the most striking:

"The Horthy regime suffered the painful result of Hungary's dismemberment at Trianon: the loss of 88 percent of her forests through heavy cuttings that abetted the spring floods and summer droughts and 83 percent of her iron ore. Then she was forced to pay reparations with Austria and Germany. Horthy ordered the Hungarian flag lowered on June 4, 1920; it was not hoisted again until 1938 with Hitler's encouragement."

Reading, I realized Hungary had become paranoid. Consciously or unconsciously, the yearning to retrieve lost territories drove all external relations, motivated all Horthy's international acts and decisions.

By the thirties they were on the road to a respected place among nations. A profusion of Hungarian plays, books and films were produced at home and abroad (I dimly recall the Hungarian prominence in Hollywood in the thirties, actresses, script writers, film producers, Lajos Biro's "Hotel Imperial" starring Pola Negri, Menyhert Lengyel's "Typhoon.") Hungarian writers, editors, composers and performers were toasts of the international art scene. The Budapest Opera and state theatre were acclaimed through the civilized world. Two Hungarian scientists received Nobel prizes; the nation's athletes took third place in the Berlin Olympics of 1936.

Horthy responded to Hitler's overbearing nationalism with a diffident pose: "'I've always held that no Hungarian should be prevented from expressing patriotism by giving his name in the Magyar form, but I oppose compulsion.'"

In 1935, Horthy's German-leaning prime-minister succumbed to his chronic kidney disease and Hitler sent Goring to the funeral in Budapest. ""I was impressed,'" Horthy exclaimed, "'since Germans were too self-centered to notice that Hungarians had borne the burden of their defeat in the war.'" German's propaganda minister was offended when Budapest newspapers doubted his story that communists set the

Reichstag fire and deplored the consequent bloodbath ordered by President Von Hindenburg.

Yet Hitler sent a warm telegram commemorating the fifteenth year of Horthy's entry into Budapest as regent. So he accepted an Austrian invitation to a chamois hunt, knowing Herr Hitler would be present. They talked later at Berchtesgaden. "Hitler shared our sorrows; Versailles had be as unjust to Germany as Trianon to Hungary. 'We were fellow victims of injustice.' Grateful that he acknowledged our dismemberment, Horthy was still tempted to say, 'You at least retained your country.' Instead a smile froze his face and he praised his gracious host. Hitler was an uneducated but wily man who had amassed considerable knowledge. He asked too many questions.

"How would your Highness set Germany's course?'

"'That question shocks me, Your Excellency . . . and honors me. But I can answer. I should try to achieve a close relationship with England. That is possible as long as Germany does not enter into naval competition. If you were to conclude a defensive alliance, Germany would have no need of a fleet.' Horthy added, 'England is the one power able to maintain order in the world.'"

Hitler shot back, "'Why should Germany not be in position to do the same?'"

They parted on friendly terms, Horthy thinking Hitler a judicious and gentle man. "'I was not the only one fooled.'"

Quite another mood dominated his meeting with Mussolini. They boarded an Italian battleship and he was overwhelmed by nostalgia and sentiment, "'carried back to our misfortune of 1918.'" Obeying Emperor Charles, he had surrendered the fleet of the Austria-Hungary Empire to Yugoslav representatives. "'Our glorious undefeated ensign was struck forever. I decided then to leave the sea. Now, eighteen years later, I once again beheld it, breathed the sea air, felt a deck beneath my feet . . . '"

Tuesday night, December 15

I trudged through thick snow, reaching the ABC just before it closed, and turned back with day-old black bread, pickled herring, and salami. The deserted street was bright; snow fell thicker before I reached the apartment. What a night for reading! I removed my damp shoes and socks, put on slippers, and in vain tried to sustain the image of a toasty fireplace.

The manuscript was poorly titled. Where were the Jews? But I had only made a dent. To finish, I'd have to skim more selectively, like a salacious voyeur at a magazine rack.

In August 1938, Horthy toasted with Hitler the launching of a heavy cruiser, but actually he participated because Germany was promising the return of Slovakia to Northern Hungary. Asked to select music for the occasion, Horthy chose a favorite, Wagner's "Lohengrin," then worried that German delicacy might be offended when the bass sang, "O Lord, protect us from the wrath of the Magyars." But the regent also basked in the reminder of Hungary's past glory.

"In a tête-à-tête, Hitler disclosed his Plan Green for Czechoslovakia. He had changed since Horthy last saw him, hair thinner, face strained, imperious movements befitting the brash master of Europe." Plan Green was simply to smash the Czechs. Hitler wanted Hungary to march into Slovakia as he entered from the west. "It was the price the Czechs would pay for falsifying maps and inventing data to steal Slovakia from us. We were to keep the piece of homeland we invaded." Horthy "assured him we preferred pressing our claim to Slovakia by more peaceful means."

I doubted it. Horthy could have said that in retrospect, having lost again in World War II. But Professor Katrona believed his regent. On the other hand, he might have made it up out of benign fidelity. He quoted Hitler's slippery reply, "'If you want to join in the meal, you must help with the cooking.'"

Festivities followed. Hitler joked about breeding of animals and delighted in ancient costumes. The Air Marshal changed costumes several times and invited Horthy to his hunting grounds, boasting, "'where all you can see belongs to me.'" Later, visiting the new party stadium in Nuremberg, Hitler told him, "'Only one person speaks here.'"

"'What? So vast and costly a rostrum for a single performer?'"

Hitler glanced at him contemptuously, "'You fail to appreciate the führer's greatness?'" The world of the Third Reich was uncomfortable. Horthy resolved that Hungary should take no part in it. "But later we were said to play the jackal. Churchill accused us of helping cook the meal in order to share it."

November 2, 1938 was a great day for Hungarians. Much of Slovakia was returned by the Axis powers. Horthy issued a proclamation: Slovaks were once more free Hungarians. "'Your days of sorrow and tribulation are past. Again, the light of glory shines upon you from the Holy Crown of St. Stephen.'"

But skies were overcast. In the plan of Lebenstraum, Hitler poorly concealed his appetite for Hungary. The regent and his votaries were committing heinous crimes by failing to accept his racial theories, continuing a friendship with Poland, even looking amiably upon England and America.

Horthy tried to ignore the "Jewish Question." The comfortable life Jews enjoyed in Hungary was a thorn in Hitler's flesh. But his obsession did appeal to many Hungarian bourgeoisies, who claimed Bela Kun had filled government with his fellow Jews. That was the reason they still earned more than twenty-five percent of the national income. In 1938, the bourgeoisie elected Bela Imredy, an advocate of Germany and virulent anti-Semite, as prime minister. Secretly, Horthy prayed for an opportunity to dismiss him.

An old friend ironically fulfilled that prayer. Count Bethlen had been informed that a Budapest newspaper was about to publish proof that Imredy's great grandfather was a Jew. "'Upset to the point of collapse, the premier asked that I accept his resignation.'"

"Count Paul Teleki, our new prime minister, informed Berlin that despite our agreement with Axis policies we could not permit German troops to march through Hungary to attack our friend, Poland, as requested. He ordered bridges blown up if German troops tramped on us. But the blitzkrieg was so swift, our land was unnecessary. We offered relief to the shocked Polish refugees."

Wednesday, December 16

I walked in the freezing cold to the bakery for my breakfast rolls. Then, out of real coffee, I washed them down with "instant." Paging through the manuscript, my eye was caught by Transylvania. It is home to two million Hungarians, Professor Katrona wrote, "hearth of the sacred flame of our nation."

The super-nationalist Arrow Cross was demanding military strikes against Romania to force the return of sacred Transylvania. Prime Minister Teleki resisted, fearing Soviet reaction. Germany, meanwhile, was "sending her troops across our land (by night in sealed wagons) to prepare for war against the Soviets." Horthy now permitted this indignity, anticipating the reward of a restored Transylvania. Then Hitler ordered both Hungary and Romania to settle the annoying little problem by negotiation, as civilized nations should.

"We sat together with the Germans mediating in Vienna and alas! most of our lost land in the north of Transylvania was restored, including the treasured Magyar towns of Koloszvar (Cluj Napoca) and Marosvasarhely (Tirgu Mures), some 51,000 kilometers square with all the people."

37. At War Once More

Thursday, December 17

Reva was back from Budapest. I promised to stop by as soon as I finished Professor Katrona's manuscript. She would be my incentive, I said. But the manuscript was by no means a bore, I was just impatient, having so much to do ending the term before I flew off. Then Tom called. Tomorrow he was heading for Paris, to establish his ground before Lily left Indiana. I had to spend lunch, say goodbye. "If I'm already in Paris," he gloated, "why would Lily come to Debrecen?" He could have figured that from the start, but I said nothing. It was late afternoon before I returned to Professor Katrona.

When Mussolini attacked Greece in December 1940, the regent saw his aim was next Yugoslavia then Hungary. Quickly he concluded a treaty with the Yugoslavs, in self-defense. Like Hungary, the Yugoslavs had been forced to sign the Three Powers Pact (Germany, Italy, Japan). "If we had hesitated Romania would be given our place and the transfer of Northern Transylvania endangered. The Pact also allowed us to retain

353

the chunk of Slovakia that had been returned, and could help us regain other lost territories." If he resisted, Horthy envisioned a hopeless, suicidal struggle. Who would help? The regent was shaken to see Great Britain fail in her guarantees to Poland. And the führer was claiming that Hungary already owed a bill for the Slovakian award.

Signing the Pact was the starting point of the Yugoslav's irreparable tragedy soon to unfold. "In no other sector of the front in World War II was the fighting more primitive or savage. Fewer Yugoslav guns were aimed at the Germans than at each other. Serbs and Croats (Ustache) unleashed fratricidal hatred.

"This conflagration upset Hitler's scheme to invade the Soviets. Instead, he ordered his army to wipe out all military and national factions in Yugoslavia. We were asked to assist in the slaughter. Our reward would be the return of land lost at Trianon to the Kingdom of Serbs, Croats, and Slovenes. For this we had merely to help Germany attack a friend with whom we had just signed a mutual defense pact.

"If Hungary refused, Germany threatened immediate occupation. Earlier, the prime minister, Count Teleki, roguishly asked an endangered Italian foreign minister if he played bridge, 'Why?' "So we might have something to do when we are together in Dachau.'

"In March 1941, Teleki heard that his chief of staff secretly pledged Hungarian participation in the proposed attack. London had also heard and threatened a declaration of war. On April 2, Horthy's Crown Council unanimously passed such a resolution, an outright double cross. Count Teleki took his life. 'We have now allied ourselves with criminals,' read his suicide note.

"That night Germany's motorized columns crossed the Hungarian frontier on the way to Yugoslavia, whose government collapsed immediately. Four days later Southern Hungary was restored and an independent Croatia proclaimed.

"The re-annexation of Croatian Hungary added 25,000 to the Jewish population. Lazlo Bardossy, the new prime minister, acted quickly to please Hitler and solve the Jewish question. He surprised and baffled the regent. 'These Jews must not be allowed to assimilate,' Bardossy announced to Parliament; they immediately demanded Jewish emigration."

But emigration was no longer the German solution. Hitler's aim was now annihilation. "While the darkest terror raged in Romania, Bulgaria, Poland and the Baltic states, Hungarian Jews suffered only economically. Their property and lives were still unmolested. Only those unable to prove Hungarian nationality were deported. But all were considered foreign elements in the life of the country. The minister of education declared them Israelites, not entitled to rights enjoyed by true Hungarians.

"The first atrocities occurred in January 1942 when Hungarian soldiers combed the restored Ujidek area of Yugoslavia for Tito partisans. Two generals notorious for fascist sympathies rounded up 3309 unfortunates including 700 Jews, and executed them. The bodies were mutilated, then stuffed through holes in the ice on the Danube to cover all traces.

"Protests over the Ujvidek massacre had little bearing on Bardossy's downfall. The direct cause was his declaration of war on the Soviet Union in support of Hitler's invasion on June 27, 1941, without consent of Parliament. Hitler had threatened unless we join the German invasion, he would take back the parts of Transylvania returned via the Vienna Awards. Horthy responded that Hitler lacked provocation. It was promptly provided. Two planes with Soviet markings bombed the Hungarian towns of Kassa and Munkacs. Only after we declared war on the Soviets did we discover what Bardossy had known; the planes were German.

"After the war, Bardossy was tried as a war criminal, imprisoned in Austria, then turned over to the Hungarian communists. 'God preserve Hungary from the rabble,' Bardossy shouted as they shot him.

"Our new prime minister, Nickolas Kallay, embodied the traditions of our race even in appearance - - high forehead, bushy eyebrows, bold cheekbones, aquiline nose and firm chin of the legendary Magyar. Though shrewd and cunning, he shared Horthy's aim to regain Hungary's freedom and state of non-belligerence.

"War fatigue was growing. Third Reich totalitarianism was now as distasteful as the postures of Western Democracies, and we were apprehensive of Soviet might. With the Communists, Smallholders, and Social Democrats, Kallay advocated withdrawal, while former Premiers

Bardossy and Imredy joined the fascist Arrow Cross in demanding intensification of the war effort.

"As Kallay surreptitiously negotiated with the West, the führer issued instruction to rid Europe of the Jewish element without further delay. 'Confiscate all Jewish property,' he demanded, 'and deport them to the conquered territories in the East.' Kallay dragged his feet. He had just concluded a secret agreement allowing Western powers to fly over Hungary if they did not bomb our towns.

"In December, Kallay categorically informed the Wilhelmstrasse that the Hungarian government rejected their demands. In January, the Wilhelmstrasse observed, 'Unquestionably, relations have deteriorated. The solution to the Jewish problem can no longer be postponed.' Kallay responded by repatriating 400 Jewish families the Germans had forced to leave.

"So Horthy was surprised to see an exhaltant Hitler at their meeting in Klessheim. It was April 16, 1943. The führer spoke of good relations enjoyed by Germans living in Hungary. Then his face clouded. He was disappointed with our troops' poor showing in the winter offensive, in spite of 200,000 Hungarian casualties at Stalingrad. His veneer began disintegrating. He reddened, the voice turned strident. 'Operatives tell us what Premier Kallay leaked to the US Ambassador at Ankara,' and he shrieked, 'that Hungary would not place a single soldier, a single rifle, at Germany's disposal!' And why, he demanded, had the prime minister not harmed the Jews in any way in spite of his anti-Semitic speeches? "Kallay must be dismissed," Hitler shouted. Then attempting to control himself, the führer huffed, 'In Poland, we settled the Jewish problem very simply. We shot them. Do you see cruelty in this? Don't we shoot deer?'

"Even as they parted, Hitler could not let go of his obsession. Somehow Jews were causing German's battlefield misfortunes, which could be reversed if they were exterminated. Not a trace of cordiality remained."

38. Hungary's "Final Solution."

Thursday, December 17

The arrow on the zoo sign at the entrance to Nagyerdi forest pointed to the left. Determined to follow it before leaving Debrecen, I hiked till nothing but trees remained at that extent of the forest. Matt's apartment building was nearby but I wasn't sure where. Anyway, he was gone to his parent's home in Sussex.

The zoo held no surprises except a catatonic elephant who kept nodding up and down. Waggishly I wondered if he had been driven to that state by all he had seen of mankind. Lions, a tiger, reptiles, a respectable zoo. I stayed about an hour and walked back reflecting on clichéd comparisons between man and beast, spirit, soul, matter, Hitler and Horthy. I was eager to finish grading my term papers. Tomorrow night I attend a farewell at CETT. So this evening, I must finish reading those satanic intricacies that curl through our century's politics.

"In September an Italian mob seized and executed Mussolini, then displayed him hanging by his heels. Italy passed over to the allies.

Germany might have also if Roosevelt had not insisted on 'unconditional surrender.' Roosevelt's cockiness prolonged the war two years.

"As Hitler's war soured, so did his Hungarian relations. He sent a special enjoy, Dr. Edmund Vassenmayer, who became fast with Hungary's far right. Vassenmayer was much concerned with Horthy's secret feelers to the West. Events moved swiftly. Italy deposed King Victor Emmanuel, Yugoslavia recognized Tito over Mahailovic, and Hungary made the Nazi's secret list of proscribed nations. Then, irony. The US Secretary of State, Cordell Hull, warned that German defeat was imminent and unless Hungary took action we would share it. Conflicts of conscience: If Germany suffered defeat, communism would triumph, and given Roosevelt's love affair with Stalin, woe betides Hungary.

"The looming disaster fed Hitler's obsession. Now he advocated a 'final solution,' and focused on Hungary. Ribbentrop observed that while the Nazis had nearly annihilated the Jewry of Central Europe, 800,000 still lived in Hungary, 'a Central European Jewish island.'

"In March, 1944, Admiral Horthy again traveled to Kleissheim. It was to be his last interview. Hitler was stooped, wrinkling, and uncertain. Searching for words, he suddenly shrieked, 'The Italians betrayed us. I will not be caught a second time.' Horthy coolly responded that Magyars are not traitors; Hitler just stared, knowing of our secret negotiations. It was a hard, silent moment. Then icily he announced that German troops were on the march to Hungary, 'to occupy it. They will be withdrawn when Kallay is replaced with a loyal government.'

"Threatening to resign, Horthy accused him of base deception, of calling him out while sending in occupation forces. Hitler cautioned the regent that if he resigned, the Slovaks, Croats, and Romanians would be given a free hand in Hungary. But the regent had no thought of resigning; he knew Hitler would then install an Arrow Cross regime and execute 800,000 Jews.

"Horthy returned to Budapest and found Germans installed at the Astoria Hotel and their sentries guarding his palace gates. Up and down the main avenues, loudspeakers blared the voice of Ferenc Szalasi, Arrow Cross leader, accompanied by German and Hungarian marches and the rumble of Tiger tanks.

"Vassenmayer proposed that Imredy be restored as premier, but accepted the regent's counter-proposal of a lesser evil, our Berlin ambassador, General Dome Sztojay. Kallay escaped through underground passages dating from the time of the Ottomans.

"Finding that airborne Germans had descended on all airfields in Budapest and the provinces, Horthy summoned the Crown Council and acerbically declared, 'We are accused of the crime of not obeying Hitler and I am charged with not permitting the massacre of the Jews.' The minister of the interior acknowledged that he no longer had much to administer since the Germans had taken over the police, and the Gestapo at that moment was busy rounding up political dissenters and Jews.

"The Israelite community of Pest had disbanded quickly that morning after a tense discussion of the German invasion and a brief tribute to Lajos Kossuth. A few still lingered when three small yellow cars bearing the letters POL drew up before their community house. They demanded to see the leaders of the Jews and said they would return the next morning at 10. 'Carry out any orders received from the Germans,' their government told them.

"The next morning, believing they would be detained, some brought small suitcases. After waiting an hour in suspense, three officers appeared with armed guards and a civilian. The tallest officer, mean-looking and dyspeptic, announced himself as Obersturmbannfuhrer Krumey. He was head of the committee that would assume all rights over Jewish affairs, as agreed with the Hungarian government in Berlin. 'If the Jews obey, no harm will come.' Krumey noticed the suitcases and smiled cryptically. "Nobody is going to be arrested.'

"'He was so cordial,' one telephoned home, 'There is nothing wrong. Germans want to collaborate with us.' They were told to form a Juden Rat (Jewish Council), and list all their institutions and property.

"The Germans had been well rehearsed. They pretended to be benefactors and made themselves inconspicuous. While Krumey had polite commands, lesser ranks thundered with maximum insult. Herr Huntshe and Herr Naumann, for example, snarled at the caretaker rabbi, "Get up when we come into the room. You are nothing but a common Jew!" They converted the synagogue on Kazincsy Ut into a stable.

"Dr. Vassenmayer informed the regent that orders of the occupation authority would now be administered by the Sztojay government; the German foreign officer had excluded Horthy from further political activity. The new premier immediately attacked the residual problem by announcing, 'All Jews will now wear the yellow star of David.' He appointed notorious anti-Semites, Lazslo Endre and Laszlo Baky, as undersecretaries of state. They had declared humanitarian considerations immaterial and were entrusted with the deportations."

"Jewish property was a bone of contention. The Germans demanded all sorts of luxury goods and big ticket items like pianos and original Watteau landscapes. The Nazis seized El Grecos, Goyas, Renoirs, Veroneses, Daumiers. They executed their Jewish collectors for illegal dealings. Even the most fertile imagination could not fathom the military need for lingerie, eau de cologne, cut crystal champagne glasses. Adolph Eichmann asked that freight bills be charged in his name, but never made a settlement.

"When he first appeared on the scene, Eichmann seemed as congenial as Krumey. Handling Jews since 1934, he claimed a fair command of the Hebrew language. Politely he inspected the Jewish museum and library and promised once victory was achieved, Jews would be freed. 'I am your protector,' he insisted. 'Executions are necessary only when you resist.'

"Eichmann grew chummy with Endre who issued a long list of prohibitions: Jews could no longer be public servants, practice law, hire Christians, belong to the Press, Stage and Film Chambers. Following the first American air raid, Eichmann ordered the evacuation of 500 Jewish apartments for the Christian victims. Instructions to the council determined where the displaced Jews would be resettled. Thus the ghetto was shaped.

"In April, 1944, Baky issued the infamous decree ordering the deportation of the Jews. He agreed with his friend Eichmann that it was time. Horthy, powerless and overwhelmed, did not object. 'Some Jews are as good Hungarians as you and me.' he insisted, 'I cannot allow them to be deported. The others? Out of mind.'"

39. Deportations

"A Hungarian Squad for the Extermination of the Jews was established at 6 Semmelweiss Utca. The entrance bore the sign, 'International Storing and Transportation Company.' Vassenmayer charged at the Nuremburg trials, "With the aid of the Hungarian government, we carried out the deportations quickly and smoothly.'

"In Debrecen, Hungarian gendarmes forced Jews to pack and drove them to the synagogue, where they were relieved of money and jewels. Those who declared nothing were beaten, some tortured with electric probes and needles beneath the fingernails. Then they were marched to the brickworks where furnaces served as temporary quarters. Thousands were squeezed into space for 300. The Jewish Council provided potato soup to these 'camps.' It was carried in bath tubs and doled a few spoonfuls to each. Water was scarce. Diseases raged.

"In Budapest, Christians queued for a half-mile to apply for the vacated flats. In Eger the archbishop protested the unchristian procedures. And the bishop in Segisvar complained that wailing from the beatings annoyed the neighborhood. In Szeged, 2000 Jews were stuffed into a salami factory to await deportation, though 200 were allowed to remain at home because they were baptized. In Kassas a well-intentioned peasant woman was caught passing food to the tormented as they entrained; she was pushed in among them and deported.

"Most ghettos were surrounded by 'Jew Extermination Squads'. Choosing dawn to avoid attention, they drove victims to the station with whips and rifle butts. When speed became necessary, they were transported in broad daylight. In the wagons Jews were ordered to exhibit manners, to raise their arms and make room for others. Each wagon was provided two buckets for sanitation.

"Baky's gendarmes lurked at railroad stations to detain fleeing Jews, and visited the Jewish cemetery where they arrested the gravediggers and undertakers. The Jewish Council provided names to the Hungarian Gestapo who scorned them for the miserable sycophants they had become. Prominent internees committed suicide, the president of the Banking Institute among them, and the chairman of the Hospital Board."

"Eichmann, always a businessman, asked 5000 Reich marks per head for transportation and board. Endry estimated Hungary paid the Germans 2.5 billion Reich marks for 'ridding the country of vermin.'"

"In August, Lajos Csatay, minister of war, who resisted measures against the Jews, learned the appalling truth about the deportation trains. He told the cabinet as though it were news, 'Their destination is the slaughterhouse.' The cabinet refused his demand for a government protest. Csatay and his wife killed themselves."

"After the Csatay suicides, Horthy informed the Reich that Hungary would no longer permit the removal of Jews from Budapest. Hitler, maintaining a pretense of Hungarian sovereignty, did not respond. He also failed to act when the Arrow Cross insisted once more that Imredy, who had returned to government as a minister without portfolio, be dismissed again because of his Jewish ancestry.

40. The Regent's End

"In early September, hearing that five Soviet armored divisions were approaching, Horthy decided to end the war at once. Paris had fallen a few days before. On September 11, we asked our Western enemies for terms of armistice. Arrogantly they referred us to their Soviet allies, converting misfortune into tragedy. The advancing Soviets were committing indescribable atrocities. Horthy sued for immediate peace. Pleading that the West take part in the occupation of Hungary, he initialed an agreement in Moscow, October 11.

"Determined to prevent a separate Hungarian armistice, Hitler resorted to kidnapping. The German security service informed Nickolas, Horthy's son and deputy, that Tito's envoys wished a conference. Intrigued but cautious, Nickolas took three guards to the designated meeting place. If they noticed anything amiss or if the meeting took more than ten minutes, they were to come running. His suspicions were justified the moment he set foot in the appointed building. Fifteen men seized him. Beaten unmercifully, he feigned unconsciousness. They rolled him into a carpet, and as they carried him to a van he managed a cry for help, alerting his guards. An open gunfight followed, one guard and a kidnapper were killed.

"Horthy received no note. He was to understand that Nickolas was hostage against the Hungarian armistice. Already the Soviets were charging into Debrecen; only days till they'd race across the flat Alfold and hammer at the palace walls. Meanwhile, Horthy was informed that the Germans had captured Kallay and taken the former premier to Dachau. The führer was offering the regent asylum if he abdicated.

"At six the next morning, Admiral Horthy was placed under the führer's protection. Taken to SS headquarters, he asked for a glass of water and was about to take an aspirin when a guard slapped the pill from his hand. 'No suicide,' he cautioned. The only visitor allowed was Ferenc Szalasi. He gave the admiral a Nazi salute, then requested appointment as prime minister.

"'Have Hitler appoint you,' Horthy spat at him. 'You are the last person I would choose.'

"When Szalasi was gone, an SS officer handed the regent a document for signature. He pushed it aside. The officer told him the paper proclaimed his abdication and the appointment of Ferenc Szalasi as premier. 'It is a question of saving your son's life.'

"Signing, the beaten admiral asked, 'What is the legality of a signature wrung from a man at gunpoint?' The next day he left his country a prisoner and arrived in Vienna in the deepest depression, while the new premier denounced the 'shameful traitor.' Then as the Soviets surrounded the city, Szalasi issued a joint communiqué with Hitler; the two nations would carry out the glorious defense of Budapest in the spirit of friendship.

"So it was that Hungary was Germany's only ally to sink all the way with her. The Eastern hordes avenged themselves by plundering and destroying our beautiful capital, stone by stone. At the bloody end, the Soviets chased the German remnants into the palace and bombarded it till only a sieve remained, Asiatic barbarians true to their past."

41. Professor Katrona's Patriotism

Friday, December 18

The centrum was wreathed for Christmas. The broad sidewalks and shops were crowded. A soft snow fell. I found gifts for Reva in the plaza crystal shop, another Szasz, a thin flower holder and a porcelain box with so many lines the scene was not decipherable - - Ah Hungary!

I had contacted Professor Katrona via Isaac Ferenc and asked that he drop by in the early evening. The affair with CETT was that night; Saturday eve, my last in Debrecen, would be devoted to Reva. She planned a dinner for two, but it was suddenly in doubt. Since her father's funeral Reva had twice run up and back to her sister's in Budapest and developed sniffles and a cough. "I wouldn't want to give you such an awful going away present."

"Christmas present," I corrected. "Going away sounds so somber and doomed. I'll be coming back to Debrecen." I said that to everyone, no one believed it.

"Maybe if we sit far apart."

"Haven't we always?"

Her deep laughter was broken with coughs and she hung up.

Friday evening, December 18

Professor Katrona brought a bottle of bull's blood. Apparently he intended to settle in. "I have an appointment later on."

He was eager, "You like it?"

"Your writing style is vivid.'

"That's the style of Isaac Ferenc. OK? Nothing to change?"

As I suspected, he hoped I would edit the manuscript. "I wouldn't presume to change anything. You probably need to list your references. But some of it is so personal, about Horthy, I mean. How can you know such detail about that aloof aristocrat?"

"In the army I played chess with Horthy's former chauffeur. You like?" He would finish in a few months. Could he send me the manuscript? Could I arrange for an American publisher?

Of course not, but I dilly-dallied. "Its curt and dramatic, like a fiction. Is it really accurate?"

Professor Katrona perceived my evasion. He smirked. His tone became resentful and huffy. "Accurate?" he asked as of a child. "You are not serious?" What history is accurate? You are a doubter of the Holocaust?"

"Sorry. I am a teacher of literature, I should know better. We tell history by making stories, but the stories are accurate in their own way."

"True to experience of the senses?" he responded. "Yes, accurate, that way."

"But elusive. Your story leaves me wanting to know a lot more."

"Example?"

"Did World War II provide no lessons to Hungary?"

Professor Katrona thought the war was merely another chapter in the vicissitudes of nations. "Hungary is accustomed to occupations and foreign despots. Horthy gave us more than two decades of stability in the face of Hitler."

"Honorable and courageous," I added, "but a bit hesitant?"

My guest nodded. "A sign of intelligence and compassion, like your Jimmy Carter. But Horthy was a much stronger leader and very popular. He had a Magyar face that inspired faith in his followers."

"I get the impression that he disdained Hitler merely because he was common. He was not horrified. Most of us thought the führer a Frankenstein monster. As you describe him, Horthy dealt with Hitler like a person of a lower order, but a person."

"You will recall the monster had a soft side which needed caressing but Dr. Frankenstein neglected him. Which was the monster?"

I rolled on. "Hungary's invasion of Yugoslavia and Teleki's suicide. What was Horthy's role? The story ignores your regent at that point; I think to preserve your noble vision of him. Teleki seems the noble one. You know that participating with Hitler in that ruthless mischief discredited the Hungarian government. Britain withdrew her diplomatic mission."

"Neutrality was Horthy's goal. Hitler forced us. You are showing your Anglo prejudice."

"Not so neat," I said. "At Nuremberg, didn't the Germans claim that Horthy's army charged into Yugoslavia to devastate the corpse the Nazis left? It's not just the British blaming Hungary for bringing tragedy on themselves."

"I write what I know. What I don't know, I don't say. Did I ennoble Horthy when I quoted his remark about the Jews? That he cared for some in Budapest but not the rest? That is ennobling?" Then the professor asked bluntly, "So you don't know where I should send it?"

"Let me think about it." This concession had a softening effect. He had risen and sat again. Most of the wine was still in the bottle. "Another question! That last phrase, the 'Asiatic barbarians." Your aristocratic regent would have relished it. Do you mean the Germans as well as the Russians?"

"All of us came from Asia, but not all have remained barbarian, like the Germans and Russians."

"And other Europeans? The British? Americans?"

"I can't say, but Americans are different."

Thoughtlessly, like a reflex, I sputtered, "We do not live in history as you do." Had this recent discovery become my unconscious theme?

367

Katrona's eyes sparkled. "Still, you are European . . .except your Indians."

"And blacks," I added.

"And all your other colors. They render a past you acknowledge only lately. For Americans yesterday does not continue today."

"That's the trouble with the Balkans."

"Hungarians too. We remember back over a thousand years. Americans are winners, they can forget."

"Even Vietnam?"

"You really don't know you were defeated. Hungarians know what they lost. They will not rest till Transylvania and Slovakia are returned."

"As Hitler promised." He ignored the sarcasm, rose, and poured himself more wine. Impatiently I burst out, "It's just such fixation that propelled you into the war. And now you justify yourself by pretending to patriotism with all its nationalist blather. What is the motive? Belong or be ostracized for a traitor? Was Horthy a traitor? You do realize his long reign legitimized Hitler's occupation? Near the end, you have Horthy tell Hitler, 'Magyars are not traitors.' It's a proud statement, but you see nothing to sneer at, nothing peculiar? In view of your schizoid history?"

Professor Katrona was visibly upset. His face reddened and I detected a tremor in the hand that retrieved his manuscript.

But instead of huffing off, he asked quietly, "What do I hear, you teach American Reform? The labor movement, the Roosevelts, Progressives, like that, great social change?" Wondering, I nodded.

"Those years were the height of America's imperialism, as I was taught, were they not? Teddy Roosevelt's big stick, ironic, no? Never losers, so now America can be generous, humanitarian." Bitterness seeped through his sudden affability.

When he had gone, I sat, exhausted. Shame crept over me for my unexpected explosion. Petty annoyance with the retired Hungarian professor was no excuse.

42. The Winter Forest

Saturday morning, December 19

Large flakes were sticking to the ground. I put on a coat and sat on my rear balcony, watching the snow stick on the red tiled roofs and cling to the leafless trees. It was a warmer winter day, flakes heavy in the wet air. No wind. Inside again, I regarded the trees on the mural, painting the barks and branches with snow. My last day in Debrecen. I must walk in the forest.

Reva called, not Milkody, Tom's Reva. She said Riedel had gone to Berlin, to meet another Fulbrighter from Finland. Reva didn't know the name. He'd be gone till after New Year's. Tom had asked her to say goodbye for him and give me his resume in case I knew of something in the USA. "You are leaving us tomorrow?" On the morning train at seven, I told her. She would drive me to the station. I protested, "Too early for you. I can arrange a taxi." She insisted.

Snow was covering the shoeprints leading into the forest. I walked around the four-figured war memorial. Each statue was

369

distinguished by headgear: the tricorner of the 18th Century, plume of the 19th, the spiked helmet of World War I, the steel bowl of II. Each soldier held his weapon at the ready in a perpetual charge, eternally threatening the quiet and peaceful snow.

I strolled past the indoor bathing pools and the still ponds, not quite frozen, dead leaves mixed in the snow on them, and through the lane of decaying great houses. The paint had flaked, colors faded; the windows were obscured with torn blinds, steps were broken. There were four houses, the last showing signs of life, washing stiffened on the line and an old car tumbled apart on the back lawn. Run-down magnificence, testimony to long-gone privilege.

Across from the frozen Copacabana pond, I re-examined the hefty female bronzes poised in cool intimacy. They were mammoth maidens, daintily gesturing to each other, not passionately, but classically, poised in peaceful and loving sisterhood. Before, I had not seen the field flowers on their carved heads. The ponderous bodies appeared more graceful and vivid in the snow.

I came to the single track that ran through to the university and hurried over it ahead of a tram approaching silently with no passengers. The meadow on the other side held a surprise. I had crossed it many times but now with the bushes bare, I beheld a standing stone slab carved as a bookcase. Approaching, I made out the books, some upright, some chiseled at a slant on the monumental shelves. Not too far from the university, surely a scholar's whimsy, the reputed Hungarian wit. In a moment I recognized the satire. It was universal, the popular neglect of learning, a stone case of books forlorn in the forest. The barrens of winter had exposed it.

Across the meadow of snow about the distance of a soccer field, I spotted the obvious explanation; another slab, this one facing the figure of a short man huddled against foul weather in a fedora and disheveled overcoat hiding his neck. Only his back could be seen. Most apparently he depicted a curmudgeon. I thought of Hawthorne, his dour old man, who had been his pure "Young Goodman Brown."

The slab bore only the simple engraving, ADY, the name of Hungary's controversial poet who died at age 42 after a syphilitic life of romantic pain and repressed hope. The Nagyerdei forest was his 'Bakony,' a legendary Sherwood Forest, his hideaway of highwaymen.

A tablet at the foot read, Endre Ady, 1877-1919. The books went with the poet. But why did the monument-maker hide his countenance? When I thrust my head into the spare space between slab and face, I confronted close-up the brooding features of Edgar Allan Poe, the same hollow cheeks, hurting eyes, and frowning mouth. Apparently, the American Gothic was destined to shadow my days in Hungary.

43. Kissing Debrecen Goodbye

Saturday night, December 18

"Ady was outrageous," Reva declared as we sat down to her casserole of veal and pork paprikas. "He came from a village near here, an impoverished family. Born with six fingers like the Arpàds who founded the country. His midwife amputated the extra, leaving two white scars he called his 'wizard marks.' He worked on Debrecen newspapers. Published his first book here."

"Nice change. Hungarians I meet are all born to the gentry, or say so."

She laughed, bringing on her cough, but managed, "Not me, but I must disappoint you about Ady. His father had a title and a small holding." Reva went on to eulogize the bombshell that burst on Hungarian literary life in 1906. "Budapest had been dormant. Ady erupted like a Walt Whitman shot out of a Brooklyn cannon." Her black eyes flashed through the congestion, "But he was more of an angry young man."

"Actually, his statue suggests Poe, not Whitman."

"He is the soul of Hungary." She sniffled, "Ady could be mystical . . . and irritating. He unleashed vicious attacks against his homeland and became the target of violent counter-attacks until he died, even after."

"The Kun period and White Terror? He as part of that?"

"He died just then, in 1919. His doctor said he died of a diseased aorta, which ruptured. He bled to death. What caused the rupture? Syphilis and alcohol, but also his many passions, sufferings, angers, his phantoms. One phantom was a tantalizing dark-skinned maiden, his beautiful gypsy princess. When his brother arrived at the death scene, he found a terribly upset girl applying cold compresses to her incapacitated lover."

Reva ran on about Ady, getting into his poetry as much as his raucous life. He was hailed a prophet by left wing radicals and attacked by right wing nationalists. The turmoil must have purified him. His later work transcended politics. He wrote about the Magyars, his people, the pain and suffering inflicted by war and the mysteries of physical love. Mostly she appreciated the curtain of mist he cast over the unchanging life of his native town near the Transylvanian Alps. "Ady even wrote religious poems, blasphemous of course, but he suspected that God was at the bottom of everything."

"As I'm sure you do." Her eyes were suddenly sad. She turned away. My remark must have disturbed the raw memory of her father's barren funeral. "Sorry," I said, though it was her sudden mood change that needed apology. Seldom did we delve into questions of spirit, though everyone asked them. "Your father was not a religious man."

"He thought all the clergy were corrupt or just plain mad. But he tolerated them, as they do the fakirs in India." Another coughing spell. Then she paused and said, "The Indian in America believes the madman speaks the truth. He is the dreamer and visionary, a holy man." Though she never mentioned Tom Riedel, his influence was apparent.

I made light of it, "The mad are all in God's keeping."

Reva fluttered a hand before her eyes as if to wave away the subject. Faint stress lines were visible on her forehead and around her mouth. She was emotionally spent. We sat wordlessly. I believe it was the first awkward moment between us.

374

"Hear from David?" I blurted.

"Yes . . .oh Daniel, don't go!" I sat at the table, wanting to hold her and said nothing. "What will I do?" She regained control. "Nothing has changed with David."

"What could change if you won't cooperate? And how will you ever satisfy your maternal drive?"

That escaped, I was taking advantage. But she refused to be offended. "We won't talk about him, or that. Its your last night."

Reva went to her piano, shoved a pile of papers to make room on the bench and began to stroke the keys.

"You've never played for me."

"And I'm not going to. I just use it to relax, when my classes go zip, when the students push me about. Next term I'll have more confidence."

"You're the teacher, Reva. Just remember you know more than they do. She smiled to acknowledge confidence, but it showed little.

"I played for hours alone when my father died. He didn't fit in very well, you know."

"Not a patriotic Magyar?"

The remark aroused a slight chuckle, "A proud Magyar, but not a patriotic anything. I try to be like him. He thought noble goals were often treacherous goals."

"And your mother?"

"The common story. Mothers and daughters. Really we have little conflict. Wants me to get married. My sister does too. We're a close family."

I ventured, "They thought you'd marry Tom Riedel?"

Reva coughed again, then laughed sadly, "My sister thought he was slimy. I'm sorry. He's your friend."

She had prepared hard little pastries with artificial sweetener. We sat on the couch, apart, a caution against her cold, and drank tea with the pastries. Reva was fighting her melancholy. "Whatever you say, I just know you won't be coming back." I could feel her restlessness. She picked up the Szasz porcelain I had brought her, rubbed it along her cheek, then put her lips to it.

"But you'll be moving about, America, Turkey. You are idealistic, Reva, eager to fly, like your Toni Morrison."

She gave a wistful smile, "I'm also Hungarian, I can stay where I was born. Dreaming usually leads nowhere, hardships mainly. But I'm not an old lady yet. I still might take a chance if a fascinating opportunity comes along."

"You want to live out your life in Hungary?"

"I do want to explore other worlds like you have. But you've come here. Hungary is jumping with people from everywhere. The world comes to you now . . . whatever you want of it."

"With all its tawdry gadgets and chintzy cheapness."

Again her hand waved before her eyes. "Why mention that." Her hand reached for mine across the couch. "I wish we didn't have to say goodbye. Isn't it a crime to catch a cold, now of all times?" Her luminous face focused directly on me, eyes shining. "I meant to kiss you tonight."

"A kiss from Hungary's heart," I said, feeling a fool.

Sunday morn, December 20

The bitter air was crystallizing our breath. Tom's Reva helped lug my bags down and stuff them in the trunk. Before we started, she handed me a present in green tissue paper. It felt mushy as I tore it open: black felt spectacle holders embroidered with a peasant design in bright red. "Just a token of Debrecen."

"Wait a minute." I raced up the stairs, opened the door, and searched about. But everything was packed and in the car trunk. This was a catastrophic parting. At the car, I opened my duffle bag, happily discovered a copy of my "Exiles at Home," signed it, and with compunction, thrust it at her. She was pleased.

My baggage was lighter going back. I hauled them into the station a piece at a time while Reva stood guard. Then up and down stairs to Platform 4: Budapest Express. How I needed her; how thankful I was. Reva's was the last friendly face I would see there. We exchanged chit-chat till she put the question, "So you know his wife?"

In a flash, this professional woman of thirty became the dusty nubile gypsy with blonde babe forlorn on the Debrecen high street. Before I found my tongue, the train came pounding in. Reva helped throw the baggage aboard, then stood as though to be kissed. I complied.

My heart plummeted as the Budapest express pulled away from the Debrecen station.

44. Afterword

Mr. and Mrs. Jozsef Czakos
Request the pleasure of your company
At the marriage of their daughter
KATALIN EVA
With
Mr. MATTHEW RICHARD PALMER
At the Cistercian Church, Eger,
On Saturday, 14th August, 1993 at 5:00 pm
And at the reception afterwards

Eger
January 3, 1994

Dear Daniel,

I was planning to go for my Transylvanian fix during the winter break but someone stole my papers and a considerable amount of money from my jacket which was hanging up in my new office here in Eger. If all goes

379

well, however, Kauty and I will make the trip over spring break.

We are now happily married and living in a small flat in the middle of Eger. We're about three minutes walk from her parents and at about the same height, so we have spectacular views over the town to the South and towards the Bukk hills to the North. One excuse for not writing is that we spent all autumn decorating and furnishing. The atmosphere is rather monastic owing to the lack of furniture.

The wedding was an incredible occasion, more pageant than a quick jaunt up the aisle. We had 38 foreign guests, who were determined to make the event "memorable." Consequently, it lasted a week, Tuesday to Tuesday, with the ceremony on the Saturday in the middle. Marvelous that the prime focus was not on the main characters, Kauty and me, but on the many supporting players and subplots.

Two of my cousins showed up with their "Comic Sausages," a frisky band who were on a European tour. Can you picture them pulling crowds of 200-300 in little Dobo Ter? The England vs. Hungary football match occurred Thursday, eleven a side, England fielding eight Palmers and the Hungarians eight Czakos. Outcome was diplomatic, yet hard-fought, 2-2 draw. An outdoor gulyas picnic followed. Cuisine brought the combatants together and bridged the communications barrier.

Some cameo roles in the monumental drama were played by people you know. My best man, Dr. Leslie Burton, came accompanied by a female who was none other than Miss Reva Milany, a gasping surprise since I went to the station expecting to pick up Les and his Polish bird. Les and Reva were going through all the flutters of a new amour, and Eger was obviously a venue of enormous promise. (Kauty suggested they stay at the Venus!)

As a result Les was a lousy best man. He didn't even get to the stag night let alone organize it. Indeed, the wedding band had to wait for Leslie, not the bride. Goeff also made it to Eger, and Alistair; unfortunately Ansca was in America. She is returning to the institute, which she all but runs. For the record, Alistair and Ansca finally got married this summer.

So Daniel, a pity you didn't hang in, though the spring term was a wretched affair. Since returning to Eger I haven't suffered any Debrecen withdrawal symptoms, but Kauty still goes, attending CETT.

Any immediate plans for visiting the States disappeared in a puff of smoke when England lost 2-0 against Holland at Rotterdam. A World Cup in America without England or Hungary lacks the mystique. So our next meeting is more likely on this side of the Atlantic. Your not so nomadic intellectual outlaw.

Matthew.

Debrecen,
January 31, 1994

Dear Daniel,
The second half of 1993 was as long as an eye-blink. I trust you will understand my long silence when you finish reading this letter. Matt's gossip about the wedding hit the nail on the head. (He should start a news agency.)

Well, Daniel, if you are standing or eating something, please sit in a comfortable armchair and make sure you don't choke. "Tremendous" changes have occurred in my life in recent months. I am married to Dr. Leslie Burton and we expect a baby in late August or early September! Daniel, I am a wife. And soon to be a mother!

Now, how it happened. To render events faithfully I will have to start last June, the time when Les and I were quite surprised to "discover" each other. While I worked on my dissertation, Les was hanging around Debrecen waiting for Matt's wedding. He began proofreading my finished copy . . . the rest I leave to your imagination.

I like to say "Les pulled it off" December 13, because there wa so much for him to arrange, all sorts of permissions and certificates. There is nothing extraordinary about our story, if not the fact itself. (One's own story is always extraordinary.) We "found" each other and have had a wonderful time together ever since.

How can I tell you what it's like to be married? I don't know. Great, unusual, especially wonderful if the basis of marriage is a desire to create a family. I am happy that I had the courage to "jump" in. When you live alone a long time and work in academia, you may become too selfish and self-centered to sacrifice your peaceful solitude.

Les is a very precious person and we have been fairly successful in learning to live together. I do not forget your casual remark, that marriage requires patience and flexibility. We are so overjoyed about the newcomer who is tiny at the moment (I am in the ninth week).

That is the private side of my life, all joy and happiness. Not so the professional one. Although I finished my dissertation on Toni Morrison, defended it, took the required exams, and was finally awarded the doctoral, it brought more trouble and pain than happiness, let alone "glory." The banana skin I slipped on was, I guess, conformity. They said the thesis was written for myself, not academic stiffs, my first "deadly sin." Andros was the worst offended, followed by our friend Steve Ruark, who also insinuated I plagiarized.

But I have the degree, though my enthusiasm has abated. Andros treats me like a student, not a colleague, humiliating me at department meetings and loading me with four different courses requiring four preparations.

I could include much gossip but this letter would never end. Instead, I enclose the lecture I read last year at the HSSE (Hungarian Society for the Study of English) conference and the intro and conclusion to the Morrison dissertation which had a shaky flight. So that's for now.

There is no danger that I will be away when you and Roberta visit here in the near future. Come see our baby!

Lots of love, Daniel
Reva

Frohliche Weihnachten
Und gluckliches Neujahr!
*

Merry Christmas
And happy 1995

Dear Daniel,

I feel like 'Absolom' returning to his good father . . . Life has been hectic and has brought me some unexpected turns which I am going to write about in a letter. I just hope I have made good decisions.

Very cryptic, eh? But I will let you know all the mysteries soon.

A blessed and peaceful Christmas and a very Happy New Year for now,

All my love,
Reva.

About the Author

Daniel Marder has been a Soros professor at the L.Kossuth University in Debrecen, Hungary, the head and professor of English at the University of Tulsa in Oklahoma, and has held professorships at The Pennsylvania State University and the University of Pittsburgh in Pennsylvania. He was Fulbright professor at universities in Macedonia and Croatia, and was visiting professor at the University of Keele and visiting scholar at Cambridge University in England. In an earlier journalistic career, he reported for *Time and Life* and established an American newspaper, the *Spanish American Courier*. In addition to rhetorics, his books have included a biography and editions of the early American Satirist, Hugh Henry Brackenridge, *Exiles at Home: A Story of Literature in Nineteenth Century America, The Arnold/Andre Transcripts: A Reconstruction,* and *A Biography of Frank Norris.* During World War II, the Chinese government honored the author with the Order of the Flying Cloud; he has received the Air Medal and his unit's Presidential Citation with Silver Cluster.

Printed in the United States
17811LVS00002B/1-30